Chastity

Presenting the Past

Central Issues in Medieval and Early Modern Studies Across the Disciplines

General Editor
Nancy van Deusen

VOLUME 1

Chastity

A Study in Perception, Ideals, Opposition

Edited by

Nancy van Deusen

BRILL

LEIDEN • BOSTON
2008

On the cover: Les Très Riches Heures du Duc de Berry, c. 1416. Courtesy of Musée Condé in Chantilly.

This book is printed on acid-free paper.

Library of Congress Cataloging-in-Publication Data

Chastity : a study in perception, ideals, opposition / edited by Nancy van Deusen.
p. cm. — (Presenting the past ; v. 1)
Includes index.
ISBN 978-90-04-16671-4 (hardback : alk. paper) 1. Chastity. I. van Deusen, Nancy (Nancy Elizabeth)
BJ1533.C4C43 2008
176—dc22

2008005744

ISSN 1875-2799
ISBN 978 90 04 16671 4

PRINTED IN THE NETHERLANDS

CONTENTS

CONTENTS

LIST OF CONTRIBUTORS

Nancy van Deusen
Director, Claremont Consortium in Medieval and Early Modern Studies, Claremont Colleges and Graduate University
Benezet Professor of Humanities, Claremont Graduate University

Frank T. Coulson
Director, Center for Epigraphical and Paleographical Studies, Department of Greek and Latin, The Ohio State University

Marcia L. Colish
Department of History, Yale University

Uta-Renate Blumenthal
Department of History, The Catholic University of America

Thérèse-Anne Druart
Department of Philosophy, The Catholic University of America

Claudia Bornholdt
Department of Germanic Languages and Literatures
The Catholic University of America

Susan L'Engle
Vatican Film Archive, Saint Louis University, St. Louis

Cristian Gaspar
Department of Medieval Studies, Central European University, Budapest

Rafael Chodos, Esq.
Los Angeles

INTRODUCTION

Nancy van Deusen

The topic of "Chastity" brings up a nexus of related considerations such as moral ambiguity, the instability of moral value and ethical choices, the inner life and its reflexive relationship to itself, of vices masquerading as virtues, or as virtues treated as vices, and the repercussions of loss of innocence; of contempt, anger, pride, all subsumed under the guise of humility, and finally, what can be seen as a certain paralysis of the soul that becomes encased, even imprisoned within, irreconcilable moral dilemmas. These are inner states—juxtapositions to be explored within the discipline of moral philosophy as well as within the development of characters in novels—involving the impact of perception upon consciousness, but cultural conventions as well. There are, in addition, legal implications of moral and cultural values, both within an historical context, as, for example, an increasing interest in the topic and issue of the celibacy of the clergy during what we commonly term the "high middle ages," as well as proscriptions against, and punishments for, prostitution. One confronts a certain "virtuous pragmatism," historically, as well as, certainly, personally and culturally, with attendant delusion and self-justification. The topic of "Chastity" is interactive; one immediately begins to add to the list of considerations.

Due to its rich internal implications as well as the fact that chastity can be viewed as an access to basic historical problems, the topic has been chosen for an interdisciplinary volume of essays that brings together some of the questions, issues, repercussions, and perhaps unsolvable problems inherent in the topic. Some of the essays can be located within a recognizable disciplinary discourse, others take an approach outside traditional academic discussion. Not all of the discordant voices can be, or indeed should be, harmonized; nor can a resolution be sought and found between all of the dichotomies presented here: between inner life and outer scruples, between intention and action, between professed spirituality and life as lived on a day to day basis, and between proscription and effect. It is the goal and challenge of this volume to focus on a topic from as many points of view as possible, also encouraging, even provoking, the reader to follow lines of thought that recur, or which all of the essays hold in common.

Frank Coulson, in his contribution to this volume, "Failed Chastity and Ovid: Myrrha in the Latin Commentary Tradition from Antiquity to the Renaissance," has explored what he describes as "the complex tapestry of Ovidian influence" upon the Latin school tradition centered upon Ovid and, in particular, the commentaries that were written on the *Metamorphoses* from 1100–1600 CE. This commentary tradition is not easy to discover, since the majority of the texts lack suitable editions, thus must be read from manuscript sources. Focusing on the story of Myrrha, one of Ovid's most extensive and "psychologically developed narratives" (occurring in Book Ten of the *Metamorphoses*), Coulson points to allusions, as well as conceptual-verbal gestures, that identify the presence and progress of this particular narrative through the "Carolingian Renaissance," the cathedral school milieux, particularly of Chartres and Orléans in the later 12th century, with writers such as Arnulf of Orléans, leading then into the thirteenth-century commentators, such as the *Integumenta Ovidii* of John of Garland, providing an alternative allegorical interpretation of the *Metamorphoses*, and a commentary on the entire Ovidian corpus, the *Versus bursarii* (*Bursarii ovidianorum*) of William of Orléans, and finally, the "Vulgate" commentary, written possibly at Orléans in the mid to later thirteenth century, a commentary that has been designated as indispensable for the study of Ovid in the Middle Ages—and beyond. Ovid's text, together with its medieval and renaissance commentators, can be seen to raise questions that provide, not only a foundation for the discussion of important—and ambiguous—moral issues for the Latin-based mental civilization of several centuries of European intellectual history, but also provide a basis for bringing into a viable connection the essays that follow within this volume. These questions include, whether a character can be interpreted as a devil or a god, and on what basis, what is the nature of "forbidden passions" (Myrrha's incestuous liaison with her father that moves on to the, in some ways, parallel relationship of her son, Adonis, with the goddess, Venus); to a consideration of the methodology of allegory and the "true" meaning of a literary work that also involves the "covering" (*integumentum*) of irony, sarcasm, and allusion.

Marcia L. Colish's essay, "Ambrose of Milan on Chastity," brings up the question of a philosophical basis for the theme of asceticism, as viewed in the frequent depictions of the Bishop of Milan and great teacher, for example, of Augustine, as exhorting his followers to flee physical pleasures. The reason given for this exhortation is an interpretation of a "Platonic" conception of human nature as dualistic. Relating this problem of asceticism, with the further implication of celibacy, to Ambrose's anthropology in terms of his creation account and life in Eden (in his commentary on the Book of Genesis, the *Hexaemeron, De paradiso*)[1] Colish points out that "In both works he [Ambrose] stresses, against Manichees, Gnostics, and Originists, that the primal parents God created and placed in Eden possessed gendered bodies as well as souls. These attributes, and a sexual mode of reproduction, were not consequences of the Fall."[2] The nature, then, of corporeal reality, of ensouled bodies, of the union of two ensouled bodies in marriage, and the meaning of self-regulation, or temperance, both within marriage and without, comprises the rich panorama of topics explored in an article that draws not only upon, and brings into an over-arching intellectual context, Ambrose's treatises dealing with creation, but also what would seem to be a lifetime of thinking and learning on topic of material reality. Paradise—the Garden of Eden—innocence and its gain or loss, seen material compared with inner substance, desire and concupiscence, are some aspects to be considered here, with a conclusion that "This high appraisal of marriage and marital sexuality is a value that Ambrose, in contrast to most of his contemporaries and predecessors who wrote on celibate vocations, refuses to cede in the treatises he produced for widows and consecrated virgins. Each of these three states of life, he argues, can be a means of salvation for those called to it."[3]

The increasingly important topic of celibacy in the eleventh century is taken up by Uta-Renate Blumenthal in her article, "The Prohibition of Clerical Marriage in the Eleventh Century," in which a long-standing ambivalence toward marriage within the early Christian church, as expressed, for example, by the Apostle Paul in his first letter to the Corinthians, is explored within, for example, the *Liber decretorum* of Bishop Burchard of Worms (ca. 1023), the *Panormia* of Bishop Ivo of Chartres (ca. 1093); which no doubt took as their sources the *Paenitentiale ad Otgarium* of Hrabanus Maurus and the *Libri duo de synodalis causis* by Regino of Prüm. Who, amongst the contemporaneous popes, was for celibacy, who ignored the topic altogether, who was against it, and on what grounds? What exactly were the issues at stake, and on what authority? The topic, for example, appears to be totally lacking

1 A topic also to be explored in the concluding essay to this volume, Rafael Chodos, "The Cry of Eden," pp. xxx, below.
2 P. xx.
3 P. xx.

in the legislation of Pope Gregory VII, "who is generally considered the unquestionable force behind the effective establishment of clerical celibacy as an unbreakable norm in the West, an establishment that is seen as one of the major accomplishments of this period of reform."[4] What then, is "reform?" These questions bring the topic of chastity into an arena of legislation, practice, institutional history, and, as Blumenthal states, into the broad stream of church history to arbitrate, negotiate, and differentiate clerical practice, a topic of relevance today.

Thérèse-Anne Druart, in her contribution to this volume, "An Arab Christian Philosophical Defense of Religious Celibacy Against its Islamic Condemnation," draws attention to the reality of the aggregation of many peoples, cultural predispositions, philosophical traditions and points of view, that must be considered in dealing with the study of philosophy in Islamic lands during the Middle Ages. Christianity had for many centuries been firmly established within the surrounding lands at the time when Muhammad emigrated from Mecca to Medina in 622. The desert landscapes were filled, to a certain extent, with Christian hermits and monks. "Islam, on the other hand, objected to monasticism, celibacy, and the eremitical life from its inception. In popular Islamic culture, celibacy be it religious or by default...is still regarded as the mother of all vices."[5] Druart examines the origin of this outspoken objection to celibacy and monasticism, looking then at a philosophical defense of monastic celibacy on the part of Yahyā ibn ʿAdī.

Susan L'Engle's opening statement in "Depictions of Chastity: Virtue Made Visible" contributes, mid-volume, a useful summarization of the preceding essays and the topics they raise, putting them, as well into a perspective. She remarks: "Today, in the twenty-first century, we all have personal takes on the meaning of the word chastity and its relevance to our individual lives, shaped by our upbringing and education and supplemented by input from various media. In the Middle Ages, however, chastity was an all-pervading and multivalent concept that regulated the lives of lay men and women, and clergy alike. The ideals of chastity were expressed verbally by churchmen, theologians, philosophers, poets, and heads of family—recorded in sermons, Saints' Lives, advice manuals for rulers, courtesy books, and poems of courtly

[4] P. xx.
[5] P. xx.

romance."[6] The study that ensues, treats again, as she states, "the various ramifications of chastity within strata of medieval society," with an exploration of how the topic of chastity could be, and was, interpreted visually; what was possible within certain, often culturally-defined, boundaries, and what circumstances provided a necessary impetus to visual representation of a concept—an important contribution to the overall structure of the volume. The crucial relationships between image and an idea or stance, such as modesty, between concept and text, and between writer, copyist, and reading audience are all factors that bring focus to, and provide resonance with, other of the essays within this volume.

In her study, "What makes a Marriage: Consent or Consummation in Twelfth-Century German Literature," Claudia Bornholdt begins her discussion with the case of the Northumbrian king and martyr saint, Oswald (d. 642) who, apparently, was a married man and the father of at least one son. By the twelfth century, however, these then perhaps embarrassing details, in view of Oswald's sanctity, had been significantly altered. What had, in the meantime, transpired, and why this transformation of an attitude toward married life and its consummation in progeny? A concept of chastity has been altered and invoked that delineates deep-seated cultural and intellectual, as well as theological, change, not only on the parts of a supposed intellectual elite, but with respect, as well, to what one could term "popular religion" and what lay people expected of their role models. Bornholdt discusses the German narrative of St. Oswald, belonging to pre-courtly German "minstrel epics" (*Spielmannsepen*), as well as other sources such as *Das Lob Salomons* (Praise of Solomon), and *Diu Hochzeit* (The Wedding), an allegorical reading of the "Song of Songs," to document what she considers to be one telling feature; they all address the idea—and clearly the positive features of—marital chastity, a feature so prominent that it can be considered a motif, and serving as models for lay audiences, in twelfth-century Germany.

Chastity's direct contrary, namely, fornication, is approached as a conceptual access to the topic of the volume in Cristian Gaspar's contribution, "'The Spirit of Fornication, Whom the Children of the Hellenes Used to Call Eros': Problematizations of Male Homoeroticism in Late Antique Monastic Milieus." The study also relates to, and provides a

[6] Pp. xx ff.

connection with, the opening study of Frank Coulson, in approaching the topic through its opposite, namely, what chastity patently is not. With a rich background of sources from Byzantine/Greek medieval monastic life, Gaspar carefully differentiates between perceived prohibition, rhetorical convention, and situations in which a literal meaning can be, with some certainty, derived to provide a complementary side to a more frequently-studied Latin monastic culture structured within a history of Latin literature and its use in the Middle Ages. Greek monks grappled with some of the same questions, and in their view, temptations, as Latin monks, with similar as well as outstandingly different approaches, both of which accessing fundamental attitudes not only to the human condition, but to legal and cultural realities that always enclose and surround the circumstances under which human beings actually live.

Finally, Rafael Chodos, in "The Cry of Eden" concludes this volume with a study of the basic concepts of purity, loss of innocence, and the law. Chodos relates the Old Testament account of the Fall and subsequent exile from Eden as related in Genesis, to other narratives, providing cross-cultural analysis, but also exploring the legal implications of "moral" conduct, with an unusual emphasis on God as landlord (of Eden), fully within His legal rights by insisting upon contractual agreements with his tenants (Adam and Eve). The volume closes then with a discussion of the legal implications of morality as founded upon, and sustained by, law.

United by title and theme, the essays also have clear internal connections, that bring together writers, sources, and situations, from several disciplinary and cultural practices; but also from antiquity, the European Latin, and Greek, Middle Ages, the Renaissance, on to the present day. Conclusions follow, namely, that there is much to be learned from historical situations, and that the questions "they" raise, though formulated in diverse manners, are nevertheless important and relevant questions. We can learn from them as well as from one another, which is the reason for the present volume.

FAILED CHASTITY AND OVID: MYRRHA IN THE LATIN COMMENTARY TRADITION FROM ANTIQUITY TO THE RENAISSANCE[1]

Frank T. Coulson

The preponderant influence of the poetry of Ovid on the artistic and cultural life of Europe from the Carolingian age to the end of the Renaissance has long been recognized, and numerous studies have documented the manner in which the tone, themes, style and ethos of both the amatory poems and Ovid's epic poem, the *Metamorphoses*, informed such vernacular poets as Dante in Italian, Chaucer and Shakespeare in English, and the poets of the *Pléiade* in renaissance France. Here, it is not my purpose to investigate such monumental works of literature as the *Commedia*, but rather to trace a slenderer, yet in my view no less important thread in the complex tapestry of Ovidian influence in the Middle Ages and Renaissance—namely, the Latin school tradition on Ovid and, in particular, the commentaries that were written on the *Metamorphoses* from 1100 to 1600. These texts, as Alastair Minnis has recently shown in his magisterial study *Medieval Literary Theory and Criticism c. 1100–c. 1375: The Commentary Tradition*,[2] are important witnesses to reading practices and literary interpretation during the medieval and humanistic periods. To date, however, these commentaries have not received the attention they deserve for several reasons. First, and perhaps foremost, the basic research necessary to uncover the manuscript witnesses of these texts and place them in their intellectual milieu is ongoing.[3] Secondly, the majority of the texts, even

---

1 I am grateful to Marjorie Curry Woods for comments on an earlier draft of this article.

2 Alastair J. Minnis and A. B. Scott, *Medieval Literary Theory and Criticism c. 1100–c. 1375: The Commentary Tradition* (Oxford, 1988, rev. ed., 1991), now supplemented by Alastair J. Minnis and Ian Johnson, eds., *The Cambridge History of Literary Criticism*, vol. 2: The Middle Ages (Cambridge, 2005).

3 For a survey of the manuscript evidence to date see Frank T. Coulson and Bruno Roy, *Incipitarium Ovidianum: A Finding Guide for Texts related to the Study of Ovid in the Middle Ages and Renaissance* (Turnhout, 2000), hereafter cited as Coulson-Roy, and Frank T. Coulson, "Addenda and Corrigenda to *Incipitarium Ovidianum*," *Journal of Medieval Latin* 12 (2002), 154–80. A team of scholars headed by Frank T. Coulson is preparing the

when known, still lack either diplomatic or critical editions and thus must be read in their original manuscript setting, often from poorly produced microfilmed copies.[4] Finally, the commentaries themselves are most frequently written in a crabbed and highly abbreviated Gothic script (usually a *textualis libraria* or *currens*),[5] often in the margins of the manuscripts of the poem, and are virtually indecipherable except by those scholars who are professionally trained to read Gothic book hands from 1200 to 1400.

In keeping with the theme of this volume of essays, I shall focus my survey of this commentary material on the interpretation of the story of Myrrha from Book Ten of the *Metamorphoses.* I have selected this particular story as the basis for my investigation for the following reasons. The narrative revolves around a young girl's failed attempt to remain chaste when confronted with an incestuous passion for her father and thus reflects the theme of this year's conference. Secondly, the story of Myrrha is one of Ovid's longest and most psychologically developed narratives, situated in Book Ten of the epic, where Orpheus, having lost his wife Eurydice, retreats to the mountains of Thrace and narrates the stories of youths loved by the gods (*pueros dilectos superis, Met.* 10.152–153) and maidens set aflame with forbidden passions (*inconcessisque puellas ignibus attonitas, Met.* 10.153–154). Myrrha's story then becomes embedded in a complexly interwoven thread of narratives that move from the story of Myrrha's incestuous liaison with her father to that of her son, Adonis, with the goddess Venus. Lastly, the Myrrha story is, from a stylistic point of view, one of Ovid's finest, in which the poet develops to perhaps the highest degree that sardonic humor that caused him to be labeled by the first-century rhetorician Quintilian (*Inst. orat.* 10.1.88) a *nimium amator ingenii sui*—"too great a lover of his own cleverness."

* * *

Ovid fascicle for publication in volume 10 of the *Catalogus translationum et commentariorum: medieval and Renaissance Latin translations and commentaries*, ed. Virginia Brown, 8 vols. (Washington, 1960-present).

[4] No complete Latin commentary on the *Metamorphoses* has to date been published. Frank T. Coulson has edited selections from the "Vulgate" commentary (discussed below, pp. 16–19). See his *The Vulgate Commentary on Ovid's* Metamorphoses: *the Creation Myth and the Story of Orpheus, edited from Sélestat, Bibliothèque humaniste, MS. 92* (Toronto, 1991).

[5] The nomenclature of Gothic scripts is a much vexed question. I follow the system proposed by Albert Derolez in his newly published *The Palaeography of Gothic Manuscript Books From the Twelfth to the Early Sixteenth Century* (Cambridge, 2003).

Let us then begin our survey of the school and commentary tradition on Ovid's transformations in late antiquity. Our knowledge of the circulation and fate of the *Metamorphoses* from the fall of Rome to the revival of learning in what Haskins has called the twelfth-century Renaissance[6] is, to state the case generously, scanty. The majority of complete manuscripts of the poem that are extant date from the 12th century onwards.[7] And unlike Virgil's corpus, Horace's poems, and the plays of Terence,[8] which benefitted from a rich commentary tradition dating from the late antique period through to the Carolingian Renaissance, only one "commentary" on the *Metamorphoses*, tentatively dated to the late antique period, survives, namely the ps.-Lactantian *Narrationes.*[9] The *Narrationes* consist of a series of *tituli*—titles—and prose paraphrases for each of the individual transformations in the epic. But the *Narrationes* are not simply a retelling in prose of the stories. Some of the accounts offer a form of the myth different from the one narrated in Ovid (so, for example, in the story of the founding of Thebes by Cadmus at the

---

[6] Charles Homer Haskins, *The Renaissance of the Twelfth Century* (Cambridge, Mass., 1939).

[7] For a complete list of manuscripts see Franco Munari, *Catalogue of the Mss of Ovid's* Metamorphoses (London, 1957); "Supplemento al catalogo dei manoscritti delle *Metamorfosi* ovidiane," *Rivista di filologia e di istruzione classica* 93 (1965), 288–97; and his "Secondo supplemento al catalogo dei manoscritti delle *Metamorfosi* ovidiane," in *Studia Florentina Alexandro Ronconi sexagenario oblata* (Rome, 1970), pp. 275–80. For updates to Munari's catalogues see Frank T. Coulson, "An Update to Munari's Catalogue of the Manuscripts of Ovid's *Metamorphoses*," *Scriptorium* 42 (1988), 111–12; "Newly Discovered Manuscripts of Ovid's *Metamorphoses* in the Libraries of Florence and Milan," *Scriptorium* 46 (1992), 285–88; "A Bibliographical Update and *Corrigenda Minora* to Munari's Catalogues of the Manuscripts of Ovid's *Metamorphoses*," *Manuscripta* 38 (1994), 3–22, and his "Addenda to Munari's Catalogues of the Manuscripts of Ovid's *Metamorphoses*," *Revue d'histoire des textes* 25 (1995), 91–127. Richard Tarrant discusses the manuscript affiliations in *Texts and Transmission: A Survey of the Latin Classics*, ed. Leighton Durham Reynolds (Oxford, 1983), pp. 276–82, and in his recently published text, *P. Ovidi Nasonis Metamorphoses* (Oxford, 2004), esp. pp. v–xxvii.

[8] See, for example, the commentaries of Servius on Virgil (edited in Georg Thilo and Hermann Hagen, eds., *Servii Grammatici qui feruntur in Vergilii carmina commentarii*, 3 vols. (Hildesheim, 1961)); Pomponius Porphyrio (edited in Wilhelm Meyer, ed., *Pomponii Porphyrionis Commentarii in Q. Horatium Flaccum* (Leipzig, 1874); and ps.-Acro on Horace (edited in Otto Keller, ed., *Pseudacronis scholia in Horatium vetustiora* [Leipzig, 1902–04], and Donatus on Terence (edited in Paul Wessner, ed., *Aelii Donati quod fertur Commentum Terenti* [Leipzig, 1902]).

[9] For a survey of published material on the *Narrationes*, see Coulson-Roy, no. 54. Alan Cameron in his most recent study attempts to redate the *Narrationes* to the second century. See his *Greek Mythographers in the Roman World* (Oxford, 2004), pp. 4–32.

beginning of Book Three of the *Metamorphoses*), and one may assume that the author was drawing upon mythological handbooks for such alternative renderings. The *Narrationes* also contain other types of comments: for example, in a dozen places the author explicitly provides the Greek source for Ovid's account. There are also a number of comments, as Richard Tarrant has demonstrated in his eloquent article on this text, which may be classified as "scholia" rather than mere prose recasting, and a few comments that may be deemed "scholia of an interpretative character".[10] These characteristics lead one to conclude (and, here, I agree with the opinion of Richard Tarrant) that the *Narrationes* probably represent material that formed part of a larger body of interpretative comment on the *Metamorphoses.*[11] The *Narrationes* are transmitted in the margins of many of the manuscripts of the *Metamorphoses* and also circulated separately as an unattributed mythographic treatise during the Renaissance.[12] Perhaps one indication of the importance of this material can be gleaned from the shear volume of manuscript copies extant. To date I have uncovered over 55 manuscript witnesses to this commentary. The ps.-Lactantian version of the myth of Myrrha differs from the Ovidian version in several important ways: First, in Ovid, no cause is given for Myrrha's incestuous love, whereas, in the *Narrationes*, the love is inspired by Venus, who seeks revenge on Myrrha's mother because she had the temerity to be preferred to the goddess. Secondly, at the conclusion of the prose paraphrase, the ps.-Lactantian *Narrationes* specifically imputes to Venus the role of transforming Myrrha into the myrrh tree, whereas, in the Ovidian version, Myrrha's prayer to the gods to be transformed is tacitly answered.[13]

---

[10] For example, the tapestry woven by Arachne and Minerva is explained in terms of an opposition between "scientia artis" and "labor." I am indebted to Richard J. Tarrant for the observations made above. See his "The *Narrationes* of 'Lactantius' and the Transmission of Ovid's *Metamorphoses*," in *Formative Stages of Classical Traditions: Latin Texts from Antiquity to the Renaissance*, eds. Oronzo Pecere and Michael D. Reeve (Spoleto, 1995), pp. 83–115, esp. p. 94. For a detailed discussion of the manuscript affiliations see Brooks Otis, "The *Argumenta* of the so-called Lactantius," *Harvard Studies in Classical Philology* 47 (1936), 131–63. Hyginus, *Fabulae*, ed. P. K. Marshall (Leipzig, 1993), p. 61 [LVIII (Smyrna)] provides a prose summary with the same changes of detail as the ps.-Lactantian *Narrationes*.

[11] Tarrant, "The *Argumenta*," 94.

[12] Complete list of manuscripts in Coulson-Roy, no. 54.

[13] I quote from D. A. Slater, *Towards a Text of the Metamorphosis* (Oxford, 1927), ps.-Lactantian *Narrationes* 10.9 (unnumbered pages). The full text is reproduced in Appendix 1.I.

Little evidence survives for the circulation and interpretation of the *Metamorphoses* in the school tradition from late antiquity through the Carolingian and Ottonian periods, but the story of Myrrha was elucidated within the mythographic traditions, particularly in the mythographic treatises of Fulgentius (entitled the *Mitologiae*) and the First Vatican Mythographer.[14] Fulgentius gives the story a naturalistic interpretation in which Myrrha's love for her father is interpreted as the love of the myrrh tree for the sun, which represents the father and engenderer of all things. The birth of her son, Adonis, reflects the fact that the bark of the myrrh tree gives forth a sap that is sweet in odor. The etymological connection between *edun* (ἡδύς)—in Greek meaning pleasant to the taste—and *suauis* in Latin is deduced to account for this interpretation. Finally, Fulgentius notes that Adonis is said to have been loved by Venus, since the sap from the myrrh tree is commonly known to be an aphrodisiac, a fact that Fulgentius proves by quoting from the comic writer Sutrius the following line spoken by the prostitute Glyco: "Give me the drink made from myrrh, so I might boldly encounter those manly arms." In addition, poets of the Carolingian period, in particular Theodulf of Orléans (and passim), who lived from 760 to 821, allude to the importance of Ovid as a curricular author. Theodulf, for example, in his famous poem on the books he was accustomed to read, makes the following claim:

Et modo Pompeium, modo te, Donate, legebam
  Et modo Virgilium, te modo, Naso loquax.
In quorum dictis quamquam sint frivola multa,
  Plurima sub falso tegmine vera latent. (*Carm.* 45.17–20)

Often I read you Pompeius, and you, Donatus, sometimes Virgil, and you, talkative Ovid. Though much in their poetry is frivolous, often truth lies hidden beneath a covering.

This reference to a covering (*tegmen*)[15] that veils the true meaning of a literary work was to find its fullest flowering in the interpretations of

---

[14] The *Mitologiae* is edited in R. Helm, ed., *Fabii Planciadis Fulgentii V. C.: Opera* (Leipzig, 1898); and the First Vatican Mythographer in Péter Kulcsár, ed., *Mythographi Vaticani I et II* (Turnhout, 1987). The full Latin text for the story of Myrrha is provided in Appendix 1.II and 1.III.

[15] Later authors also use the terms *integumentum* and *volucrum*.

the *Metamorphoses* espoused by schoolmasters during the high Middle Ages.[16]

The history of Latin commentary on the *Metamorphoses* in its traditional sense[17] resurfaces in the 12th century. A series of manuscripts in the Bayerische Staatsbibliothek, the Universitätsbibliothek in Freiburg im Breisgau, and the Stiftsbibliothek St. Peter in Salzburg preserve *accessus* and commentaries on the *Metamorphoses* that represent the earliest true scholia yet uncovered.[18] The commentary found in Munich, Clm 4610 has been extensively studied by Karl Meiser in an article published in 1885.[19] Meiser tentatively linked this commentary with Manegold of Lautenbach, an important German humanist who lived 1035–ca. 1103.[20] These earliest commentators on the Myrrha story tend to be rather sparse in their comments on individual lines, in the main restricting their comments to questions of grammar and mythology. But a more detailed study of these earliest commentators, which still remains to be done, could unearth illuminating details. In the commentaries which I examined in preparation for this study, I noted a recurring interest in details of the structure of the poem (usually labeled by the commentator with the term *continuatio*) and in providing background to abstruse mythological allusions.

With the advent of the cathedral schools in the Loire valley, and particularly those at Chartres and Orléans in the later 12th century,[21]

---

[16] The best article on this concept is still Edouard Jeauneau, "L'usage de la notion d'*integumentum* à travers les gloses de Guillaume de Conches," *Archives d'histoire doctrinale et littéraire du Moyen-Âge* 32 (1957), 35–120.

[17] I use the term "commentary" or "scholia" to refer to exegetical material that provides a lemma (the words from the text to be commented upon) and comment upon that lemma in a continuous fashion. I use the more general term "school material" to refer to additional explanative and accretive materials, such as prose paraphrases, that accompanied the text.

[18] The relevant manuscripts are Munich, Bayerische Staatsbibliothek, Mss Clm 4610, 14482 and 14809; Salzburg, Stiftsbibliothek St. Peter, Ms a. V. 4; and Freiburg im Breisgau, Universitätsbibliothek, Ms 381.

[19] C. Meiser, "Über einen Commentar zu den *Metamorphosen* des Ovid," in *Sitzungsberichte der Königlichen bayerischen Akademie der Wissenschaften, philosophisch-philologisch- und historische Classe* (Munich, 1885), pp. 47–89.

[20] See also Michael Herren, "Manegold of Lautenbach's Scholia on the *Metamorphoses*—Are There More?," *Notes and Queries* N.S. 51 (2004), 218–22, and Claudia Villa, "Tra *Fabula e Historia*: Manegoldo di Lautenbach e il 'Maestro di Orazio'," *Aevum: Rassegna di scienze, storiche, linguistiche e filologiche* 70 (1996), 245–56.

[21] The literature on masters at these cathedral schools is vast. See, in particular, Paul Dutton, *The 'Glosae super Platonem' of Bernard of Chartres* (Toronto, 1991); Lodi Nauta, ed., *Guillelmi de Conchis Glosae super Boetium* (Turnhout, 1999); and William of Conches, *Glosae super Platonem*, ed. Edouard Jeauneau (Paris, 1965).

we find a flourishing of commentary material on Ovid's epic. Two commentators from this period may be singled out for particular commendation: first, the *Orléanais* commentator, Arnulf of Orléans, who worked at Orléans in the late 12th century and who is known to have written commentaries on many of the other poetic works in Ovid's corpus, specifically the *Fasti*[22] and the amatory works,[23] in addition to a commentary on Lucan's *Bellum civile*;[24] and secondly, the Orleanais commentator, William of Orleans, who wrote a commentary ca. 1200 on the entire poetic corpus of Ovid entitled the "*Versus bursarii*".[25]

Arnulf of Orléans composed both a series of allegories on the *Metamorphoses* and a separate philological commentary on the epic[26] (more on the philological commentary below, pp. 8–9). The allegories themselves are of some importance for the history of medieval interpretation of the *Metamorphoses*, since they usher in a form that was to have a long history, beginning with Arnulf, developed by Giovanni del Virgilio[27] and Pierre Bersuire[28] in the 14th century, and culminating in a series of allegorizations on the poem composed by northern European humanists in the sixteenth century.[29] Arnulf's *Allegorie* are transmitted widely throughout the thirteenth and fourteenth centuries, both in the margins of manuscripts of the *Metamorphoses* and separately, often combined with the poetic interpretation of John of Garland called the

[22] Now edited in Jörg Rudolf Ricker, ed., *Arnulfi Aurelianensis Glosule Ovidii Fastorum* (Florence, 2005).

[23] Arnulf's glosses to the *Remedia amoris* are edited in Bruno Roy and Hugues V. Shooner, "Arnulfi Aurelianensis *Glosule de Remediis amoris*," *Journal of Medieval Latin* 6 (1996), 135–96.

[24] For Arnulf's glosses on the *Bellum civile* see Berthe M. Marti, ed., *Arnulfi Aurelianensis Glosule super Lucanum* (Rome, 1958). The best general study of Arnulf is still Fausto Ghisaberti, "Arnolfo d'Orléans: un cultore di Ovidio nel secolo XII," *Memorie del Reale Istituto Lombardo di Scienze e lettere* 24 (1932), 157–234.

[25] William's commentary was first identified by Hugues V. Shooner, "Les *Bursarii Ovidianorum* de Guillaume d'Orléans," *Mediaeval Studies* 43 (1981), 405–24. The glosses are edited in Wilken Engelbrecht, *Filologie in de Dertiende eeuw: De Bursarii super Ovidios van Magister Willem van Orléans (fl. 1200 AD)*, 2 vols. (Olomouc, 2003). See further Ernst H. Alton and D. E. W. Wormell, "Ovid in the Mediaeval Schoolroom," *Hermathena* 94 (1960), 21–38 and 95 (1961), 67–82, and *Cambridge History of Literary Criticism*, vol. 2, p. 188.

[26] The allegorical interpretation is edited in Ghisalberti, "Arnolfo." Excerpts from Arnulf's philological commentary to the *Metamorphoses* are edited in Frank T. Coulson and Krzysztof Nawotka, "The Rediscovery of Arnulf of Orléans' Glosses to Ovid's Creation Myth," *Classica et Medievalia* 44 (1993), 267–99.

[27] For Giovanni del Virgilio, see below, footnote 51.

[28] For Pierre Bersuire, see below, footnote 44.

[29] For northern humanists of the Renaissance, see below, footnote 64.

Integumenta Ovidii.[30] The *Allegorie* interpret the stories historically, morally and allegorically.[31] Arnulf gives an explicitly natural interpretation to the Myrrha story, one which appears to be drawn largely from Fulgentius's *Mitologiae*. Myrrha is said to have loved her father and been turned into the myrrh tree, since the myrrh tree that grows in India is burnt by the heat of the sun, which is the father of all living things. Myrrha is said to have given birth to Adonis, since the tree drips sap from its bark. *Adon* in Greek means *suauis* in Latin. And as the juice that flows from the tree is naturally sweet, the tree's offspring is called Adonis.[32]

The *Integumenta Ovidii* of John of Garland,[33] written in the early thirteenth century, provides an alternative allegorical interpretation of the *Metamorphoses* in elegiac verse that has some similarities with the *Allegorie* of Arnulf of Orleans. John claims in his introduction that "the meaning of the poem will be unlocked by the little key of John. It unknots the secrets, it reveals hidden facts, it scatters the mist of obscurity, it sings of hidden truths".[34] Alas far from elucidating the poem, the singularly abstruse vocabulary employed by John serves to obfuscate its meaning. The story of Myrrha is here given an explicitly moral interpretation in an elegiac couplet that highlights the alliterative strain in John's poetic technique:

> Rem miram mirare novam Mirram per amorem
> In mirram verti quam dat amarus amor. (ll. 413–414)

> You marvel at a new wonder, Myrrha, turned into the myrrh tree through love, which bitter love produced.

In addition to this strongly developed allegorical interpretation on the *Metamorphoses* nascent in the late 12th century, there exists a second, more purely philological strain of interpretation represented by the commentaries of Arnulf of Orléans and William of Orléans. As was mentioned earlier, as a companion to his allegorical exposition, Arnulf

---

30 Complete list of manuscripts in Coulson-Roy, no. 257.

31 "Modo quasdam allegorice, quasdam moraliter exponamus, et quasdam historice." Ghisalberti, "Arnolfo," 201.

32 For the full Latin text, see below, Appendix 1.IV.

33 The *Integumenta Ovidii* is edited in Fausto Ghisalberti, *Integumenta Ovidii, poemetto inedito del secolo XIII* (Messina/Milan, 1933), and in Lester K. Born, "The *Integumenta* on the *Metamorphoses* of Ovid by John of Garland—First Edited with Introduction and Translation." Ph.D. diss., University of Chicago, 1929. Quotations from the *Integumenta Ovidii* in this article follow the edition of Ghisalberti.

34 "Morphosis Ovidii parva cum clave Iohannis/ Panditur et presens cartula servit ei./ Nodos secreti denodat, clausa revelat/ rarificat nebulas, integumenta canit." (ll. 5–9)

of Orléans wrote a more standard philological commentary on the *Metamorphoses*. I should like to point out, perhaps as an apologia for my own extensive manuscript research on the commentary tradition to this poem, that prior to my own work, Arnulf's philological commentary was known in a single manuscript in the Biblioteca nazionale Marciana in Venice (Marc. Lat. XIV.222 (4007)), a manuscript that had lost a folio containing Arnulf's glosses on Ovid's creation myth (*Met.* 1.1–150). Through much painstaking research in European and North American collections, I have been able to uncover 26 copies containing either complete or partial copies of Arnulf's philological commentary and/or *accessus*.[35] Arnulf's philological commentary contains no allegories[36] but rather provides synonyms or brief explanations for unusual words in the text; it also furnishes background on mythological material and deals with astronomy and geography. Arnulf's real interest, however, seems to lie in the grammar of the text and, when required, he can discourse at length on a given passage. All these interests are in evidence in Arnulf's explication of the story of Myrrha.[37] For example, the unusual adjective *Ismariis* (10.305) is explicated as a synonym for Thracian; the allusive reference to the Eumenides at 10.349 (*sorores crinitas*) is explained; and various ellipses are provided for the reader (such as at 10. 412 where the participle *instanti* is glossed with *anui*). Arnulf also pays particular attention to outlining the meaning of particular passages where the structure of the Ovidian sentence might not be properly understood by the reader, either because of antithesis or ellipsis. For example, at 10.318–19 Ovid employs a complex web of antithesis and repetition to warn Myrrha: Ex omnibus unum/elige, Myrrah, uirum, dum ne sit in omnibus unus—"Myrrha select a single man from all, provided that one may not be amongst them!" Arnulf comments thus: *dum ne sit unus* id est pater—"*provided that one man is not amongst them*, namely her father." Similarly, at 10.424 Ovid employs a delicious interjection to underline the horror of the nurse—sensit enim—"for then she truly understood"—and Arnulf observes: *sensit*

[35] See Coulson-Roy, no. 257.

[36] This aspect may in part be explained by the fact that in the earliest manuscript copies (Venice, Biblioteca nazionale Marciana, Ms Marc. Lat. XIV.222 (4007) and Munich, Bayerische Staatsbibliothek, Ms Clm 7205) the text of the philological commentary is transmitted in tandem with the *Allegorie*. See Coulson-Roy, no. 257.

[37] Quotations are taken from St. Omer, Bibliothèque de la ville, Ms 678, fols. 77r–79v.

enim eam amare Cinaram patrem suum.—"*then she realized* that Myrrha loved Cinyras, her father."

Our second philological commentary is the work of William of Orléans, who in the early 13th century wrote a commentary on the entire Ovidian corpus called the *Versus bursarii* (or *Bursarii ovidianorum*). William's commentary seems to be a relatively original work, since a perusal of extant glosses dating from the period prior to 1200 reveals no verbatim correspondences. William has, however, consulted previous scholarship on the poem as the *Versus bursarii* is replete with references to "secundum sententiam aliorum," "alii dicunt," and the ubiquitous "dicunt quidam." William's approach to explicating the poem contains no allegorizations, nor does he show much interest in literary matters. Rather he is a straightforward philologist, who is primarily concerned with construing the grammar, clarifying word meanings, showing students the connection between loose strands of the story line, providing etymologies for words, as well as furnishing mythological background. His commentary on the Myrrha story contains only a single long gloss to *Met.* 10.304., where Orpheus, in his introduction to the story proper, warns the audience not to believe the story, or if they give credence to it, to believe in the punishment that followed (10.301–303):

> [*Met.* 10.304] *Si tamen admissum sinit hoc natura videri*: Continua et construe: *tamen*, quamuis dixerim non credite facta, *tamen si natura sinit hoc admissum*, id est hoc peccatum, *videri*, ab aliquo et fieri. Vel aliter fiet continuacio et constructio: Credite, quod ille qui hoc fecit meruit puniri, et *tamen*, quamuis hoc dixerim, *si natura sinit hoc*, scilicet quod filia concubuit cum patre, *videri admissum*, id est delictum et offensio iuris, quasi dicat: Si natura reputat hoc peccatum quod non videtur esse peccatum secundum ipsam, immo secundum leges, si, inquam, hoc est, *gratulor* etc. [Berlin, Deutsche Staatsbibliothek-Preussischer Kulturbesitz, Ms Lat. Qu. 219, fol. 132r]

> *If however nature allows this to happen*: Make the connection and construe the grammar so: *yet*, although I said do not believe it, *yet if nature allows this*, namely this sin, *to be seen* and done by anyone. Or the connection and grammatical construction can be made so: Believe that he who has committed this deserved to be punished *and yet*, although I said this, *if nature allows this*, namely that a daughter sleep with her father, *to happen*, namely this sin and offense against the law, as though he were to say: if nature deems this sin not to be a sin in its eyes, but only according to man-made laws, if, I say, this is so, *I congratulate* etc.

Our last example of the Latin commentary tradition on the *Metamorphoses* from the Loire valley is that of the "Vulgate" commentary, written possibly at Orléans in the mid to later 13th century.[38] As early as 1920, Luigi Castiglioni signaled the importance of the "Vulgate" commentary for any proposed study of Ovid in the Middle Ages.[39] He wrote:

> Whoever should study attentively the exemplars of this commentary could write a page that would not be insignificant both for the medieval Latin culture of the West and for the diffusion of the text of the poem itself during this period.[40]

No single, unified method characterizes the approach of the "Vulgate" commentator. Rather he adopts a highly varied and eclectic approach to the text, dealing with the most rudimentary questions of grammar and syntax; more advanced problems related to mythography and science; and most interestingly, matters of more literary import. The "Vulgate" commentary was evidently intended as a teaching tool to explicate the text of the poem at its most basic level. So, for example, the interlinear gloss in the commentary provides synonyms or explanations for words in the text that posed problems for the medieval reader. Yet it is undoubtedly for its literary sensitivity revealed in the marginal commentary surrounding the text that the "Vulgate" commentary may claim a unique position among the hundreds of commentaries and random glosses transmitted in the margins of the manuscripts of the *Metamorphoses* during the 13th and 14th centuries. Herein the "Vulgate" commentator shows remarkable insights into Ovidian style, poetic technique, structure, characterization, and Ovidian influence on the poetry

---

38 For the Vulgate commentary, see, in particular, Frank T. Coulson, "MSS. of the *Vulgate* Commentary on Ovid's *Metamorphoses*: A Checklist," *Scriptorium* 39 (1985), 118–29; "MSS. of the *Vulgate* Commentary on Ovid's *Metamorphoses*: Addendum," *Scriptorium* 41 (1987), 263–64; and "The *Vulgate* Commentary on Ovid's *Metamorphoses*," *Mediaevalia: A Journal of Medieval Studies* 13 (1987), 29–62. Its *accessus* is edited in Frank T. Coulson, "Hitherto Unedited Medieval and Renaissance Lives of Ovid (I)," *Mediaeval Studies* 49 (1987), 152–207. No complete edition of the commentary has yet been undertaken, though portions of the commentary edited from Sélestat, Bibliothèque humaniste, Ms 92 are available in *The Vulgate Commentary on Ovid's Metamorphoses: The Creation Myth and the Story of Orpheus* (Toronto, 1991). Kathryn McKinley discusses aspects of the Myrrha story in her article "The Medieval Commentary Tradition 1100–1500 on Metamorphoses 10," *Viator* 27 (1996), 117–49.

39 Luigi Castiglioni, "Spogli riccardiani," *Bollettino di filologia classica* 27 (1920), 162–66.

40 "Chi volesse attentamente studiarne gli esemplari, potrebbe scrivere una pagina non insignificante sia per la coltura latina medievale nell'estremo occidente, sia per la propagazione del testo stesso del poema nei secoli sopra accennati." Luigi Castiglioni, "Spogli," 165.

of the 12th-century Renaissance, particularly Alan of Lille, Bernard Silvester, and Walter of Châtillon. Space prevents me from providing detailed examples of these traits, but I draw the reader's attention to my own studies of the "Vulgate" commentary and to those studies of Kathryn McKinley for more detailed analysis of the literary qualities of the "Vulgate".[41] The story of Myrrha in the "Vulgate" commentary is analyzed from a variety of perspectives, including the philological, the literary, and the allegorical. The "Vulgate" interprets the story in accordance with the earlier exposition of Fulgentius, in which a natural reading is given to the story.[42] In addition, however, the "Vulgate" commentator spends much time outlining how various narrative strands within the story fit together. Interestingly, he is vitally concerned with the way in which Ovid imparts narrative unity to his entire epic, labeling this concept *continuatio*. Lastly, as is his wont throughout the commentary, the "Vulgate" commentator stresses character portrayal and the manner in which features of Ovidian style and usage have influenced the poets of the twelfth century, particularly Walter of Châtillon's epic, the *Alexandreis*. To give two examples from the story of Myrrha where the "Vulgate" draws apposite comparisons: as the nurse is leading Myrrha to her father's bedroom, Ovid provides a description of the heavenly bodies: the moon flees the sky, black clouds cover the stars that are in hiding. The "Vulgate" aptly compares the description to Walter's description in Book 7 of the *Alexandreis*:

> [*Met.* 10.448–49] FUGIT AUREA CELO LUNA: simile habetis in *Alexandreide*:
>
> > Et tantum uisura nefas Latonia terris
> > uirgo morabatur roseos ostendere uultus. (*Alex.* 7.4–5) (Vatican City, Biblioteca Apostolica Vaticana, Ms Vat. lat. 1598, fol. 106v)
>
> *The Golden Moon flees from the sky*: Walter of Châtillon uses a similar description in his *Alexandreis*: The moon about to look upon such abomination hesitated to show its pale face to the earth.

A few lines later in the poem, Ovid stresses that the darkness of night lessens one's chastity. Our commentator explicates the line thus:

---

[41] Frank T. Coulson, "The *'Vulgate'* Commentary on Ovid's *Metamorphoses*," *Mediaevalia: A Journal of Medieval Studies* 13 (1987), 29–62, and Kathryn McKinley, *Reading the Ovidian Heroine: Metamorphoses Commentaries 1100–1618* (Leiden, 2001).

[42] See Appendix 1.V, below for full text.

[*Met.* 10.454] TENEBRE ET MINUUNT NOXQUE ATRA PUDOREM: De nocte siquidem nullus habetur pudor. Unde in *Alexandreide*:

> Distulit ergo nefas in ydonea tempora noctis
> Noctis quando solent patrari turpia, noctis quando
> impune placent que sunt dum luce pudenda. (*Alex.* 6.535–537)
> (Vatican City, Biblioteca Apostolica Vaticana, Ms Vat. lat. 1598, fol. 106v)

Shadows and dark night lessen her chastity: Night and chastity are not compatible. Thence we have in the *Alexandreis*:

> He put off the abomination till the dark of night,
> when evils are brought to completion, when it is pleasing
> to perform without punishment what would be shameful in daylight.

During the 14th century, Ovid's *Metamorphoses* became widely used among the clerical elite as a pre-eminent handbook from which to draw exemplars. In part, this function of the *Metamorphoses* has been explored by Beryl Smalley in her monograph, *English Friars and Antiquity in the Early Fourteenth Century*,[43] in which she studies how such authors as Thomas Waleys, John Ridewell and Robert Holcot drew upon Ovid for their inspiration. Perhaps the most celebrated of such interpretations is the allegorical *Ovidius moralizatus* written by Pierre Bersuire.[44] Bersuire composed at least two redactions of the work: the first was written at Avignon between 1337 and 1340, the second revised version, wherein Bersuire makes use of the vernacular *Ovide moralisé*,[45] was composed at Paris before 1362. In the introduction to the work proper, Bersuire alludes to the use made of myth in scripture and its use in poetry:

[43] Beryl Smalley, *English Friars and Antiquity in the Early Fourteenth Century* (Oxford, 1960). Smalley's work is now greatly supplemented by James Clark, *A Monastic Renaissance at St. Albans. Thomas of Walsingham and his Circle c. 1350–1440* (Oxford, 2004).

[44] For editions and bibliography on Bersuire, see Coulson-Roy, no. 2. I quote from the editions of the text by J. Engels, *Petrus Berchorius, Reductorium morale*, liber XV, cap. ii–xv, *"Ovidius moralizatus" naar de Parijse druk van 1509* (Utrecht, 1962), and his *Petrus Berchorius, Reductorium morale, Liber XV: Ovidius moralizatus; cap. i*: De formis figurisque deorum. *Textus e codice Brux., Bibl. Reg. 863–9 critice editus* (Utrecht, 1966). The best summary discussion of Bersuire's methodology is Ann Moss, *Ovid in Renaissance France* (London, 1982). For a stimulating discussion of the purpose behind the work, see Ralph Hexter, "The *Allegari* of Pierre Bersuire: Interpretation and the *Reductorium morale*," *Allegorica* 10 (1989), 51–84.

[45] For the *Ovide moralisé*, see C. de Boer, ed., *Ovid moralisé. Poème du commencement du 14ième siècle* (Amsterdam, 1915–38); J. Engels, *Études sur l'Ovide moralisé* (Groningen-Batavia, 1945); and Paule Demats, *Fabula: trois études de mythographie antique et médiévale* (Geneva, 1973), esp. chapter II.

> Sacra enim Scriptura hiis et similibus fabulis et fixionibus solet uti, ut exinde possit aliqua veritas extrahi vel concludi. Simili modo fecerunt poete qui in principio fabulas finxerunt, quia scilicet per huiusmodi figmenta semper aliquam veritatem intelligere voluerunt. (Fol. 1ra, *Prologus*, ll. 16–21)

> For sacred scripture is accustomed to use these and similar stories so that from them a certain truth may be extracted. The poets acted in like fashion, since through fictions of this type they wished a certain truth to be perceived.

Bersuire goes on to give an explicitly moral purpose to his work:

> Congruum michi visum est.... eciam ad moralizandum fabulas poetarum manum ponere, ut sic per ipsas hominum ficciones possim morum et fidei misteria confirmare. (Fol. 1ra–rb, *Prologus*, p. 2. ll. 1–5)

> So I thought it appropriate..to ply my hand at moralizing the stories of the poets so that through these fables I might strengthen the mysteries of the faith.

For Bersuire, there are four senses: 1) natural or physical; 2) historical or euhemeristic; 3) tropological, whereby Ovid's characters become personifications of good and evil; and 4) allegorical, by which is generally meant spiritual allegory, which refers to matters of faith and interprets fabulous persons and events as episodes in the life of Christ or in the spiritual life of the Christian soul.[46] Bersuire goes on in his introduction to mention that he will concentrate on the moral and allegorical senses of his fables, which are more germane to his exposition than the physical and historical senses:

> Verum quia de litterali fabularum intellectu iam plurimi tractaverunt, scilicet Fulgencius, Alexander, et Servius et alii nonnulli, quia eciam naturalis intellectus non est presentis propositi, ubi scilicet non agitur nisi de reductione morali....Hinc est quod in presenti opusculo quod huius mei voluminis particulam esse volo, non intendo nisi rarissime litteralem sensum fabularum tangere, sed solum circa exposicionem moralem et allegoricam laborare...(*Prologus*, fol. 1rb, p. 2, ll. 10–26)

> But because many authors, such as Fulgentius, Alexander and Servius, have already dealt with the literal sense of the fables, and because the literal sense is not relevant here, where our only subject is the extraction of moral meanings,...I propose only occasionally to touch on the literal sense of the fables and to concentrate solely on the moral sense and on allegorical exposition, which is the focus of my treatise.

---

[46] I adopt these classifications from Moss, *Ovid in Renaissance France*, p. 24.

It may also be important to remember that Bersuire conceived the *Ovidius moralizatus* as part of a larger work, the *Reductorium morale super totam bibliam*, which allegorizes spiritual scripture as well. That a single story might offer various interpretations that were logically inconsistent seemed not to bother Bersuire. The *Ovidius moralizatus* was perhaps the most widely disseminated of interpretations of the *Metamorphoses*, surviving wholly or partially in at least 85 manuscript copies;[47] and unlike many of the medieval commentaries that never made it into print, the *Ovidius moralizatus* was printed by Badius in France in 1509 under the name of Thomas Waleys and was reprinted in Paris in 1511, 1515, and 1521.[48] Further, excerpts from Bersuire's interpretation appeared in French in 1484 in the vernacular compilation usually entitled *la Bible des poètes*, a work that enjoyed a wide circulation.[49] In his exposition of the story of Myrrha, Bersuire first produces a prose paraphrase that serves to recapitulate the essential points. The interpretation that follows contains multifaceted levels of meaning. Bersuire provides four different allegories for the myth: one which is historical, two which are tropological, and a final one which is specifically spiritual in focus.[50] I reproduce here the final spiritual allegory for the myth of Myrrha:

> Vel dic quod ista filia est beata virgo quae de patre concepit et in myrram, id est amaritudinem, est mutata et in odoris fragantiam conuersa. Eccl. XXIIII. Quasi Myrra electa dedi suauitatem odoris. Ista igitur a patre suo filium concepit, id est Christum, et ipsum intra lignum et corticem, id est intra vterum castum et intactum sine corruptione continuit, et post ea eum non caro, <set> lignum existens, id est non carnalis set virgo permanens, peperit. Esa. VII Ecce virgo concipiet et pariet filium. Figuratur in virga Aaron quae sicca floruit Numeri XVII.
>
> (Engels, p. 154)

> Or say that this daughter is the Blessed Virgin who conceived by her father and was changed into the myrrh tree—that is bitterness and transformed into a good-smelling odor. Ecclesiasticus 24.20 "I yielded a sweet odor like the best myrrh". By her father she conceived a son—that is Christ—and kept him within wood and bark—that is to say within her chaste and intact womb which was without corruption—and afterwards

47 Fully catalogued in Coulson-Roy, *Incipitarium*, no. 2.

48 For the history of print editions of the *Ovidius moralizatus* in France, see Ann Moss, *Ovid in Renaissance France* (London, 1982).

49 Colard Mansion. *Cy commence Ovide de Salmonen son livre intitule Methamorphose* (Bruges, 1484), slightly revised and republished as *La Bible des poètes. Methamorphoze* (Paris, 1493).

50 For the full text, see Appendix 1.VII.

> bore him though she was not flesh but wood, that is not carnal but still a virgin. Isaias 7:14 "Behold a virgin will conceive and bear a son". She is figured in the rod of Aaron which flowered though it was dry.

Two other commentators, both Italian, form an important link between the medieval tradition of commentary on the *Metamorphoses* and its humanistic school tradition that begins with the edition of the commentary on the *Metamorphoses* composed by Raphael Regius and printed in Venice in 1493. These two commentators are Giovanni del Virgilio[51] and Sozomeno (or Zomino) of Pistoia.[52] About 1321/22, Giovanni del Virgilio, an intimate of the poetic circle of Dante,[53] composed at Bologna two interpretations of the *Metamorphoses*: the one, entitled the *Allegorie*, is a prosimetric, allegorical interpretation following in the earlier tradition of Arnulf of Orléans and John of Garland's *Integumenta Ovidii*, in which Giovanni first interprets the story allegorically in prose and then summarizes it in verse. The majority of the allegorical interpretations in Giovanni are ethical in nature, and the author himself explicitly alludes to this aim in his introduction.[54] Often Giovanni elaborates an earlier allegory found in Arnulf in a specifically Christian sense. So, while for Arnulf Athena's tapestry from Book Six symbolizes virtue and love of God and Arachne's tapestry symbolizes vice (*Allegorie*, 6.1), Giovanni refashions this into an explicit statement of Christian piety (*Allegorie*, 6.27). Likewise, characters from the *Metamorphoses* are often interpreted as the devil or god. In compiling his work, Giovanni was not only indebted to his predecessors Arnulf and John of Garland; he also drew upon a variety of classical sources in order to make comparative judgments concerning the validity of interpretations. Giovanni uses the Vatican Mythographers and Fulgentius, and he is sufficiently knowledgeable to cite Horace's view of Circe from *Epistles* 2.23–26 and to allude to Boethius's opinion that whoever lives in the manner of a beast is changed into one (both in the allegory to 14.7). Giovanni gives a purely literal interpretation to the Myrrha myth within his

---

[51] For Giovanni, see, in particular, Fausto Ghisalberti, "Giovanni del Virgilio, espositore delle *Metamorfosi*," *Giornale dantesco* 34 (1931), 1–110.

[52] The fullest treatment of this commentator is to be found in Lucia Cesarini Martinelli, "Sozomeno maestro e filologo," *Interpres* 11 (1991), 7–92.

[53] See in particular P. H. Wickstead and G. G. Gardner, *Dante and Giovanni del Virgilio* (Westminster, 1902), and Ettore Bolisani and Manara Valgimigli, eds., *La corrispondenza poetica di Dante Alighieri e Giovanni del Virgilio* (Florence, 1963).

[54] ...ideo unaqueque transmutatio in hoc libro descripta merito ad mores est penitus reducenda.—"Therefore each transformation enumerated in this book is rightly reduced to ethics." (*Allegorie, Praefatio*)

Allegorie (10.11). He says, "Verum fuit quod iacuit cum patre"—it is the truth that she lay with her father. Her transformation into the myrrh tree reflects her suicide from the branches of the tree. Adonis's birth from the bark indicates that a midwife found Myrrha while she was hanging and extracted the youth from her womb. All of this is neatly summarized in four elegiac verses:

> Mirra suum nomen plante suspensa reliquit
> Conscia decepto concubuisse patri.
> Cuius ab execta tractus puer extitit alvo
> Quem scit amorosum fertur amasse Venus. (10.11)

> Mirra hanged herself and gave her own name to the tree,
> guilty of having slept with her father who was unawares.
> Her son drawn from her cut womb survived
> whom Venus is said to have loved.

Giovanni also narrates Fulgentius's earlier allegorization (see above, p. 11) wherein the mythographer gave an explicitly natural interpretation to the story. Once again, the allegorization is summarized in four lines of elegiac verse:

> Plantarum pater est sol cuius texta calore
> Exudat succi mirra suave genus
> Nomen Adonis habens. Veneri quod fertur amatum
> Pigmentum venerem concitat illud enim. (10.11)

> The sun is the father of plants through whose warmth the myrrh tree produces a sweet type of sap bearing the name Adonis. And Adonis is said to be loved by Venus since this sap serves as an aphrodisiac.

Giovanni's second interpretation of the *Metamorphoses* is a most curious work indeed. Entitled the *Expositio*, it begins as a traditional commentary with lemma followed by comment, but at line 623 of book one the commentary switches its approach to one that might be termed a prose paraphrase of the *Metamorphoses*—a paraphrase noteworthy for its use of dramatic dialogue and which the late Judson Boyce Allen, in a conversation with me, viewed as a precursor to the Italian novella genre. Like most of the commentary material on the *Metamorphoses*, the *Expositio* is unedited, though Gelinda Huber-Rebenic of the University of Jena is at work on a critical edition.[55] The *Expositio* provides

---

[55] See her "Die Metamorphosen-Paraphrase des Giovanni del Virgilio," in *Gli Umanesimi medievali: Atti del II Congresso dell' "Internationales Mittellateinerkomitee" Firenze, Certosa del Galluzzo, 11–15 settembre 1993*, ed. Claudio Leonardi (Florence, 1993), pp. 215–29.

a simplified prose paraphrase of the Myrrha story. Yet in sections it does much more than this. For example, Ovid has the nurse intervene with Myrrha's father, Cinyras, in order to set up the assignation. Ovid provides few details about the interchange, except to inform the reader that Cinyras's wife is absent at a religious rite and that when asked by Cinyras about the girl's age, the Nurse replies "par est Myrrhae" (*Met.* 10.441)—oh just Myrrha's age. Giovanni's *Expositio* develops this scene with extended dialogue between the nurse and Cinyras:

> Set interim celebrabatur festum Cereris, in quo festo statutum erat quod quilibet deberet sibi cauere a tactu coniugali per nouem dies et noctes. Vnde omnes domine ibant ornate ad illud festum. Similiter vxor regis Cinare etiam iuerat illuc. Dum autem Cinaras mansisset sine coniuge quinque uel sex diebus, illa nutrix iuit ad eum et dixit "Quomodo potestis manere tot diebus sine muliere?" Dixit ille, "Ego multum agrau[au]or." Dixit nutrix, "Ego congnosco quandam virginem pulcerimam que multum diligit uos. Si uel<l>etis, ego facerem uos eam habere." Dixit Cinaras, "Quotenis est illa?" Dixit nutrix, "Ipsa est par Mire." Dixit Cinaras, "Duc eam ad me hac nocte." Dixit nutrix, "Factum est. Sed ego ducam sine lumine quia non uult cognosci." Iuit ergo ad Miram et dixit, "Gaude quia hodie explebitur uotum tuum." Tunc Mira cepit condolere in mente. Videns tantum scelus tamen gauisa est quantum ad <a>petitum sensitiuum. (Oxford, Bodleian Library, Ms Canon. Misc. 457, fol. 48v)

> The festival of the goddess Ceres was being observed, in which women were forbidden to have intercourse for nine days and nights. So all the women went to this celebration, including Cinyras's wife. On the seventh day, after Cinyras had been without wifely commiserations for five or six days, the nurse went to him and said, "How are you able to last for so long without intimacy?" He replied, "I am much vexed." To which the nurse replied, "I know a most beautiful girl, much enamoured of you, and if you wish, I shall bring her." To which Cinyras asked, "How old?"—Oh just Myrrha's age.—"Bring her to me"—"Yes I shall, but without a torch as she does not wish to be revealed." And so the nurse returned to Myrrha saying, "Rejoice for today your wish is fulfilled." Then was Myrrha much aggrieved in mind since she realized what a great crime she was committing and yet she rejoiced that her desire was being fulfilled.

Our last named commentator before the age of the printing press is the Italian humanist scholar Sozomeno of Pistoia,[56] better known

[56] Sozomeno's place within the tradition of scholia on classical authors is discussed in Martinelli, "Sozomeno". His *accessus* to the commentary on the *Metamorphoses* is edited in Frank T. Coulson, "Hitherto Unedited Medieval and Renaissance Lives of Ovid (I)," *Mediaeval Studies* 49 (1987), 152–207.

perhaps as a scribe, whose hand has been studied in the exemplary work of the late and much lamented paleographer Albinia C. de la Mare,[57] and as a writer of the historical work, the *Chronicon universale*.[58] Sozomeno, however, was also an ardent commentator of classical texts, glossing not only Ovid's *Metamorphoses* but also the *Tragedies* of Seneca (extant in Pistoia, Biblioteca Forteguerriana, Ms A.46), Juvenal's *Satires* (extant in Pistoia, Biblioteca Forteguerriana, Ms A.35), Persius (extant in London, British Library, Ms Harl. 3989), Horace (extant in London, British Library, Harl. Ms 6512), and the *Orationes* of Cicero (extant in Berlin, Deutsche Staatsbibliothek- Preussischer Kulturbesitz, Ms Diez B. Sant. 149). Sozomeno's commentary on Ovid reveals a certain interest in Platonic philosophy, particularly in its exposition of Ovid's creation myth at the beginning of the epic. And Sozomeno follows directly in the footsteps of his mythographic predecessors, most notably Fulgentius, providing the reader with alternative accounts drawn from Boccaccio's work, the *Genealogia deorum gentilium*, Macrobius, and Fulgentius for each myth developed by Ovid. In his exposition of the story of Myrrha, for example, Sozomeno is at pains to compare the account of the myth as found in Boccaccio, Fulgentius, and Macrobius's *Saturnalia.* Sozomeno, moreover, helps his reader through the intricacies of grammar in Myrrha's rhetorical set speeches, as well as detailing learned and unusual allusions.

The age of the printing press ushered in a new type of commentary, one that reflected the pedagogical concerns of Italian humanists and accorded more closely with the precepts of the Latin rhetorician Quintilian. The most important example of this newly conceived commentary is that of Raphael Regius, who composed his commentary on the *Metamorphoses* while teaching in Venice in 1492.[59] In his preface to the work, Regius expounds his reasons for reading the *Metamorphoses*: first, its comprehensive material provides the basis for a sound liberal education and will ensure a knowledge of geography, astrology, music, rhetoric and moral and natural philosophy:

> Non solum enim veteres historie que propter antiquitatem fabularum loco habentur ex vetustissimis autoribus collecte eleganter ab Ovidio

[57] Albinia C. de la Mare, *The Handwriting of Italian Humanists* (Oxford, 1973).

[58] The *Chronicon universale* is now edited in Guido Zaccagnini, ed., *Sozomeni pistoriensis presbyteri Chronicon universale* (Città del Castello, 1908).

[59] Regius's commentary is discussed by Ann Moss in her *Ovid in Renaissance France* (London, 1982), especially pp. 28–31.

> describuntur, set ita et geographie et astrologie et musice et artis oratorie et moralis naturalisque philosophie ratio exprimitur vt cui Ouidii Metamorphosis bene percepta sit, facillimum ad omnes disciplinas aditum habiturus neque difficultatis quicquam in vllo fere poeticorum operum inuenturus esse videatur. (Regius, *Praefatio*)
>
> For not only does Ovid elegantly transcribe records of distant history, which had been collected from very ancient authors and were regarded as fables because of their antiquity, but the disciplines of geography, astrology, music, oratory, and moral and natural philosophy are expounded in such a way that anyone who has a good understanding of Ovid's *Metamorphoses* is promised easy access to all branches of learning and is unlikely to find any difficulty in reading almost any work of poetry.

Regius procedes through a list of 25 poets including many Greek references.

Secondly, the *Metamorphoses* allows the student to develop a polished Latin style; and finally the *Metamorphoses* is to be commended for the moral virtues it inculcates.

> Iam ciuiliter viuendi rationes vnde facilius sumamus autorem inuenies neminem. Ex eis enim qui statim in operis initio de mundi origine, gigantum aduersus deos temeritate, aliorumque impietate narrantur, aperte colligimus deum mundi ipsius opificem fabricatoremque fuisse ac eum in primis colendum atque venerandum. (Regius, *Praefatio*)
>
> Moreover, you will find no author from whom we may more easily learn how to conduct our lives as citizens. For from those fables at the beginning of the work about creation, the Giants' rash boldness against the gods, and other examples of impiety, we are clearly led to conclude that God was the creator and maker of the world and that He must be revered and worshipped above all else.

The commentator's role then is vital in translating abstruse and elliptical allusions found in the epic into prosaic factual information. Regius's annotations do this, with paraphrases and explanations of proper names and references to ancient geography, history, and philosophical theories drawn from a wide selection of classical and post classical authors.[60] One other unique feature of Regius's commentary is its intense interest in matters of more literary import.[61] And finally Regius comments extensively on the various literary devices Ovid employs. Interestingly

---

[60] A felicitous summary of Regius's methodology which I have paraphrased from Ann Moss, *Ovid in Renaissance France*, p. 29.

[61] A point made by McKinley, *Reading the Ovidian Heroine*, p. 144.

enough, though Regius in his introduction purports to deal with questions of a textual nature, deriding the inadequacies of medieval commentators, there is in the commentary proper little or no comment on textual readings. Indeed of all the commentaries I have read, the only one from the late fifteenth century that takes an interest in the text of the *Metamorphoses* is that of Jacobus a Cruce, whose comments have been preserved in the 1518 edition of the *Metamorphoses* printed at Lyon[62] and whose acerbic wit and vitriol can rival that of Housman or a J. B. Hall. Regius's glosses on the Myrrha story first and foremost outline unusual words and allusions for the reader, often with reference to such encyclopedists as Pliny the Elder. In addition, Regius is particularly concerned, as was the earlier Vulgate commentary, with underlining the subtleties of the character portrayal of Myrrha and the rhetorical embellishments that Ovid uses to heighten that portrayal. Ovid describes Myrrha's feelings before she attempts to commit suicide with a rhetorical tour de force:

> at uirgo Cinyreia peruigil igne
> carpitur indomito furiosaque uota retractat.
> Et modo desperat, modo uult temptare, pudetque
> et cupit et quid agat non inuenit. (*Met.* 10.369–372)
>
> But the daughter of Cinyras lay awake consumed by a passion she could not subdue. She reflects again and again on her mad wish, now despairing, now wanting to try, now feeling shame, now desiring but not knowing what to do.

Regius succinctly comments:

> Eleganter autem ut omnia poeta exprimit puelle amore ardentis cogitationes atque affectus. (fol. 135v)
>
> The poet in his usual manner elegantly expresses the thoughts and reflections of a girl captured by love.

A few lines later, Myrrha, while slipping the noose around her neck, intones: "Care, uale, Cinyra" (dearest Cinyras, farewell) [*Met.* 10.380]. Herein, Regius astutely points out that the name of *pater*—father—is eschewed as one that prohibits sexual union:

[62] See *Metamorphoseos: Lyon, 1518* (New York, 1976) (reprint of the 1518 edition published by J. Huguetan, Lyon). The comments of Jacobus are indicated by the heading Jacobus Bononiensis in the margin. For Jacobus's biography and a bibliography of studies relevant to this commentator, see *Catalogus translationum et commentariorum*, ed. Virginia Brown, 8, pp. 249–50.

> *Chare vale Cinyra*: amatorie Myrrha Cinyram nomine proprio appellat. Patris enim nomen proprio odio habebat vt quod sibi esse impedimento putabat ne optato concubitu potiretur. (Fols. 135v–136r)
>
> *Farewell, dear Cinyras*: In love Myrrha address Cinyras by his proper name. For she holds in hatred the name of father as one which stands in the way of her desired union.

During the sixteenth century, Regius's commentary became the Renaissance equivalent of a best seller in Italy and in France. Indeed, Regius himself claims, one suspects perhaps hyperbolically, that 50,000 copies of the work are in print.[63]

The commentary tradition on the *Metamorphoses* that flourished from 1500–1600 in northern Europe has already been extensively treated by Ann Moss in her stimulating and unrivalled survey of Ovid in Renaissance Europe.[64] Moss's work reveals several tendencies that link Renaissance commentators with their medieval predecessors. In particular, she underlines their fondness for allegorizing the various stories in a spiritual sense, and for providing mnemonic verse summaries for each of the myths. There remains, however, one important late figure in our survey of commentators on the *Metamorphoses*—that of Hercules Ciofanus, a hometown boy, so to speak, who like Ovid was a native of the hill town of Sulmona situated in the Appenines about 90 miles east of Rome. Ciofanus published his *Observationes* on the entire Ovidian corpus in Venice in 1575, and they represent one of the most sophisticated analyses of the poem from the later sixteenth century.[65] Our commentator draws from an extensive array of Greek and Latin literature for information and examples of linguistic usage

---

[63] Venice, 1513 edition, Ioannes Tacuinus de Tridino. In a new dedicatory letter to Philippus Cyulanus, maior, Regius writes: "Nam Ovidii Metamorphosis, praeclarum in primis opus, postquam enarrationibus nostris fuit illustrata, sic ubicunque Romana est in usu lingua, lectitatur, ut in quinquaginta milia exemplarium et amplius iam dicantur fuisse descripta…" "For that renowned work of Ovid, the *Metamorphoses*, after it was equipped with our commentary is read wheresoever Latin is spoken, so that 50,000 or more exemplars are said to have been printed…"

[64] Ann Moss, *Latin Commentaries on Ovid from the Renaissance* (Signal Mountain, 1998). Moss treats in particular the northern European humanists Jacobus Micyllus, Johannes Sprengius, and Georgius Sabinus.

[65] Ciofanus's commentary is discussed in Giuseppe Papponetti, "Per la biografia di Hercole Ciofano," *Misura* 4 n.s. 2 (1982–1985), 13–26, and his "Geminazioni della memoria: l'*Ovidio* di Hercole Ciofano," in *Ovidio, poeta della memoria: Atti del Convegno internazionale di studi: Sulmona, 19–21 ottobre 1989*, ed. G. Papponetti (Rome, 1991), pp. 143–79. I quote from *Herculis Ciofani Svlmonensis in omnia P. Ovidii Nasonis opera obseruationes. Vna cum ipsius Ovidii vita et descriptione Sulmonis* (Antwerp, 1581–1583).

in order to suggest emendations to the text. In his introduction to the work, Ciofanus is at pains to stress that he has given due credit to any emendations made by earlier scholars, and that many of his proposed emendations have been made on the basis of manuscript authority. While Ciofanus is particularly interested in providing variant readings for the reader and in discussing textual *cruces*, he nonetheless also furnishes many literary parallels, frequently selected from Greek as well as Latin authors, to illustrate dramatic situations in the *Metamorphoses* or to authenticate readings in the text. I provide two such examples drawn from the Myrrha story.

Ovid concludes his story of Myrrha with her transformation into the myrrh tree and the subsequent birth of Adonis. At *Met.* 10.501–502, Ovid writes:

> Est honor et lacrimis, stillataque robore murra
> nomen erile tenet nulloque tacebitur aeuo.
>
> Her tears are not without honor, for that distillation still keeps her name,
> no age will forget her

Our commentator Ciofanus aptly compares these lines to *Ars* 1.285 where similar sentiments are expressed:

> *Met.* 10.501 EST *honor et lacrimis: stillataque cortice Myrrha Nomen herile tenet*] De Myrrha sic ipse alibi:
>
> Myrrha patrem, sed non ut filia debet, amauit:
> Et nunc obducto cortice pressa latet.
> Illius lacrimis, quas arbore fundit odora,
> Vnguimur, et dominae nomina gutta tenet. [*Ars* 1.285–88] (*Observ. In Met.*, Antwerp, 1583, p. 201.)
>
> Honor remains for those tears and the myrrh distilled in the bark retains the name of her mistress

Ovid speaks similarly about Myrrha elsewhere:

> Myrrha loves her father, but not as a daughter should.
> And now she lies beneath the bark that covers her;
> we are annointed with these tears poured forth from that fragrant tree,
> and the drops keep the name of the mistress.

Likewise, at 10.512 Ciofanus decides between two variant readings by drawing a comparison with a similar reading at line 67 of the pseudo-Ovidian *Nux*. The relevant line at *Met.* 10.512 reads: "the tree cracked open and the bark split". Two readings in the Latin text are possible: either *scisso cortice* or *fisso cortice*. Ciofanus opines:

[*Met.* 10.512–13] ARBOR *agit rimas et scisso cortice viuum reddit onus*] Superius dixi, tum ex veteribus libris, tum auctoritate versus, qui est in elegia *De Nuce*:

> At cum maturas fisso noua cortice rimas
> Nux agit. (*Nux* 67–68)

Legendum esse, *Et fisso cortice.* (Ciofanus, *Observ. In Met.*, p. 201)

> The tree cracked open and the bark was split and gave birth to a living child.

Above I stated that here must be read *fisso*, both on the authority of ancient manuscripts and on the authority of that verse from the *Nux* [67] that reads: "and when the covering of the new nut cracks and splits showing that it is ripe."

* * *

Our survey, then, of the medieval and renaissance school tradition on the story of Myrrha from Book Ten of the *Metamorphoses* has ranged chronologically from the German schools of the 11th century, through the cathedral schools of the Loire valley in the 12th and 13th centuries, to the Italian and northern European humanists of the later 14th and 15th centuries. We have identified four important strands of commentary: the purely philological, which was interested in elucidating the literal meaning of the text of the poem for its readers; the prose paraphrase, which in the case of the Italian humanist, Giovanni del Virgilio, became a virtual recasting of the narrative of the poem itself; the literary, best exemplified by that commentary known as the "Vulgate" which demonstrates an intense and relatively sophisticated interest in elucidating character portrayal, Ovidian influence, and narrative structure in the poem. And finally, the allegorical tradition on Ovid's epic, inititiated by Arnulf of Orleans in the 12th century, enriched by Bersuire in the 14th century, and still very much a force in the interpretation of the poem in the later 16th century.

Latin text of selected mythographers and commentators treated in the article

I. ps.-Lactantian *Narrationes* (10.9) 4th century
Myrrha, Cinyrae et Cenchreidis filia, iracundia Veneris, quod mater eius praeferretur deae, patrem impio more dilexit: nec viam potiendi inveniens cogitur suspendium experiri. Cuius nutrix intra cubile gementis excepit vocem: et signis cognitis nefariae mortis, dum diligentius

scrutatur, causam poscit. Consolata ergo puellam in praesentia ei pollicetur, se effecturam, ut parenti sine ulla infamia iungatur: +cuius illa orationem in promissum tempus differt.+ At anus die sollemni Cereris, quo mater eius operata a viro secubabat, alumnam noctu deducit ad Cinyram, praedicans forma eius impulsam sibi se concredidisse: qui sedata cupiditate lumen inferri iussit, ut speciem eius notam haberet, cognitusque filiae pater stuprator coactus est pudore ferro stricto eam insequi. Quae duplici metu territa in silvam profugit ibique misericordia eiusdem deae in arborem, quae eius nomen indicaret, mutata est.

II. Fulgentius, *Mitologiae* (3.8) 5th–6th century
Mirra patrem suum amasse dicitur, cum quo debriato concubuit; cumque eam pater utero plenam rescisset, crimine cognito euaginato eam coepit persequi gladio. Illa in arborem myrram conuersa est; quam arborem pater gladio percutiens, Adon exinde natus est. Quid uero sibi haec fabula sentiat edicamus. Mirra genus est arboris, de qua sucus ipse exsudat; haec patrem amasse dicitur. Istae enim arbores in India sunt, quae solis caloribus crementantur, et quia patrem omnium rerum solem esse dicebant, cuius opitulatu cuncta germinum adolescit maturitas, ideo et patrem amasse dicitur; dumque iam grandioris fuerit roboris, solis ardoribus crepans ragades efficit, per quas sucum desudat—quod mirra dicitur—et redolentibus lacrimosa guttulis fletus suaues scissuris hiantibus iaculatur. Unde et Adonem genuisse fertur; adon enim Grece suauitas dicitur; et quia haec species odore suauis est, Adonem dicitur genuisse. Ideo autem Venerem eum amasse dicunt, quod hoc genus pigmenti sit ualde feruidum; unde et Petronius Arbiter ad libidinis concitamentum mirrinum se poculum bibisse refert; nam et Sutrius comediarum scriptor introducit Gliconem meretricem dicentem "Murrinum mihi adfers quo uirilibus armis occursem fortiuscula."

III. Vatican Mythographer I (1.197) Merovingian period
Myrra patrem suum amasse dicitur cum quo inebriato concubuit. Cumque eam pater utero plenam rescisset, crimine cognito eam euaginato gladio cepit persequi. Illa in arborem mirram uersa est, quam arborem pater gladio percutiens Adon exinde natus est, quem Adonidem Venerem amasse dicunt. Ideo hoc fingitur quod mirra, uidelicet arbor generet adonem, quod Grece suauitas dicitur, quia mirre gumma suauis est odore. Vnde et a Venere amatur, quia huiusmodi pigmenti sit ualde feruidum.

IV. Arnulf of Orléans, *Allegorie* 10.10–11 (ca. 1180)

Mirra patrem suum amavit cum quo inebriato concubuit. Cumque pater eam utero plenam fecisset, crimine cognito, evaginato cepit persequi gladio. Illa in arborem mirram mutata est, qua arbore gladio percussa, Adon exinde natus est. Quod de hac fabula sentiat videamus. Mirra est genus arboris de qua succus exudat. Hec patrem amasse dicitur quia huiusmodi arbor est in India et solis ardore crematur et quia solem patrem omnium rerum esse asserit cuius opitulatu cuncta germinum adolescit maturitas, ideo patrem amasse dicitur. Que cum grandioris fuerit roboris solis ardoribus crepans, ragades id est fixuras facit per quas succus desudat qui mirra dicitur, et redolentibus lacrimosa rivulis vel guttulis fletus suaues scissuris hiantibus iaculatur, unde et Adonim genuisse dicitur. Adon enim grece suavitas dicitur et hec species suavis esse dicitur, inde Adonem genuisse dicitur. Hunc autem Venerem amasse dicunt quia hoc genus pigmenti sit valde fervidum, unde et Petronius Arbiter ad libidinis incitamentum mirrinum se bibisse poculum refert. Nam et Sutrius commediarum scriptor introducit Gliconem meretricem dicentem: mirrinum affers quo virilibus armis occursem fortiuscula. Hic etiam Adonis venatione[66] extinctus postea in florem est mutatus, omnis siquidem amoris dulcedo aut labore venationis aut alterius officii extinguitur unde in Ovidio: otia si tollas periere cupidinis arcus. Extincta igitur veneris dulcedine pre labore, mutatur in florem sui nominis id est qui adonim, quia dulcius foret amor caritativus quam amor venereus.

V. "Vulgate" Commentary (ca. 1250)

Quid sentiat hec mutatio uideamus. Mirra est genus arboris de qua succus exundat. Hec patrem amasse dicitur quia huiusmodi arbor est in India que solis ardore crematur quem patrem omnium rerum asserunt, cuius opitulatu omnium germinum procedit maturitas. Vnde patrem amasse dicitur. Cum autem hec arbor grandioris sit roboris, solis ardoribus crepans, quasdam facit rugales, id est fixuras, per quas succus desudat. Igitur mirra dicitur et est mire fragrancie et sic ad naturam spectat hec mutatio. (Leiden, Bibliotheek der Rijksuniversiteit, B.P.L. 95, fol. 98r)

[66] Ghisalberti, "Arnolfo," p. 223 prints: "Hoc etiam Adonis venans" which I emend.

VI. Giovanni del Virgilio, *Allegorie* 10.11 (1322–23)
Undecima est de Mirra conversa in arborem sui nominis. Verum fuit quod Mirra iacuit cum patre per modum in fabula contentum. Quod dum pater scivisset, voluit filiam interficere sed illa abiit. Et cum iam tempus partus adesset suspendit se ad arborem que vocata est mirra. Sed dum esset suspensa, quedam mulier vidit quod erat pregnans et omnia scindit per medium et filium extraxit qui vocatus fuit Adonis. Unde dictum est:

Mirra suum nomen plante suspensa reliquit
   Conscia decepto concubuisse patri.
Cuius ab execta tractus puer extitit alvo
   Quem scit amorosum fertur amasse Venus.

Set Fulgentius allegorizat eam naturaliter dicens quod Mirra est quedam arbor in Arabia cuius pater est sol. Nam sol generat omnia. Dicit enim philosophus: homo hominem generat et sol. Multo ergo fortius generat plantas. Et dicitur precipue Mirra filia solis quia ex beneficio solis magis nascitur in una parte quam in alia. Et dicitur iacere cum patre, quia sol in vere gravidat eam quodam succo, demum in estate desiccat sic eam quod scinditur cortex et stilat quoddam gumi, quod vocatur adonis. Adon enim grece, suavitas latine. Sed domina Venus capitur amore eius, quia ex isto adone quod dicitur latine mirra fit quedam confectio que incitat ad Venerem. Et introducit Fulgentius Petronium expertum fuisse qui quondam scripsit super hoc libro. Unde dictum est:

Plantarum pater est sol cuius texta calore
   Exudat succi mirra suave genus
Nomen Adonis habens. Veneri quod fertur amatum
   Pigmentum venerem concitat illud enim.

VII. Pierre Bersuire, *Ovidius moralizatus* (ca. 1360) [J. Engels, *Ovidius moralizatus*, pp. 152–154]
Cinaras fuit quidem rex magnus et potens qui filiam habuit mirrham virginem admodum speciosam. Ista igitur insano amore patrem diligens, sed de concubitu desperans secum flendo pulcherrime disputabat, et nunc pro se nunc contra se allegabat et prohibitionem paterni concubitus in naturae et deorum inuidiam retorquebat. Cum igitur prae desperatione se suspendere vellet, nutrix eius causam doloris cognoscens, apponere remedium ei promisit. Regina igitur quadam die absente nutrix patrem de tradendo ipsi quandam iuuenculam alloquitur. Ipsam tamen nullo modo velle videri attestatur. Et sic fit quod patre ignorante

patri pluries myrrha supponitur et impraegnatur ab eo. Rex tamen lapsu temporis cognoscens filiam prae facti turpitudine ne fit infamis, et euiginato gladio filiam persequitur fugientem. Mirrha igitur proprium crimen abhorrens deos vt ipsam mutent in arborem interpellat ne si forte in mundo remaneat, vivos violet vel si moriens ad inferos descendat mortuos violet siue corrumpat. Et ecce vota suos habuere deos. Nam ipsa praegnans in arborem sui nominis mutatur quae prae doloris amaritudine adhuc lachrymas amarissimas fundit. Ouidius: Sanguis it in succos, in magnos brachia ramos, in paruos digiti. Duratur cortice pellis. Quae quamquam amisit veteres cum corpore sensus, flet tamen et tepidae manant ex arbore guttae. Puer vero genitus intra ipsum lignum sub cortice perficitur, et tandem completo tempore ab arbore nascitur qui puer adonis nuncupatur.

Dic si vis quod iste rex significat Christum, vel praelatum, cuius vxor immediate coniuncta significat quemlibet ecclesiasticum virum. Mala vero et impudens filia significat ambitiosum. Igitur dico quod plaerumque accidit quod aliqua mala filia, id est aliqua persona ambitiosa, cupit patri suo Christo in aliquo beneficio ecclesiastico coniugari, et ad eius connubium exaltari, quae quamuis imperfectione meritorum suorum et contra dictamen rationis hoc posse vel debere fieri desperat. Solet tamen quando videt quod mater sua est absens, id est quando praelatus est mortuus et vacat aliqua sedes, statim se occulte supponere et in lectum patris, id est in ecclesiam Christi se ingerere, et per auxilium nutricis, id est per adiutorium alicuius mali fautoris, prece vel precio subintrare. Sed talis a patre Christo eiicitur et tribulationibus et infortuniis fatigatur, et in myrrham amarissimam mutari dicitur pro eo quod finaliter qui sic intrat eccelesiam solet in amaritudinem terminari et in arborem, id est in infernum, transformari, ita quod talis potest finaliter dicere: vocate me mara, id est amaram, quia amaritudine valde me repleuit omnipotens. Rut. I. Vel dic quod ista filia significat animam peccatricem quae Cinarae, id est diaboli, dicitur esse nata quia ista a patre suo diabolo cum quo est fornicata et male delectata et vitiis impregnata fuit finaliter ab ipso persequitur et morti et inferni tribulationibus exponitur. Et sic fit quod in myrrham, id est in amaritudinem, vertitur inquantum in inferno damnatur et mortua existens parturit inquantum errores et vitia ad alios mittit post mortem per mala exampla et documenta quae dimisit. Tunc enim puer de matre mortua in arborem conuersa extrahitur quando peccatum ex mortui dictis et exemplis concipitur et per imitationem ad alios fertur. Vel dic quod quando deus pater persequitur malam filiam, id est animam peccatricem, solet plerumque in myrram mutari, id est per poenam in amaritudinem conuerti . Ista igitur sic mutata et iam tribulationibus arbor effecta medicinalis solet filium pulchrum, id est opus bonum, sub cortice humilitatis parere et liquorem medicinalem, qui myrra dicitur, fundere, id est bonam doctrinam vel elemosinam propinare. Canti. V Manus meae distillauerunt myrram et digiti mei pleni myrra probatissima. Vel dic quod ista filia est beata virgo quae de patre concepit et in myrram, id est amaritudinem, est mutata et in odoris fragantiam conuersa. Ecclesiastici XXIIII. Quasi myrra electa dedi suauitatem odoris. Ista igitur a patre suo filium concepit, id est Christum, et ipsum intra lignum et corticem, id est intra vterum castum et intactum sine corruptione continuit et post ea eum non caro sed lignum existens, id est non carnalis sed virgo permanens, peperit. Esa. VII Ecce virgo concipiet et pariet filium. Figuratur in virga Aaron quae sicca floruit. Numeri XVII.

AMBROSE OF MILAN ON CHASTITY

Marcia L. Colish

Ambrose of Milan is frequently depicted as an advocate of asceticism, basing his exhortations to flee physical pleasures on a dualistic, Platonic conception of human nature.[1] Some scholars have applied this

---

[1] The leading advocate of this position is Pierre Courcelle, "Plotin et saint Ambroise," *Revue de philologie, de littérature, et d'histoire anciennes* 76 (1950), 29–56; idem, "Nouvelle aspects de platonisme chez saint Ambroise," *Revue des études latines* 34 (1956), 220–39; idem, "L'humanisme chrétien de saint Ambroise," *Orpheus* 9 (1962), 21–34; idem, "Anti-Christian Arguments and Christian Platonism," in *The Conflict between Paganism and Christianity in the Fourth Century*, ed. Arnaldo Momigliano (Oxford, 1963), pp. 165–66; idem, *Recherches sur les Confessions de S. Augustin*, 2nd ed. (Paris, 1968), pp. 106–17, 122, 124–38; idem, *Late Latin Writers and Their Greek Sources*, trans. Harry E. Wedek (Cambridge, Mass., 1969), pp. 137–38; idem, "Ambroise de Milan, 'professeur de philosophie'," *Revue de l'histoire de philosophie* 181 (1972), 147–55; idem, *Recherches sur saint Ambroise: "Vies" anciennes, culture, iconographie* (Paris, 1973), p. 16; idem, *Connais-toi toi-même de Socrate à saint Bernard*, 2 vols. (Paris, 1974), 1:122–23, 125; idem, "Saint Ambroise devant le précepte delphique," in *Forma futuri: Studi in onore del cardinale Michele Pellegrino* (Turin, 1975), pp. 185–86. See also Raymond Thamin, *Saint Ambroise et la morale chrétienne au IVe siècle: Étude comparée des traités 'Des devoirs' de Cicéron et de saint Ambroise* (Paris, 1895), p. 324; W. Willbrand, "Ambrosius und Plato," *Römische Quartalschrift* 25 (1911), *42–*49; Lorenzo Taormina, "Sant'Ambrogio e Plotino," in idem, *Miscellanea di studi di letteratura cristiana antica* (Catania, 1954), pp. 41–85; Pierre Hadot, "Platon et Plotin dans trois sermons de saint Ambroise," *Revue des études latines* 34 (1956), 203–20; Aimé Solignac, "Nouvelles parallèles entre saint Ambroise et Plotin (Le *De Jacob et vita beata* et le Περὶ εὐδαιμονίας, (Ennéade I, IV)," *Archives de philosophie*, n.s. 19 (1956), 148–56; Wolfgang Seibel, *Fleisch und Geist beim heiligen Ambrosius* (Munich, 1958), pp. 15–50, 97–99, 119–22, 129–45, 194–97; Heinrich Dörrie, "Das fünffach gestufte Mysterium: Der Aufstieg der Seele bei Porphyrios und Ambrosius," in *Mullus: Festschrift Theodor Klauser*, eds. Alfred Stuiber and Alfred Herman (Münster, 1965), pp. 83–92; Ernst Dassmann, *Die Frömmigkeit des Kirchenvaters Ambrosius von Mailand: Quellen und Entfaltung* (Münster, 1965), p. 17; Helen North, *Sophrosyne: Self-Knowledge and Self-Restraint in Greek Literature*, Cornell Studies in Classical Philology 35 (Ithaca, N.Y., 1966), pp. 312–23, 328–60; André Loiselle, "'Nature' de l'homme et histoire de salut: Étude sur l'anthropologie d'Ambroise de Milan," Ph.D. diss., Université de Lyon, 1970, pp. 1–4, 12, 24–25, 31, 35–39, 44–46, 48–49, 77–78, 90, 117–20, 127, 143, 168; Peter Brown, *The Body and Society: Men, Women, and Sexual Renunciation in Early Christianity* (New York, 1988), pp. 348–49; Robert A. Markus, *The End of Ancient Christianity* (Cambridge, U.K. 1990), pp. 34–38, 49; Elizabeth A. Clark, *Reading Renunciation: Asceticism and Scripture in Early Christianity* (Princeton, 1999), p. 89; John Moorhead, *Ambrose: Church and Society in the Late Roman World* (London, 1999), pp. 56–59, 172–73; Ilario Tolomio, "'Corpus carcer' nell'Alto Medioevo: Metamorfosi di un concetto," in *Anima e corpo nella cultura medievale*, Atti del V convegno di studi della Società italiana per lo studio del pensiero medievale, Venezia, 25–28 settembre 1995, eds. Carla Casagrande and Silvana Vecchio

interpretation even more stringently to the works Ambrose dedicated to Christians with celibate vocations.[2] This paper seeks to challenge that position. While Ambrose certainly cites Platonic motifs in his anthropology and ethics, he appropriates them in the light of non-Platonic philosophy and Christian thought. The anthropology he actually develops is hylomorphic, not dualistic. His ethics, including ethics for the celibate, is one of moderation, not extremism. After describing Ambrose's anthropology as found in his *Hexaemeron, De paradiso*, and treatises on the four Old Testament patriarchs, we will consider his views on chastity for three of the groups of Christians to whom he writes: married couples, widows, and consecrated virgins.

Ambrose gives his broadest treatment of anthropology in his account of creation and life in Eden in his *Hexaemeron* and *De paradiso*. In both works he stresses, against Manichees, Gnostics, and Origenists, that the primal parents God created and placed in Eden possessed gendered bodies as well as souls. These attributes, and a sexual mode of reproduction, were not consequences of the Fall.[3] Ambrose shares the consensus view that human souls are made in the image and likeness of God, a condition which, in his view, applies equally to men and

(Florence, 1999), pp. 5–6, 10–11, 13. Although Carole Hill, "Classical and Christian Tradition in Some Works of Saint Ambrose of Milan," Ph.D. diss., Oxford University, 1980, pp. 150–76, generally portrays Ambrose as a Stoic, she sees him teaching a Platonic body-soul dualism.

[2] See, in particular, Franco Gori, introduction to his translation of Ambrose, *Verginità e vedovanza*, ed. Ignatius Cazzaniga, Sancti Ambrosii episcopi mediolanensis opera [hereafter SAEMO] 14/1–2 (Milan, 1989), 1:74, 76–78, 91; Jan N. Bremmer, "Pauper or Patroness: The Widow in the Early Christian Church," in *Between Poverty and the Pyre: Moments in the History of Widowhood*, Jan Bremmer and Lourens van den Bosch, eds. (New York, 1995), pp. 43–45; Domingo Ramos-Lissón, "En torno al alegorismo bíblico del tratado *De virginitatis* de San Ambrosio: Los préstamos de los clásicos y cristianos," in *Stimuli: Exegese und ihre Hermeneutik in Antike und Christentum. Festschrift für Ernst Dassmann*, Georg Schöllgen and Clemens Schotten, eds., Jahrbuch für Antike und Christentum, Ergänzungsband 23 (Münster, 1996), pp. 455–56, 459, 460–61. Even more extreme are John Bugge, *Virginitas: An Essay on the History of a Medieval Ideal* (The Hague, 1975), pp. 31–66 and Calogero Riggi, "Fedeltà verginale e coniugale in S. Ambrogio," in *"Humanitas" classica e "sapientia" cristiana: Scritti offerti a Roberto Iacoangeli*, ed. Sergio Felici (Rome, 1992), pp. 180–83, who see in Ambrose the idea that the primal parents were pure spirit when first created and that embodiment and human sexuality are consequences of original sin.

[3] Ambrose, *Hexaemeron* 6.9.6.39, ed. Karl Schenkl, trans. Gabriele Banterle, SAEMO 1 (Milan, 1979); idem, *De paradiso* 1.5, 10.47–11.49, ed. Karl Schenkl, trans. Paolo Siniscalco, SAEMO 2/1 (Milan, 1984). Noted by Loiselle, "'Nature' de l'homme," pp. 20–26; Luigi Franco Pizzolato, "La coppia umana in Sant'Ambrogio," in *Etica e matrimonio nel cristianesimo delle origini*, ed. Raniero Cantalamessa (Milan, 1976), pp. 190–208; Moorhead, *Ambrose*, pp. 45–46. Cf. Bugge and Riggi in n. 2 supra.

women.[4] The human body, made up of parts well adapted to their functions, is the vesture of the soul and the temple of the Holy Spirit, at least when it is illuminated and guided by the eyes and other sense organs located in the head. It is only when the head, containing both reason and the sense organs, fails to inform and rule the body that the body can be thought of as the soul's prison.[5] While Ambrose sees male and female as equal in ontological status, they are still hierarchically ordered in the prelapsarian state. Man represents the mind; woman represents the mind's sensory functions, which the mind needs in order to operate. These attributes fail to interact harmoniously only when we sin.[6] The four rivers of paradise illustrate how they interact in the service of virtue. Each river stands for one of the cardinal virtues, as well as a particular age of human history. The river Geon stands for temperance, of which one subdivision is chastity, a good not only *per se* but also because chastity "removes all passions from the body" ("ita corporis passiones abolere consuevit").[7] This is a theme to which we will return. But it is worth flagging here that, rather than viewing the other modes of temperance as guardians of chastity, Ambrose sees chastity as engendering other forms of temperance. Historically, the river Geon stands for the age of the Old Testament patriarchs, "in whom there shone a chaste and pure temperance inspired by religion" ("in quibus casta et pura quaedam temperantia religionis effulsit").[8]

Now, the patriarchs were all husbands and fathers. In his treatises on these biblical worthies Ambrose offers further reflections on human nature, on ethics in general, and on sexual ethics for the married. Drawing expressly on Aristotelianism and the Bible, he states that we are an integral union of body, as our matter, and soul, as our form. This is how we were created, this is how we function in this life, and this is how we will be saved: "For the human person is saved, in body and in soul, not just one part" ("Iam enim non ex parte sed totus homo salvatur, in corpore, salvatur in anima").[9] It follows that the body as

[4] Ambrose, *Hex.* 6.9.7.40–6.9.8.50.

[5] Ibid. 6.9.6.39, 6.9.9.55–74.

[6] Ambrose, *De par.* 2.11–3.12, 4.29, 11.51, 14.72, 15.73.

[7] Ibid. 3.16; my translation unless otherwise indicated.

[8] Ibid. 3.20.

[9] Ambrose, *De Abraham* 1.4.29, ed. and trans. Franco Gori, SAEMO 2/2 (Milan, 1984). See also ibid. 2.6.28; idem, *De Isaac vel anima* 2.3, 3.6, ed. Karl Schenkl, trans. Claudio Moreschini, SAEMO 3 (Milan, 1982). Noted by Silvester Stenger, "Das Frömmigkeitsbild des hl. Ambrosius nach seinen Schriften *De Abraham, De Isaac*, und

such is not the source of our moral problems. The decision to sin, or to follow virtue, is made by the soul through the faculty of free will, which Ambrose staunchly defends. The body merely executes the soul's commands, "for the body is the servant of the will" ("caro autem voluntas ministra").[10] When body and soul work together to achieve virtue, the body can be viewed, as in the *Hexaemeron*, as the soul's clothing, not in the sense that we can put it on or remove it at will but because, just as clothing protects the body, so the soul needs to protect its own physical clothing and keep it in good condition.[11] Further, for Ambrose, the passions drawing us away from reason and into sin can arise in the body, in the soul, and in both, a position that reworks the theory of the passions found in all schools of Greek philosophy.[12] At the same time, he analogizes both body and soul to fields that yield vice or virtue, depending on how we cultivate them.[13]

It is in the light of the theory of human nature just described that we need to understand both Ambrose's frequent advice that we distance ourselves from physical pleasures and his use of two Platonic themes, the body as the prison of the soul and the soul's flight to virtue in the craft of the *Phaedrus* charioteer. While he cautions his audience on the need for detachment from physical pleasures, his norm for so doing is moderation, not extremism; i.e. we should abandon the vices in worldly goods, not their use. Temperance is the key to virtue, for it produces both the self-control and the decorum in action that govern the exercise of other virtues.[14] The opposite of temperance is

---

De bono mortis," Inaugural-diss., Universität Tübingen, 1947, p. 8; Stanis-Edmund Szydzik, "*Ad imaginem dei*: Die Lehre von der Gottebenbildlichkeit des Menschen bei Ambrosius von Mailand," Inaugural-diss., Freie Universität Berlin, 1961, p. 44; Mechthild Sanders, *"Fons vitae Christus": Der Heilsweg des Menschen nach der Schrift De Isaac et anima des Ambrosius von Mailand*, Münsteraner theologische Abhandlungen 42 (Altenberg, 1996), pp. 179–81.

[10] Ambrose, *De Jacob et beata vita* 1.3.10, ed. Karl Schenkl, trans. Roberto Palla, SAEMO 3 (Milan, 1982); trans. Michael P. McHugh in Ambrose, *Seven Exegetical Works*, Fathers of the Church 65 (Washington, D. C., 1972), p. 51. See also ibid. 1.1.1.

[11] Ambrose, *De Isa.* 7.60. Noted by Szydzik, "*Ad imaginem dei*," pp. 50–51.

[12] Ambrose, *De Jac.* 1.1.1, 1.2.5.

[13] Ambrose, *De Isa.* 3.7, 7.60, 8.68–70. This position represents an advance over that of *De Abr.* 2.6.26, where Ambrose states that virtue can be cultivated only in the soul.

[14] On detachment, see Ambrose, *De Isa.* 1.1, 1.2, 2.3, 2.4, 2.5, 3.6, 3.7, 3.8, 4.11, 4.13, 4.16, 4.23, 4.25, 4.27, 4.34, 5.46, 6.52, 7.59, 7.60, 7.61, 8.78, 8.79; idem, *De Jac.* 1.4.15, 1.5.17, 1.5.19–1.6.20, 1.7.27, 1.7.29, 1.7.32–1.8.39, 2.3.12, 2.6.28, 2.6.29–2.7.30, 2.9.37–39, 2.10.42–2.12.57; on moderation, see idem, *De Abr.* 1.4.26, 1.7.59, 2.2.7, 2.6.31, 2.6.34, 2.8.46, 2.10.68, 2.11.82; idem, *De Isa.* 3.5, 7.61, 8.65,

concupiscence, which Ambrose defines as irrational desire of any kind. By no means does he foreground sexual desire in this definition; the example he offers after giving it is King David's desire for water from a well behind enemy lines, although he places at risk the men whom he orders to obtain it, when good water is available where he stands.[15] As for the Platonic images, citing Romans 7.23, Ambrose states that the real prison of our souls is not "the body" but "the flesh." By "the flesh" he means human sinfulness, wherever in our constitution it may arise: "Where 'flesh' is applied to a human being, a sinner is meant" ("ubi autem caro pro homine nuncupatur, peccator exprimitur").[16] Ambrose conflates the Phadrean charioteer motif in *De Abraham* with Ezekiel's winged chariot, with the four creatures in the prophet's vision standing for the subdivisions of the soul and the cardinal virtues; returning to this theme in *De Isaac*, he conflates it with another biblical chariot, that of Aminidab, mentioned in the Song of Songs. Here, reason drives the chariot's eight horses, representing the cardinal virtues and their opposing vices, yoked by faith and charity as well as by moderation and justice, so as to win the race, and Christ, its prize. In both cases, the *Phaedrus* charioteer has been Christianized, with the cardinal virtues

---

8.79; idem, *De Jac.* 1.2.5–1.3.9, 1.8.37, 2.1.4, 2.4.15, 2.5.21, 2.6.27, 2.10.43; idem, *De Joseph* 2.5, ed. Karl Schenkl, trans. Roberto Palla, SAEMO 3 (Milan, 1982). Noted by Stenger, "Das Frömmigkeitsbild," pp. 14–19; Raymond Berton, "Abraham dans le *De officiis ministrorum*," *Revue des sciences religieuses* 54 (1980), 312–13, 316–17; Sanders, *"Fons vitae Christus"*, pp. 25–29, 99–102.

15 Ambrose, *De Jac.* 1.1.1–3, 1.2.5.

16 Ambrose, *De Isa.* 2.3; see also ibid. 6.52; idem, *De Jac.* 2.9.28; idem, *De Jos.* 6.31. Scholars recognizing Ambrose's Christianization of this theme in the light of Pauline theology include Szydzik, *"Ad imaginem dei,"* p. 44; Dassmann, *Die Frömmigkeit*, pp. 41–44, 181–84; R. H. Otten, "Caritas and the Ascent Motif in the Exegetical Works of St. Ambrose," *Studia Patristica* 8/2 (1966), 442–48; Goulven Madec, "L'Homme intérieure selon saint Ambroise," in *Ambroise de Milan*, XVIe centenaire de son élection épiscopale, ed. Yves-Marie Duval (Paris, 1974), pp. 296–306; Roberto Iacoangeli, "Anima ed eternità nel *De Isaac* di Sant'Ambrogio," *Morte e immortalità nella catechesi dei Padri del III–IV secolo*, ed. Sergio Felici (Rome, 1985), pp. 108–11; Sanders, *"Fons vitae Christus"*, pp. 23–25, 179–91. For the view of Ambrose as an unreconstructed Platonist on this theme, see Pierre Courcelle, "L'Âme en cage," in *Parusia: Studien zur Philosophie Platons und zur Problemgeschichte des Platonismus. Festschrift J. Hirschberger* (Frankfurt am Main, 1965), pp. 103–16; idem, "Tradition platonicienne et tradition chrétienne du corps-prison," *Revue des études latines* 43 (1965), 406–43; idem, "Le corps tombeau (Platon, *Gorgias* 493a; *Cratyl* 400c; *Phèdre* 250c)," *Revue des études augustiniennes* 68 (1966), 101–22; North, *Sophrosyne*, p. 365; Loiselle, "'Nature' de l'homme," p. 143 (he also fails to see the Pauline distinction between "body" and "flesh" in Ambrose, pp. 32–34); Tolomio, "'Corpus carcer'," pp. 5–6, 10–11, 13.

intact.[17] It is true that Ambrose also invokes the *Phaedrus* charioteer in two of his works for consecrated virgins.[18] But, the addressees of the patriarch treatises, lay adult converts being prepared for baptism, were, like the patriarchs themselves, not celibates but people who were, or were likely to be, married. In this respect, in addition to expanding on the anthropology and ethics he develops in the *Hexaemeron* and *De paradiso*, the patriarch treatises also provide rich insights into Ambrose's view of chastity within marriage.

À propos of marital chastity, there are three main agendas that Ambrose develops in his patriarch treatises. On one level, and this message is particularly vital to the male members of his audience, baptism will require a mode of sexual behavior far different from the freedoms accorded to men in Roman law and social custom, which found prostitution, concubinage, and a master's sexual use of his slaves acceptable whether a man was married or not. This is an argument developed most fully in *De Abraham*, which traces the learning curve of a convert not only from Chaldean polytheism and star-worship and from the false philosophy of Egypt but also from pagan sexual mores. Abraham must dismiss his Egyptian slave-concubine Hagar and her son once he learns what marital chastity requires. The Christian norm that Ambrose retrojects onto Abraham is that male sexual behavior must observe the same rules as female sexual behavior. For both, the only licit sexual

[17] Ambrose, *De Abr.* 2.8.54, 2.10.68–70; idem, *De Isa.* 8.65–68. For scholars recognizing Ambrose's Christianizing of this theme, see those cited first in n. 16 supra, to whom may be added Gérard Nauroy, "La méthode de la composition et la structure du *De Jacob et beata vita*," in *Ambroise de Milan*, XVIe centenaire de son élection épiscopale, ed. Yves-Marie Duval (Paris, 1974), pp. 115–53; Luigi F. Pizzolato, *La dottrina esegetica di sant'Ambrogio* (Milan, 1978), pp. 68–75; Roberto Palla, introduction to his trans. of Ambrose, *De Jac.*, pp. 218–19; Iacoangeli, "Anima ed eternità," pp. 103–37. For those treating his use of this motif as straightforward Platonism, see Courcelle, "Plotin et saint Ambroise," pp. 31–35, 45; idem, "Anti-Christian Arguments and Christian Platonism," pp. 165–66; idem, *Recherches sur les Confessions*, pp. 106–17, 122; idem, "Ambroise de Milan, 'professeur de philosophie'," pp. 147–55; idem, *Recherches sur saint Ambroise*, p. 16; Taormina, "Sant'Ambrogio e Plotino," pp. 41–85; Hadot, "Platon et Plotin," pp. 203–10; North, *Sophrosyne*, p. 365; Moreschini, intro. to his trans. of Ambrose, *De Isa.*, pp. 9–13, 20–25; Roberto Iacoangeli, "'Humanitas' classica e 'sapientia' cristiana in S. Ambrogio," in *Crescita dell'uomo nella catechesi dei padri (età postnicena)*, ed. Sergio Felici (Rome, 1988), pp. 132–42; Moorhead, *Ambrose*, pp. 172–73; Volker Henning Drecoll, "Neuplatonismus und Christentum bei Ambrosius, De Isaac et anima," *Zeitschrift für Antikes und Christentum* 5 (2001), 107–9, 129–59.

[18] Ambrose, *De virginibus* 1.10.61, 2.4.30, 3.2.8, 3.7.34, SAEMO 14/1; idem, *De virginitate* 17.108–18.118, SAEMO 14/2. Noted by Angela Russell Christman, "Ambrose of Milan on Ezekiel and the Virtuous Soul's Ascent to God," in *L'esegesi dei padri latini dalle origini a Gregorio Magno*, 2 vols. (Rome, 2000), 2:547–59.

relations are those between spouses. Ambrose concedes that, in some respects, Abraham's values are compatible with Roman law. His son Isaac, being his only child by a legitimate union, is his only legitimate heir, Ambrose notes, "as we accept according to our law" ("et nos hunc morem accepimus").[19] Similarly, Ambrose applauds Abraham's spousal *pietas*. When his wife Sarah dies, he mourns her with "marital affection" ("adfectio maritalis,") the term of art in Roman law denoting the honor, respect, and esteem granted to a lawful spouse with whom one engenders legitimate offspring, in contrast to the more casual attitude one might display toward a partner in a transitory relationship.[20]

On the other hand, Ambrose insists that the double standard of sexual ethics enshrined in Roman law is not acceptable for Christians. *Stuprum*, the legal term denoting the sexual delicts of men, is far from isomorphic with *adulterium*, a crime gender-specific to women. Cognizant of this distinction, Ambrose seeks to annihilate it. As he puts it, "Every *stuprum* is *adulterium*; nor is it lawful for the man what is not lawful for the woman" ("Omne stuprum adulterium est, nec viro licet quod mulieri non licet").[21] Further reclassifying and renaming what Roman law permits as a sin for Christians, Ambrose argues that divorce and remarriage, for both husbands and wives, counts as *adulterium*. While, for pagans, this practice may be licit, for Christians, "it is illegal" ("non licet").[22] Ambrose reminds his audience, especially its male members, that pagan sexual behavior in which they may have indulged before conversion, and as catechumens, will be forgiven them in baptism. But, from here on, he adjures them, "go, and see that you sin no more" ("vade, et post haec vide non pecces").[23]

It is true that, in order to depict the convert Abraham as having internalized the norms of Christian marital chastity, Ambrose has to edit the account of the patriarch's life given in the Book of Genesis, which relates that, after Sarah's death, Abraham took a concubine, Keturah, by whom he had six sons (Gen. 25:1–3). No such exercise of selective omission is needed in his depiction of Joseph, whose paramount

---

19 Ambrose, *De Abr.* 2.11.89.

20 Ibid. 1.9.80. On this term, see Adolf Berger, *Encyclopedic Dictionary of Roman Law*, Transactions of the American Philosophical Society, n.s. 43/2 (Philadelphia, 1953), s.v. *affectio maritalis*. Also noted by Gori, intro. to his trans. of *De Abr.*, p. 113 n. 1.

21 Ambrose, *De Abr.* 1.4.25. On these terms, see Berger, *Encyclopedic Dictionary*, s.v. *adulterium, stuprum*.

22 Ambrose, *De Abr.* 1.4.23. Noted by Clark, *Reading Renunciation*, pp. 236–37.

23 Ambrose, *De Abr.* 1.7.59; see also ibid. 1.4.23.

virtue of chastity shines forth from the outset of his story. Joseph is a model of both pre-marital and marital chastity; living faithfully with his wife once married, he remains celibate as a bachelor, resisting Potiphar's wife. Not only are his sexual purity and abhorrence of adultery laudable in themselves, the second point about marital chastity that Ambrose wants to make, they also bring with them other virtues, his third major point. In Joseph's case these include forbearance, in his refusal to accuse Potiphar's wife of would-be seduction as a means of exculpating himself from her false charge against him, and his gratitude and sense of obligation to his master, Potiphar, who has placed Joseph in charge of his household.[24]

This connection between Joseph's chastity, as a personal and domestic virtue, and his social responsibility, is not accidental. For, not only is pre-marital and marital chastity for those who marry an improvement on Roman law and pagan practice, it is also good because it promotes other virtues. This is a point, touched on in *De paradiso*, which Ambrose elaborates in *De Abraham* and *De Isaac* as well as *De Joseph*. As he explains in *De Abraham*, marital chastity goes well beyond what transpires in the marriage bed. Mutual fidelity and mutual consideration in their sexual relations, he argues, will lead spouses to develop selflessness and mutual respect in other aspects of their common life. Marital chastity will inspire temperance more generally, promoting modesty and moderation in the use of food and drink. It will empower its possessors to avoid egotism, petulance, and insolence, sustaining the vigilant attention needed to discipline the self against these and other departures from temperance that would undermine domestic harmony as well as the harmonious relationship between the soul and body of each of the spouses.[25]

In *De Isaac*, the impact of marital chastity includes these values but goes beyond the domestic sphere. This work, like *De Abraham*, is about conversion. The convert is Rebecca, Isaac's wife. A Chaldean like her kinsman Abraham, she must be instructed by Isaac in monotheism, the covenant, and its moral requirements, so that she can take her place as a matriarch in the people of God. Ambrose presents the ethical *paideia* undergone by Rebecca according to two schemata. One is the threefold precepts of the Delphic Oracle: know thyself, nothing in excess, thou art. She must acquire self-knowledge and self-discipline before she can

[24] Ambrose, *De Jos.* 1.1, 5.6, 5.23–24, 6.31.
[25] Ambrose, *De Abr.* 2.5.17–18.

encounter and unite with the Other, her spouse. Ambrose takes his second scheme from the Bride's dialogue in the Song of Songs. The Bride, awakened by the Bridegroom's kiss, seeks him in various locales before finding and uniting with him.[26] For Ambrose, there is a final stage in the biblical scheme not found in that of the Delphic Oracle. Union with the Other is the end point of the Oracle's instruction. But in the model Ambrose takes from the Song of Songs, the one-on-one union of the Bridegroom and Bride is not the end point of their relationship. For the Bride encourages the Bridegroom to leave their nuptial chamber and go out to assist those who still need his help.[27] Regarding marital chastity, there are two points that Ambrose accents in *De Isaac*. First, moderation in the pleasures of the bridal chamber is fully acceptable. Rebecca is not being trained to be an ascetic but to be a wife and mother in the flesh. In this connection, and remarkably so, Ambrose sees no difficulty in applying the Song of Songs to a real, flesh-and-blood marriage, treating that text not merely as an allegory of the relationship of the Christian soul, or the church, with Christ.[28] The second point is that the wedded bliss of spouses, far from encouraging them to treat their union as a perpetual honeymoon, inspires them to concern themselves with the needs of others. *Eros* does not prescind from *caritas*, for Ambrose; rather, the consummation of *eros* engenders *caritas*.

This high appraisal of marriage and marital sexuality is a value that Ambrose, in contrast to most of his contemporaries and predecessors who wrote on celibate vocations, refuses to cede in the treatises he produced for widows and consecrated virgins. Each of these three states of life, he argues, can be a means of salvation for those called to it. Chastity is a virtue that applies, in its own way, to each of these callings. As Ambrose observes in *De viduis*,

> Thus we are taught that the virtue of chastity is threefold: first that of marriage, second that of widowhood, and third that of virginity. For we do not praise one so as to exclude the others. Each of them pertains to its

---

[26] Ambrose, *De Isa.* 3.7–5.49, 6.50–8.77.

[27] Ibid. 4.11, 4.19, 5.43–46, 7.57, 8.69.

[28] This feature of Ambrose on the Song of Songs in *De Isaac* is missed by commentators on patristic interpretations of the Song of Songs such as Elizabeth A. Clark, "The Uses of the Song of Songs: Origen and the Later Latin Fathers," in eadem, *Ascetic Piety and Women's Faith: Essays on Late Ancient Christianity* (Lewiston, N.Y., 1986), pp. 401, 404–5; E. Ann Matter, *The Voice of My Beloved: The Song of Songs in Western Medieval Christianity* (Philadelphia, 1990), p. 36.

> own particular calling. In this regard the discipline of the church is rich, since she has those whom she prefers but none whom she rejects... Thus, we have preached on virginity so as not to reject widows, and thus, we honor widows so as to preserve the honor due to marriage.
>
> Docemur itaque triplicem castitatis esse virtutem: unam coniugalem, aliam viduitatis, tertiam virginitatis; non enim sic aliam praedicamus, ut excludamus alias. Suis quibusque professionibus ista conducunt. In hoc ecclasiae est opulens disciplina, quod quos praeferat habet, quos reiiciat non habet... Ita igitur virginitatem praedicavimus ut viduas non reiceremus, ita viduas honoramus ut suus honos coniugio reservetur.[29]

Following up on that point, Ambrose adds that all three states of life describe the church, which offers to all Christians pertinent lessons and examples of virtue in each state: "Therefore, all have an example to imitate: virgins, married women, and widows. And for this reason, indeed, the church is a virgin, a married woman, and a widow, for they are all one body in Christ" ("Habent itaque omnes quod imitentur exemplum, virgines, nuptae, viduae. Et fortasse ideo ecclesia virgo, nupta, vidua, quia unum corpus in Christi sunt").[30]

It is actually in one of his treatises for virgins that Ambrose gives his classic definition of marriage: "Marriage is made not by physical consummation but by marital consent" ("non enim defloratio virginitatis facit coniugum, sed pacto coniugalis").[31] It has been noted that Ambrose follows almost verbatim the classic Roman legal definition of marriage formation as based on mutual consent.[32] And, while he introduces this definition, in its present context, to defend the marriage of Mary and Joseph as a valid and indissoluble union, although it was a *mariage blanc*, part of his argument for Mary's perpetual virginity, its wider effect is to stress the intentionality of the spouses, their wish to create a conjugal society, over the physical facts of their relationship.

---

[29] Ambrose, *De viduis* 4.23, ed. Ignatius Cazzaniga, trans. Franco Gori, SAEMO 14/1 (Milan, 1989). On all three states as means of salvation, see Pizzolato, "La coppia umana," p. 199. Cf. Raymond d'Izarny, "La virginité selon Saint Ambroise," Ph.D. diss., Institut Catholique, Lyon, 1952, 2 vols., 1:52–68, 71–72, who thinks Ambrose regards marriage and childbearing as forms of ritual impurity.

[30] Ambrose, *De viduis* 3.16.

[31] Ambrose, *De inst. virg.* 6.41.

[32] *Digesta* 23.1.4, 23.2.2, 24.1.32.13, 35.1.15, 50.17.30, ed. Theodor Mommsen (Berlin, 1893). Noted by Brian Dooley, *Marriage according to St. Ambrose*, Studies in Christian Antiquity 11 (Washington, D.C., 1948), pp. 1–3; Susan Treggiari, *Roman Marriage: Iusti Coniuges from the Time of Cicero to the Time of Ulpian* (Oxford, 1991), pp. 54–55, 146–47, 161, 167, 170–80.

This principle of intentionality is one that he also applies to widowhood and consecrated virginity.

In addressing widowhood, therefore, Ambrose marks a sharp departure from previous Christian writers on that subject who adopt a rigorist ascetic tone, dismissing marriage and, *a fortiori*, the remarriage of widows, as incontinence. Instead of focusing merely, or preclusively, on their sexual abstention, he accents the positive virtues and opportunities to serve the Christian community possessed by widows.[33] Ambrose repeatedly states that it is the widow's virtuous intentionality, her inner life, and a wide range of external virtues, that define her chastity, not her physical state: "For a widow is defined not so much by her physical abstinence as by her virtue.... The fortitude of a widow lies not in physical chastity but is a great and abundant exercise of virtue;...a widow proves her chastity not by the testimony of the midwife but by her manner of life" ("Ergo vidua non abstinentia corporis tantum definitur sed virtute designatur....Nec sola tamen castitas corporis viduae fortitudo est, sed magna et uberrima disciplina virtutis;...non in voce obstetricis, sed in suis moribus habet castitatis examen").[34] To hammer in the point that it is not the widow's sexual abstinence that defines her calling, Ambrose contrasts favorably the widow with true inner chastity with the eunuch, abstinent willy-nilly.[35]

If a life lacking sexual expression is not the real essence of the widow's chastity, what is? In response, Ambrose notes that the absence of a new husband and of the maternal trials and duties that may arrive with remarriage should be seen not as a sacrifice but as an opportunity. The decision not to remarry grants the widow independence, the freedom from entanglements that gives her the time and energy to carry on

---

33 This point is brought out well by Ernst Bickel, *Das ascetische Ideal bei Ambrosius, Hieronymus und Augustin: Eine kulturgeschichtliche Studie* (Leipzig, 1916), pp. 21–23, 27, 37; Linus Bopp, *Das Witwentum als organische Gliedschaft im Gemeinschaftsleben der alten Kirche: Ein geschichtlicher Beitrag zur Grundlagen der Witwenseelsorge in der Gegenwart* (Mannheim, 1950), pp. 45–50, 53–67; Antonio V. Nazzaro, "La vedovanza nel cristianesimo antico," *Annali della facoltà di lettere e filosofia dell'Università di Napoli* 26, n.s. 14 (1983–84), 103–32; idem, "Il *De viduis* di Ambrogio," *Vichiana*, n.s. 13 (1984), 274–98; Gori, intro. to his trans. of *De viduis*, pp. 65–66. Cf. Bremmer, "Pauper or Patroness," pp. 43–45, who reads this text as a call to asceticism.

34 Ambrose, *De viduis* 2.7, 2.11, 4.26 for these respective passages; see also ibid. 1.1, 1.4.

35 Ibid. 13.75–77.

the host of activities in which he thinks widows should engage.[36] He expects them to manifest a range of virtues, classical and Christian. These include faith,[37] the four cardinal virtues with particular emphasis on modesty under the heading of temperance,[38] sobriety,[39] filial piety toward parents and children,[40] forbearance, and the willingness to forgive injuries.[41] A widow should pray, keep the fasts of the church, and weep, although she should not become so preoccupied with mourning her husband's death that she neglects her other duties.[42] Equally if not more important are the virtues widows display in an array of public functions serving the Christian community. Ambrose describes these functions generically as works of mercy, with mentoring consecrated virgins as a service that he regards widows as particularly well positioned to undertake.[43] Also high on his list are hospitality[44] and almsgiving.[45] With respect to poor relief, those widows lacking in wealth can offer their wisdom, righteousness, and abstinence to God, while those rich in worldly goods should also alleviate the needs of the poor and suffering.[46] In aid of that virtue, widows endowed with property should manage it efficiently. Ambrose dismisses categorically the notion that widows need to remarry in order to have husbands to manage their

[36] Ibid. 1.1–2, 2.10, 11.69, 13.81–14.82, 15.86–88. Noted by Bopp, *Das Witwentum*, pp. 45–50; Nazzaro, "Il *De viduis* di Ambrogio," p. 280; Clark, *Reading Renunciation*, pp. 275, 364.

[37] Ambrose, *De viduis* 5.30, 5.32, 13.75.

[38] Ibid. 5.31, 6.36, 7.39, 7.42, 8.51, 9.57–58.

[39] Ibid. 5.30, 7.37–42, 10.64. Noted by North, *Sophrosyne*, p. 365.

[40] Ambrose, *De viduis* 2.7, 2.11, 6.33–34.

[41] Ibid. 9.58.

[42] Ibid. 2.8, 2.11, 4.21–22, 6.35–36, 7.38, 9.59, 10.62–63. On mourning the deceased husband at 9.59, Ambrose, in addition to counseling against prolonged mourning, exceeding the standard year after the husband's death, criticizes equally the swift shedding of the widow's weeds and their replacement with a new wedding veil. For Roman practice in this area, see Percy Ellwood Corbett, *The Roman Law of Marriage* (Oxford, 1931), pp. 248–51; Gori, intro. to his trans. of *De viduis*, p. 293 n. 123; Treggiari, *Roman Marriage*, pp. 493–95.

[43] Ambrose, *De viduis* 2.11, 5.27–32, 9.53, 10.60, 10.66; on instructing virgins, see ibid. 1.1.

[44] Ibid. 1.4–6, 2.11. Noted by Bopp, *Das Witwentum*, pp. 45–50; Michele Renee Salzman, *The Making of a Christian Aristocracy: Social and Religious Change in the Western Roman Empire* (Cambridge, Mass., 2002), p. 172.

[45] Ambrose, *De viduis* 1.4–6, 2.11, 3.16, 4.21, 5.27–28, 5.32, 6.33–34, 9.54, 13.75. Noted by Bopp, *Das Witwentum*, pp. 45–50; Antonio V. Nazzaro, "Metafore e immagini agricole del *De viduis* di Ambrogio," *Vetera Christianorum* 28 (1991), 278–79; Salzman, *The Making of a Christian Aristocracy*, p. 207.

[46] Ambrose, *De viduis* 5.27–28, 5.30, 6.33–34.

property for them. Women, he argues, are perfectly competent to manage their own affairs. If a widow has any hesitations on this account, she can always call on a son, a son-in-law, or some other male relative for help. Indeed, Ambrose sees the faintheartedness of widows in this connection as the single biggest temptation leading them to remarry, far more important than the desire for an active sex life or additional children.[47]

Ambrose's chosen method for making the above case is the citation of biblical examples. In supporting his initial assertion that marriage, widowhood, and virginity are all praiseworthy callings, he presents the figures of Mary the virgin, Anna the widow, and Susanna the wife.[48] That point made, he focuses on biblical widows, or biblical women he thinks were widows, to develop his concrete advice. As these examples clarify, Ambrose does not expect widows to be passive recipients of charity but rather to be active and engagée, collaborating with the clergy in a wide range of public services.[49] Along with Ambrose's emphasis on temperance, this activist orientation obviates an ascetic or contemplative approach to widowhood. Only one of his examples, Anna, fasting and praying daily in the Temple and recognizing the infant Christ as the Messiah,[50] displays what we might call self-mortification and religiosity. His other exemplary widows are all doers. There is the poor woman contributing her widow's mite to the Temple fund. She recognizes the apodictic obligation of almsgiving and expresses true generosity, measured by intention not the size of her donation.[51] Then, there is Naomi, who ministers to her widowed daughter-in-law, Ruth, helping her to survive, and who also illustrates the notion that a woman who raises her children well will not suffer want on their account.[52] Ambrose also

[47] Ibid. 8.44–51, 9.52–59, 10.66, 11.67. On the competence of widows to manage property, see Nazzaro, "La vedovanza," pp. 119–20; idem, "Il *De viduis*," p. 279; Virginia Burrus, "'Equipped for Victory': Ambrose and the Gendering of Orthodoxy," *Journal of Early Christian Studies* 4 (1996), 473–74; Domingo Ramos-Lissón, intro. to his ed. and trans. of Ambrose, *Sobre las vírgenes y Sobre las viudas* (Madrid, 1999), p. 36.

[48] Ambrose, *De viduis* 3.24. Noted by Bopp, *Das Witwentum*, p. 47.

[49] This point is brought out well by Bopp, *Das Witwentum*, pp. 32, 45–50; Ramos-Lissón, intro. to his ed. and trans. of *Sobre las vírgenes y Sobre las viudas*, p. 26; Salzman, *The Making of a Christian Aristocracy*, p. 207.

[50] Ambrose, *De viduis* 2.12, 4.21–22, 4.24.

[51] Ibid. 5.27, 5.29.

[52] Ibid. 6.33–34.

presents the mother-in-law of St. Peter, whom Christ heals so that she can rise from her sickbed and serve Him and His disciples.[53]

Taking a considerably larger leap into the public sphere, he cites Judith, the chaste widow who does not hesitate to present herself as available to Holofernes so that she can ply him with wine and kill him, thereby defending the faith and saving her people. For Ambrose, Judith's virtues include wisdom, temperance, and modesty after her victory. But her chief virtue is courage, and the chief lesson she teaches is that chastity is an internal state, which she maintains notwithstanding the seductive appearance she assumes in aid of her mission.[54] Even more impressive is the example of Deborah. Like Judith, she is a warrior woman, but more, a military commander and policy-maker and judge, a leader of men in war and peace. Deborah is the high card Ambrose plays in rebuking widows who despair of managing property independent of husbands. Deborah's case demonstrates that this claim is pure rubbish:

> For she taught not only that widows do not need the help of men, but also that they are even a help to men. For she, not held back by the weakness of her sex, took on the duties of men and, having taken them on, brought them to completion.... And I think the story of her judgeship has been told and her deeds described so that women should not be held back from the duty of virtue because of the weakness of their sex.... It is not [women's] nature that is the guilty party or that is subject to weakness. It is not sex but virtue that makes people strong.
>
> Haec enim docuit non solum viri auxilio viduas non egere, verum etiam viris esse subsidio: quae nec sexus infirmitate revocata, munia virorum obeunda suscepit, et suscepta cumulavit.... Et ideo lectum istius puto esse iudicium et gesta eius arbitror esse descripta, ne mulieres a virtutis officio muliebris sexus infirmitate revocentur.... Non ergo natura est rea culpae nec infirmitati obnoxia: strenuos non sexus, sed virtus facit.[55]

Ambrose's widows are thus to be exponents of the active life of service. What chastity means, for them, is that celibacy, and the property at their disposal, will free them from domestic duties and empower them to take up the broad range of roles in the lay ministry which

[53] Ibid. 9.53, 10.60, 10.66.

[54] Ibid. 7.37–42. On Judith's valor, see Burrus, "'Equipped for Victory'," pp. 473–74.

[55] Ambrose, *De viduis* 8.44. For the whole passage on Deborah, see ibid. 8.44–51, 9.52–59, 10.66, 11.67. On Deborah as a leader, see the scholars cited in n. 49 supra.

Ambrose envisions for them. What is likely to draw them away from the widow's calling, in his estimation, is not the lure of an active sex life or the desire for children but the cowardly disinclination to take charge of their own lives and fortunes. With distaste Ambrose compares self-indulgent widows with soldiers who, having completed their tour of active duty, retire to their farms to live strictly private lives.[56] While he does not want widows to return to the marital fray, neither does he want them to go into retirement. Their chastity should equip them to engage in public service; it should not license them to detach themselves from it.

If fourth-century mores made it possible for matrons to engage in many of the public roles that Ambrose imagines for widows, how does he distinguish the calling of the consecrated virgin from the life-style of her unmarried secular sister, who also lived at home with her parents? In responding to this question, Ambrose distances himself from contemporaries and predecessors who wrote on virginity, just as he does with respect to widowhood. To begin with, many of these other authors reflect the view that human sexuality is a consequence of the Fall, and that the virgin's sexual innocence enables her to recover the prelapsarian nature of the primal parents.[57] Also, many of them prescribe a detailed regime of ascetic self-mortification for virgins, seen as weakening the sex drive, and in some cases as a preparation for the contemplative life. While Ambrose borrows from these authors, he is far less ascetic, far less dismissive of marriage, and in no sense an advocate of a contemplative program.[58]

---

56 Ambrose, *De viduis* 14.84. Noted by Nazzaro, "Metafore," pp. 284–88.

57 See scholars cited in nn. 1 and 38 supra.

58 The best general considerations of Ambrose on virginity in relation to his sources are Pierre Thomas Camelot, *Virgines Christi: La virginité aux premiers sieclès de l'église* (Paris, 1944), pp. 373–92; Yves-Marie Duval, "L'Originalité du *De virginibus* dans le mouvement ascétique occidental: Ambroise, Cyprien, Athanase," in *Ambroise de Milan, XVI*e centenaire de son élection épiscopale, ed. Yves-Marie Duval (Paris, 1974), pp. 15–66; Vittorio Grossi, "La verginità negli scritti dei padri: La sintesi di S. Ambrogio. Gli aspetti cristologici, antropologici, ecclesiali," in *Il celibato per il regno* (Milan, 1977), pp. 141, 146–63; Gori, intro. to his trans. of *De virginibus*, pp. 20–58; Luciana Mirri, *Il monachismo femminile secondo sant'Ambrogio di Milano* (Vicenza, 1991). Comparing Ambrose with Jerome, scholars who take the same line include Bickel, *Das asketische Ideal*, pp. 21–23, 27, 37; Franca Ela Consolino, "Il *De exhortione virginis* di Ambrogio: Dagli *exempla* ad un esempio di comportamento cristiano," *Rivista storica italiana* 94 (1982), 455–77; Ramos-Lissón, intro. to his ed. and trans. of *Sobre las vírgines y Sobre las viudas*, pp. 29–30; David G. Hunter, "The Virgin, the Bride, and the Church: Reading Psalm 45 in Ambrose, Jerome, and Augustine," *Church History* 69 (2000), 289–303. Opting for Ambrose's independence from other authors who also cite the Song of Songs as a

As with his treatment of widowhood, in writing to and about virgins Ambrose does not disparage other callings. While in praising virginity he does not neglect to point out the inconveniences of marriage, he repeatedly states, in this segment of his oeuvre, that marriage is good and necessary for the continuity of the human race, a great mystery in that it signifies the union of Christ and the church, the state to which most people are called, and a state in which they can be virtuous. As he sums up this point, he concludes, "I do not therefore discourage marriage if I enumerate the fruits of virginity. For the latter is a gift given to few while the former is given to all... I am comparing good things with good things, so as to clarify more easily the things that are better" ("Non itaque dissuadeo nuptias, si fructus virginitatis enumero. Paucarum quippe hoc munus est, illud omnium... Bona cum bonis comparo, quo facilius quid praestat eluceat").[59]

At the same time, Ambrose observes, having elected not to marry, virgins thereby gain freedom. There are three aspects of their choice that he stresses. One is the virgin's freedom from the travails of marriage. This is a topic which Ambrose also airs in *De viduis*, but with a difference. Having experienced marriage, widows do not need an elaborate recitation of its inconveniences. But more detail is required in describing them to the inexperienced. Ambrose makes much of the etymological connection between *coniugum*, marriage, and *iugum*,

---

model for the virgin as a bride of Christ is Franca Ela Consolino, "*Veni huc a Libano*: La *sponsa* del Cantico dei Cantici come modello per le vergini negli scritti esortatori di Ambrogio," *Athenaeum* 62 (1984), 399–415. And, while scholars such as Louis Theophile Lefort, "Athanase, Ambroise, et Chenoute 'Sur la virginité'," *Le Muséon* 48 (1935), 355–72; Michel Aubineau, "Les écrits de saint Athanase sur la virginité," *Revue d'ascétique et de mystique* 31 (1955), 163–69; Ramos-Lissón, intro. to his ed. and trans. of *Sobre las vírgines y Sobre las viudas*, pp. 22, 27, have accented Ambrose's dependence on Athanasius (cf. Athanasius, *Letter to Virgins, Precepts for Virgins* 2.1–3 in *Lettres festales et pastorales*, ed. and trans. Louis Theophile Lefort, Corpus scriptorum christianorum orientalium 151, Scriptores coptici 20 [Louvain, 1955]), others have accented his departures from Athanasius; see Luigi Dossi, "S. Ambrogio e S. Atanasio nel *De virginibus*," *Acme* 4 (1951), 274–98; Giuseppe Rosso, "La 'Lettera alle vergini', Anastasio e Ambrogio," *Augustinianum* 23 (1983), 421–52; Hervé Savon, "Un modèle de sainteté à la fin du IVe siècle: La virginité dans l'oeuvre de saint Ambroise," in *Sainteté et martyre dans les religions du Livre*, ed. Jacqueline Marx (Brussels, 1989), pp. 23–28.

[59] Ambrose, *De virginibus* 1.7.35; see also ibid. 1.6.24, 1.7.34; idem, *De virginitate* 6.26–27. 6.29, 6.31, 6.33–34, 9.56; idem, *De exhortione virginitatis* 6.36; idem, *De institutione virginis* 3.24; idem, *Ep.* 63.10, 63.40, ed. Otto Faller, *CSEL* 79 (Vienna, 1964). Noted by Pierre Thomas Camelot, "Les traités 'De virginitaté' au IVe siècle," in *Mystique et continence*, Travaux du VIIe congrès international d'Aven (Bruges, 1952), pp. 279–81; Duval, "L'Originalité," p. 17; Savon, "Un modèle," p. 23.

or yoke. He sees marriage as binding the wife into servitude to the husband, rather than seeing the bond as mutually yoking both spouses to each other.[60]

The second feature of the virgin's veiling is that it constitutes a real choice, a lifelong commitment made with her full knowledge and consent. The chastity of the virgin is thus a sign of her personal autonomy, her "unconquered mind" ("invictum animum"),[61] her capacity for self-rule, which Ambrose contrasts pointedly with the condition of the Vestal Virgins. These priestesses of Vesta, chosen between the ages of six and ten by the *pontifex maximus*, were bound to celibacy in order to keep alive the sacred flame at the temple of Vesta day and night. They were not required to practice asceticism in any other respect. They enjoyed many exemptions and privileges. The Vestals served for a fixed term, after which they were free to marry. If, however, they broke their vow of continence while on duty, they were put to death. This institution of pagan Rome remained on the books, supported by tax funds, until it was formally abolished by Theodosius I in 392. In Ambrose's view, the Vestals, in comparison with Christian virgins, are not truly chaste. For him, the issue is not the high-profile and luxurious life-style of the Vestals or their entitlements but rather the motives for their continence. As he puts it, "She is not modest who is bound by the law, nor is she immodest who is set free by the law.... She is not chaste who is constrained by fear" ("Sed nec illa pudica est quae lege retinetur, et illa impudica quae lege dimittitur... Itaque nec casta est, quae metu cogitur").[62] In contrast, the Christian virgin's chastity is not imposed, but chosen by her own free will, reflecting her internally chaste state of mind, and it is a permanent commitment.[63]

---

[60] Ambrose, *De inst. virg.* 17.108–109; idem, *De ex. virg.* 3.17, 4.19–25, 5.29, 5.31, 6.40–7.42, 7.46, 7.50. Noted also by Duval, "L'Originalité," p. 18; Gori, intro. to his trans. of *De virginitate*, pp. 52–56; Riggi, "Fedeltà verginale," p. 177; Savon, "Un modèle," p. 23; Moorhead, *Ambrose*, pp. 51–52, 62, 67–68; Ramos-Lissón, intro. to his ed. and trans. of *Sobre las vírgenes y Sobre las viudas*, pp. 30–31; idem, "Le binôme liberté-virginité dans les écrits exhortatifs de saint Ambroise sur la virginité," *Studia Patristica* 38 (2001), 468–74; this last citation provides an excellent guide to the literature on this theme in the author's notes.

[61] Ambrose, *De virginibus* 1.7.37; see also ibid. 1.4.15, 1.5.23; idem, *De ex. virg.* 3.17; idem, *De virginitate* 3.10, 3.13, 12. 74.

[62] Ambrose, *De virginibus* 1.4.15.

[63] Ambrose, *De virginitate* 3.13. This contrast with the Vestal Virgins is noted by Camelot, *Virgines Christi*, p. 29; Izarny, "La virginité," 1:15–18; M. Olphe-Galliard, "La virginité consacrée dans l'occident latin," in *La chastité* (Paris, 1953), pp. 76–77; Robert Schilling, "Vestales et vierges chrétiennes dans la Rome antique," *Revue des*

A third feature of Christian virginal chastity that Ambrose also contrasts with the life-style of the Vestals is the notion that the virgin's abstinence from human marriage qualifies her, above all other kinds of Christians, to be a bride of Christ. Aside from sparing her the inconveniences of marriage in the flesh, this bond of spiritual love, expressed in terms of the relationship between the Bride and the Bridegroom in the Song of Songs, brings with it incomparable advantages of its own. The virgin receives from her divine spouse, Himself a virgin born of a virgin, the supreme model for her to imitate. As the bride of Christ, she provides her parents with a son-in-law of the highest imaginable character and status, without their having to pay a dowry or to lose the company of their daughter. Best of all, the virgin becomes the daughter-in-law of God the Father and is welcomed into the inner life of the Trinity.[64] While still *in via*, she thus enjoys the privileges of the saints *in patria*. The virgin's nuptial union with Christ makes her body a temple of the Holy Spirit in a special way.[65] This union will be a fruitful one, since the virgin will be fecund with virtues, which she will have the time and energy to cultivate, not being faced with the hazards

---

sciences religieuses 35 (1961), 118–25; Calogero Riggi, "La verginità nel pensiero di S. Ambrogio," *Salesianum* 42 (1980), 798–99; Gori, intro. to his trans. of *De virginibus*, pp. 17–19; Domingo Ramos-Lissón, "'Referamus ad Christum' comme paradigme aux vierges dans les *Traités sur la virginité* de Saint Ambroise," *Studia Patristica* 38 (1993), 65–74; idem, intro. to his ed. and trans. of *Sobre las vírgines y Sobre las viudas*, p. 24. On virginity as a state of mind, see Camelot, "Les traités 'De virginité'," pp. 290–91; Grossi, "La verginità," pp. 147, 156.

64 Ambrose, *De ex. virg.* 5.28, 9.58–59, 10.62; idem, *De virginibus* 1.3.11–13, 1.5.21–22, 1.7.32, 1.7.36–37, 1.8.52, 1.11.62, 1.11.65; idem, *De virginitate* 12.74–13.77, 13.79–80. Noted by Camelot, *Virgines Christi*, p. 60; idem, "Les traités 'De virginitaté'," pp. 290–91; Raymond d'Izarny, "Marriage et consécration virginale au IVe siècle," *La Vie Spirituelle*, supplément 24 (1953), 92–118 (emphasizing parallels with earthly marriage); Grossi, "La verginità," pp. 146, 152–55; Duval, "L'Originalité," p. 18; Riggi, "La verginità," pp. 790–94; Gori, intro. to his trans. of *De virginitate*, pp. 46–48; Ramos-Lissón, "'Referamus ad Christum'," pp. 65–74; idem, "Las tipologías de Cristo en el 'Cantico Canticorum' según el tratado ambrosiano 'De virginitate'," in *Biblia, exegesis, y cultura: Estudios en honor del Prof. D. José María Casciaro*, eds. G. Aranda, C. Basevi and J. Chapa (Pamplona, 1994), pp. 534–40; idem, intro. to his ed. and trans. of *Sobre las vírgenes y Sobre las viudas*, pp. 26–27; Hunter, "The Virgin, the Bride," pp. 285–90. On the other hand, Izarny, "La virginité," 1:11–29, 58–64, ignores these aspects of the Bride of Christ theme.

65 Ambrose, *De inst. virg.* 17.105; idem, *De virginibus* 2.2.18, 2.4.26; idem, *De virginitate* 17.111. Noted by Dossi, "S. Ambrogio," pp. 274–98; Gori, intro. to his trans. of *De virginibus*, pp. 42–44; Joyce E. Salisbury, *Church Fathers, Independent Virgins* (London, 1991), p. 38; Clark, *Reading Renunciation*, pp. 212–14, 219; Ramos-Lissón, intro. to his ed. and trans. of *Sobre las vírgenes y Sobre las viudas*, p. 28.

and burdens of physical maternity.[66] And, as brides of Christ, virgins, while still in this life, will function as eschatological signs, forecasting the angelic life in the resurrection, where there will be no marrying or giving in marriage.[67]

The traits just considered are manifestations or consequences of the virgin's physical chastity. But, just as chastity, for married couples and for widows, has effects that go well beyond the issue of sexuality, so too, in the case of virgins, Ambrose regards their sexual abstinence as only one aspect of their lives. He thinks that they also need to express their calling in other ways, some private and some more public. As with other Christians, he enjoins virgins to practice the virtues of faith, hope, and charity[68] as well as the cardinal virtues of wisdom, temperance, courage, and justice.[69] Ambrose's handling of the cardinal virtues, as displayed by virgins, has much in common with his treatment of this theme as applied to married lay people. Here, too, he invokes the image of the *Phaedrus* charioteer much as he does in *De Isaac*, only shifting the prize attained by the charioteer to the heavenly banquet.[70] As with other Christians, virgins need to be guided by reason, which counsels other virtues in addition to those enumerated. Some of them Ambrose classifies as ornaments of the virgin's inner life.[71] These include a clean conscience;[72] self-knowledge;[73] prayer, both to meditate on God's word, to seek a fuller understanding of the sacraments, to lament for

---

66 Ambrose, *De inst. virg.* 17.108–109; idem, *De virginatate* 16.98–99. Noted by Izarny, "La virginité," 1:26–27; Olphe-Galliard, "La virginité consacrée," p. 82; Riggi, "Fedeltà verginale," p. 179; Gori, intro. to his trans. of *De virginitate*, p. 56; Ramos-Lissón, intro. to his ed. and trans. of *Sobre las vírgines y Sobre las viudas*, p. 28.

67 Ambrose, *De virginibus* 1.8.51–52; idem, *De virginitate* 17.111. Noted by Izarny, "La virginité," 1:38–51; Duval, "L'Originalité," pp. 27–29; Riggi, "La verginità," pp. 794–98; idem, "Fedeltà verginale," p. 176; Gori, intro. to his trans. of *De virginibus*, pp. 44–46; Ramos-Lissón, intro. to his ed. and trans. of *Sobre las vírgenes y Sobre las viudas*, pp. 25–26.

68 Ambrose, *De ex. virg.* 10.70; idem, *De inst. virg.* 16.102, 17.110, 17.111, 17.113; idem, *De virginibus* 2.2.7, 2.2.12–15; idem, *De virginitate* 16.110. Noted by Riggi, "La verginità," pp. 802–5.

69 Ambrose, *De ex. virg.* 5.32, 7.50, 8.54, 12.81; idem, *De inst. virg.* 16.102, 17.109, 17.110; idem, *De virginibus* 2.2.7–9; idem, *De virginitate* 15.95–96, 17.108–109, 18.112–115, 8.118, 18.121. Noted by Grossi, "La verginità," p. 147.

70 Ambrose, *De virginitate* 15.95–96, 17.108, 18.112–115, 8.118. Noted by Christman, as in n. 18 supra. Scholars who read this passage Platonically include Gori, intro. to his trans. of *De virginitate*, pp. 74, 76–78; Ramos-Lissón, "Entorno al alegorismo bíblico," pp. 455–56, 459.

71 Ambrose, *De ex. virg.* 10.64.

72 Ibid. 10.65; idem, *De inst. virg.* 1.7.

73 Ambrose, *De ex. virg.* 10.68.

her own sins and those of the world, and simply to render to God the glory He deserves;[74] the tranquillity of mind and the constancy of soul needed to endure trials and temptations;[75] and an inner harmony resulting from the virgin's success in overcoming the Pauline battle of flesh and spirit.[76]

At the same time, Ambrose counsels virtues manifested externally in the virgin's social interactions. The one to which he adverts the most frequently is modesty, by which he means decorum in the virgin's demeanor and external appearance; outside of banning jewelry, he is unspecific regarding the virgin's hygiene and clothing.[77] Closely allied to modesty are humility,[78] patience,[79] and forbearance.[80] While enjoined to practice justice as a cardinal virtue, the virgin must go beyond rendering to each his own; as a Christian, she must also forgive her enemies, render good for evil, and be merciful.[81] She should observe the church's fast days and not seek delicate food at other times.[82] She should engage in good works, including almsgiving, which takes the virgin out of a purely domestic environment.[83] In his catalogue of virginal virtues, Ambrose mentions continence sparingly, subordinating it to modesty and sobriety of demeanor.[84] In singling out the virgin's greatest temptation, he focuses on gossip and idle chatter. If widows may be tempted by cowardice, virgins are inclined to loquaciousness, in his view, and this without reference to the already burgeoning theological *topos* of silence as a monastic virtue and as an approved mode of prayer.[85] While

---

[74] Ambrose, *De ex. virg.* 9.58, 10.70, 11.75, 11.78; idem, *De inst. virg.* 1.7, 2.8–9, 15.93, 16.100, 16.103, 17.110, 17. 112; idem, *De virginibus* 3.4.18–20, 3.5.21–23.

[75] Ambrose, *De inst. virg.* 2.10, 9.61; idem, *De virginitate* 16.98–99.

[76] Ambrose, *De inst. virg.* 2.11–3.16.

[77] Ibid. 1.5, 9.58, 9.60, 9.62, 9.66, 16.102, 17.109, 17.111, 17.113; idem, *De ex. virg.* 5.29, 6.35, 10.62, 10.71, 11.76, 12. 81–82, 13.86; idem, *De virginibus* 2.2.12–15, 3.3.9–10, 3.7.35; on jewelry, ibid. 1.6.29–30, 1.10.55; idem, *De virginitate* 16.100.

[78] Ambrose, *De inst. virg.* 15.93, 16.102.

[79] Ibid. 16.102.

[80] Ambrose, *De ex. virg.* 11.77.

[81] Ambrose, *De ex. virg.* 13.85; idem, *De inst. virg.* 2.8–9; idem, *De virginibus* 2.2.7.

[82] Ambrose, *De ex. virg.* 12.79; idem, *De virginibus* 1.8.53, 2.2.8, 3.2.8, 3.4.15.

[83] Ambrose, *De ex. virg.* 9.58, 10.70, 12.80; idem, *De inst. virg.* 17.111, 17.113; idem, *De virginibus* 1.8.42, 2.2.7.

[84] Ambrose, *De inst. virg.* 7.109.

[85] Ibid. 1.5; idem, *De ex. virg.* 10.72–73, 13.86–90; idem, *De virginibus* 1.3.10, 2.2.7, 2.2.11, 3.2.8–3.3.14. Noted by Duval, "L'Originalité," pp. 14–15; Michele Pellegrino, "'Mutus...loquar Christum': Pensieri di sant'Ambrogio su parola e silenzio," in *Paradoxos politeia: Studi patristici in onore di Giuseppe Lazzati*, eds., R. Cantalamessa and L. F. Pizzolato, (Milan, 1979), pp. 447–57; Moorhead, *Ambrose*, p. 69. On the monastic

Ambrose urges virgins to lament for their sins and those of the world, he also counsels cheerfulness.[86] He also prescribes daily reading and Bible study, suggesting that, since his virgins are wealthy and literate, this intellectual work is the only work they need to do.[87]

As with widows, Ambrose illustrates the points he makes with examples, post-biblical as well as biblical. Following a general trend in the post-Constantinian church, he assimilates martyrdom to the celibate calling.[88] He has no lack of actual virgin martyrs to call upon; we will focus here on two of those he cites, Agnes and the virgin of Antioch. Agnes, like Ambrose's target audience, was young when she met her fate, only twelve years old. Yet, she demonstrates the faith, courage, and commitment he seeks to inspire in those who take the veil.[89] The virgin of Antioch reinforces the point about true inner chastity made in Ambrose's critique of the Vestal Virgins. As he narrates her story, when she is haled before the magistrate and told that she will be placed in a brothel if she does not worship the pagan gods, she chooses the brothel after mulling over these options in an interior monologue that Ambrose ascribes to her.[90] She considers two biblical

---

tradition of silence, see Edith Claudia Kunz, *Schweigen und Geist: Biblische und patristische Studien zu einer Spiritualität des Schweigens* (Freiburg, 1996), pp. 15–182, 318–93, 401–682. Cf. Savon, "Un modèle," p. 25, who thinks that Ambrose sees boredom as the virgin's chief temptation.

[86] Ambrose, *De virginibus* 2.2.7.

[87] Ibid. 2.2.7, 3.4.16. The emphasis on reading is noted by Consolino, "Il *De exhortatione virginis*," pp. 463–65; Savon, "Un modèle," p. 28; Clark, *Reading Renunciation*, pp. 56–57; Moorhead, *Ambrose*, pp. 68–70.

[88] See, on this point, Edward Malone, *The Monk and the Martyr: The Monk as Successor to the Martyr*, Studies in Christian Antiquity 12 (Washington, D. C., 1950); Ernst Dassmann, "Ambrosius und die Märtyrer," *Jahrbuch für Antike und Christentum* 18 (1975), 61–65, 67–68; Gori, intro. to his trans. of *De virginibus*, pp. 51–52; Markus, *The End of Ancient Christianity*, pp. 65–88; Mirri, *Il monachismo femminile*, pp. 165–88; Gérard Freyburger, "De l'*amicitia* païenne aux vertus chrétiennes: Damon et Phintias," in *Du héros païen au saint chrétien*, Actes du colloque organisé par le Centre des Rhétoriques Religieuses de l'Antiquité (C.A.R.R.A.), Strasbourg, 1–2 décembre 1995, Gérard Freyberger and Laurant Pernot, eds. (Paris, 1997), pp. 83–93; Clark, *Reading Renunciation*, pp. 214–15; Ramos-Lissón, intro. to his ed. and trans. of *Sobre las vírgenes y Sobre las viudas*, pp. 29, 51–52.

[89] Ambrose, *De virginibus* 1.2.5–9. Other figures he mentions include Thecla and Pelagia and her sisters, at ibid. 2.3.19–21 and 3.7.33–35, respectively. As Virginia Burrus, "Reading Agnes: The Rhetoric of Gender in Ambrose and Prudentius," *Journal of Early Christian Studies* 3 (1995), 25–33, 43–46, notes, by associating Thecla with Agnes, Ambrose in effect makes Thecla a martyr as well, although she was not one.

[90] Ambrose, *De virginibus* 2.2.22–33. The real model for this tale is Theodora of Alexandria, as is noted by Gori, intro. to his trans. of *De virginibus*, pp. 84–85; Ramos-Lissón, intro. to his ed. and trans. of *Sobre las vírgines y Sobre las viudas*, p. 34. On the

cases, Rahab of Jericho and Judith. Rahab, she notes, washed away her prior life as a harlot by giving Joshua's scouts military intelligence that helped the Israelites conquer Jericho and by then converting to Judaism; Judith did better by putting her chastity at risk to defend the faith and save her people than had she protected it. The conclusion the virgin draws is that, even if subjected to a life of prostitution, she can preserve her virginity of mind: "It is better to preserve a virgin mind than a virgin body. Both are good, if it is possible to have both. But if it is not possible, let us at least remain chaste, not in the eyes of men but in God's sight" ("Tolerabilius est mentem virginem quam carnem habere. Utrumque bonum, si liceat. Si non liceat, saltem non homini castae, sed deo simus"). As chance would have it, the virgin's first client, a soldier, reveals that he is a secret Christian and that he has jumped to the head of the line in order to save her. In a passage that has escaped the attention of scholars in the burgeoning field of medieval cross-dressing, they exchange clothes and slip from the brothel initially undetected. But, the authorities eventually hunt them down and, happily, they are martyred together.[91]

Further, mere physical purity is far from the whole story in Ambrose's major biblical example, the Virgin Mary. For it is not just Mary's lifelong virginity, much as Ambrose extols it, but her daily activities and interactions with people around her that makes her a prime exemplar for his own consecrated virgins.[92] As with Miriam, the sister of Moses

---

example of Judith, see Jean Doignon, "La première exposition ambrosienne de l'*exemplum* de Judith (*De virginibus* 2.2.24)," in *Ambroise de Milan*, XVIe centenaire de son élection épiscopale, ed. Yves-Marie Duval (Paris, 1974), pp. 220–28. The quotation is at *De virginibus* 2.2.24. This passage echoes the consolation that Lucretia's husband and father seek to offer her on discovering that she has been raped, in Livy, *Ab urbe condita* 1.58.9: "Mentem peccare, non corpus."

[91] Ambrose, *De virginibus* 2.2.27–33. Not noted by Valerie Hotchkiss, *Clothes Make the Man: Cross-Dressing in Medieval Europe* (New York, 1996); Kerstin Losert, "Weibliches 'Cross-Dressing' in mittelalterliche Hagiographie: Zur Legende der heiligen Euphrosyna von Alexandria," in *Exil, Fremdheit, und Ausgrenzung in Mittelalter und früher Neuzeit*, Andreas Bihrer, Sven Limbeck, and Paul Gerhard Schmidt, eds., Identitäten und Alteritäten 4 (Würzburg, 2000), pp. 75–89, with extensive bibliography at pp. 87–89; nor by Laila Abdalla, "Theology and Culture: Masculinizing the Woman," in *Varieties of Devotion in the Middle Ages and Renaissance*, ed. Susan Karant-Nunn, Arizona Studies in the Middle Ages and the Renaissance 7 (Turnhout, 2003), pp. 17–37. To date, the only previous scholar who has noted this passage is Virginia Burrus, *Sex Lives of the Saints: An Erotics of Ancient Hagiography* (Philadelphia, 2004), p. 134, but she is interested in it primarily from the standpoint of queer theory.

[92] Ambrose, *De inst. virg.* 5.33, 5.35, 6.44–45, 13.82, 16.103; idem, *De virginibus* 1.8.53, 2.2.6–15, 2.2.18, 3.2.8–3.6.31. This accent on the Virgin's activities is drawn from

and Aaron who led the Israelite women through the Red Sea, Ambrose presents Mary as an activist as well as a person with many private virtues.[93] Mary is humble, prudent, modest, courageous, reticent in speech, strong in faith, zealous in reading and the desire to understand the things of God. She is also zealous and abundant in good works, helpful, benevolent, putting up with family members who fail to grasp her role in God's plan. She observes the stipulated fasts scrupulously and at other times eats for nutrition not gastronomy. She is frugal with sleep. She remains at home, except when on missions of mercy or when attending church, always accompanied by parents or other relatives. She receives the Eucharist. She comports herself without ostentation but with dignity and decorum. She avoids wedding feasts and parties, where guests indulge in rich food, wine, and dancing; but she is no spoil-sport. Her manner is both cheerful and urbane. As Hervé Savon has noted,[94] this picture is a better description of the upper-class consecrated virgins whom Ambrose is advising than of a busy first-century Jewish craftsman's wife. It is also worth noting, with Savon, that Mary's temperance with respect to food and sleep is not cited as a medically-inspired strategy for dampening down the sex drive. Rather, it is an expression of moderation and self-discipline in general.

This last point is a good point on which to conclude Ambrose's understanding of virginal chastity, and of chastity in general. As we have seen, he does not focus exclusively, or obsessively, on the virgin's physical integrity. Her physical state, and its external presentation, cede pride of place to her virginity of mind and her freely given commitment. The other virtues she possesses are less a *cordon sanitaire* erected to guard her physical purity than expressions of the virtues appropriate to her state, which her freedom from earthly marriage and her incorporation into

---

Ambrose's model, Athanasius, as is noted by scholars cited in n. 58 supra. See also Camelot, *Virgines Christi*, pp. 62–63; E. Joussard, "Un portrait de la sainte Vierge par saint Ambroise," *La Vie Spirituelle* 90 (1954), 477–89; Charles William Neumann, *The Virgin Mary in the Works of Saint Ambrose*, Paradosis 17 (Fribourg, 1962), pp. 38, 43–47, 181–83; Grossi, "La verginità," pp. 160–61, 163. Izarny, "La virginité," 1:65–68 and Riggi, "Fedeltà verginale," p. 179, stand alone in seeing the importance of Mary for Ambrose here as lying purely in her physical virginity.

[93] Ambrose, *De virginibus* 1.3.12, 2.2.17 on Miriam. Noted by Consolino, "Il *De exhortatione virginitatis*," pp. 463–65. Jean Doignon, "Miryam et son tambourin dans la prédication et l'archéologie occidentales au IVe siècle," *Studia Patristica* 4 (1961), 72–74, observes that Ambrose is the first Latin Christian thinker to make this Miriam/Mary connection.

[94] Savon, "Un modèle," p. 24.

the inner life of the Trinity as the bride of Christ make possible. In this respect, there are real parallels uniting the chastity of consecrated virgins, as Ambrose understands it, with the chastity he prescribes for widows and for married couples. Underlying his counsels for all three groups of Christians is a view of human nature that refuses to see the body, and human sexuality, as the chief obstacles in the path of those seeking virtue. In all three cases, his keynote is conscious commitment and moderation, as well as the placement of all three callings in a social context in which serving one's neighbors, and not merely pursuing one's own perfection and pleasures, be they physical, spiritual, or both, define the vocation of the individual Christian.

THE PROHIBITION OF CLERICAL MARRIAGE IN THE ELEVENTH CENTURY

Uta-Renate Blumenthal

By the eleventh century the prohibition of marriage for clerics of most ranks and not only monks—whose very name implied the solitary life—was very old. One could go back as far as the letters of St. Paul who, it is well known, exhibited a deep ambivalence towards marriage.[1] Ascetic, monastic, and cultic tendencies inherited from antiquity by the young Christian church led early on to attempts to require clergy to lead celibate lives, especially in the West. Indicative of such efforts in the context of ecclesiastical legislation are the canons of Elvira (306–314).[2] Despite the passage of time they were by no means forgotten in the 11th century. They were taken up in the widely known and influential *Liber decretorum* of Bishop Burchard of Worms of ca. 1023. Through Burchard's collection they reached the *Panormia* of Bishop Ivo of Chartres (of ca. 1093), the one collection that rivaled Burchard's influence in the 11th and early 12th centuries.[3] Burchard's sources, as far as they could be determined, were the *Paenitentiale ad Otgarium* of Hrabanus Maurus and the *Libri duo de synodalis causis* by Regino of Prüm, who in his turn was also heavily dependent on the penitentials.[4] The influence of the penitentials on the history of celibacy cannot be overestimated,

---

[1] See I Corinthians 7.25–40 as example.

[2] For this church council see J. Vives, *Concilios Visigóticos e hispano-romanos* (Barcelona, 1963), pp. 5, 6, 13 and J. A. Brundage, *Law, Sex, and Christian Society in Medieval Europe* (Chicago, 1987), pp. 69f. (especially n.102 regarding the disputed date of the Elvira meeting), 75, 110f., 150ff., and 205.

[3] For the canonical collections of Burchard and Ivo see P. Fournier and G. LeBras, *Histoire des collections canoniques en occident*, 2 vols. (Paris 1931 and 1932), vol. 1, pp. 364–421 and 2, pp. 55–114; H. Fuhrmann, *Einfluss und Verbreitung der pseudoisidorischen Fälschungen*, Monumenta Germaniae Historica [abbreviated below MGH], Schriften 24 (Stuttgart 1972–1974), part 2, pp. 442–85 and pp. 542–62; L. Kéry, *Canonical Collections of the Early Middle Ages* (Washington, D.C. 1999), pp. 133–155 (Burchard) and pp. 253–60 (Ivo's Panormia); L. Fowler-Magerl, *Clavis Canonum: Selected Canon Law Collections Before 1140*: Access with data processing, MGH Hilfsmittel 21 (Hanover, 2005), index p. 279 and 281.

[4] Burchard's sources are identified in H. Hoffmann and R. Pokorny, *Das Dekret des Bischofs Burchard von Worms*, MGH Hilfsmittel 12 (Munich, 1991).

although efforts at enforcement were sporadic at best and had very little success until we come to the 11th century.

Given the influence in particular of Burchard in the 11th century, and especially at the time of the Gregorian reform in the second half of the century, it is all the more remarkable that such influence appears to be totally lacking in the legislation of Pope Gregory VII, who is generally considered the unquestionable force behind the effective establishment of clerical celibacy as an unbreakable norm in the West, an establishment that is seen as one of the major accomplishments of this period of reform.[5] As this paper will show the eleventh-century ecclesiastical reform was by no means limited to the reign of Pope Gregory VII (1073–1085). We have to look to the pontiff's predecessors rather than Gregory himself in order to uncover the roots of the legislative strands of the new emphasis on the prohibition of clerical marriage and the reasons for its effectiveness. This will be the focus of this paper, whereas other important developments such as the formation of a matrimonial law under ecclesiastical jurisdiction or changing concepts of consanguinity, in other words marriage and the laity, will be disregarded here.

The historiographical discourse does not yet acknowledge the differences between the moralistic, popular and cultic emphases found in the 11th-century treatises of an Abbo of Fleury, of the cardinals Humbert of Silva Candida and Peter Damian, for instance, and the entirely different emphasis in papal legislation dealing in the first place with the social and economic consequences of clerical marriage and concubinage, with cultic considerations in the far-background. Intriguing precursors for the condemnation of clerical marriage in the 11th century are the writings of Abbo of Fleury (d. 1004), oblate, student and eventually teacher at this powerful abbey, formally known as Saint-Benoît-sur-Loire. His arguments, as represented in his *Liber Apologeticus* which he composed for kings Hugh Capet and Robert the Pious around the year 993, supported claims to a privileged status for monks within the Christian community by virtue of the virginity and sexual purity of monks. In a neo-Platonic sense of progression toward perfection monks assumed the highest possible rank in Abbo's scheme, designed not to promote virginity which was seen as a given, but rather in order to exempt monasteries from the discipline and visitation rights of the

[5] J. Lynch, "Marriage and Celibacy," *The Jurist* 32 (1972), 189.

episcopacy.[6] It is a short step from virginity and moral purity to the ideas presented by monastic writers half a century later, such as St. Peter Damian (d. 1072). Damian insistently demanded the prohibition of clerical marriage for reasons of cultic purity. He argued, for example, that "because Christ's natural body was formed in the temple of a virgin's womb, He looks to his ministers nowadays to be continent and clean in the presence of His sacramental body," and stated with regard to bishops that "hands that confer the Holy Spirit should not touch the genitals of harlots."[7] It is noteworthy that ecclesiastical legislation and monastic arguments such as those of St. Peter Damian could not be more different from each other as will be seen. Any inquiry into possible antecedents for the decrees of Gregory VII and his successors is bound to begin with the synod of Pavia, held in 1022 jointly by Pope Benedict VII and Emperor Henry II.[8] Its initial two canons exceed the severity of c. 3 of the Ecumenical Council of Nicaea in 325.[9] At Pavia all women were excluded from the houses of priests, and all married clergy, including bishops, was to be deposed. Their children and possibly wives—c. 2 of the imperial edict is unclear—are to become serfs of the manor of the cleric concerned. The imperial confirmation of the decisions of Pavia called unchastity of the clergy "the root of all evil", and unfree clerics who father sons with free women are described as "the worst enemies of the church."[10] Up to this point it is readily

[6] D. C. van Meter, "Eschatological Order and the Moral Arguments for Clerical Celibacy in Francia Around the Year 1000," in: *Medieval Purity and Piety*, ed. M. Frassetto (New York/London, 1998), pp. 149–175, here p. 154.

[7] H. E. J. Cowdrey, "Pope Gregory VII and the Chastity of the Clergy," ibid., pp. 269–302, here p. 271; see p. 270 for the similar arguments of Humbert of Silva Candida in 1054.

[8] MGH *Legum sectio IV*: *Constitutiones et acta publica imperatorum et regum*, vol. 1, ed. L. Weiland (Hanover, 1893), [cited below as: MGH Const. 1], no. 34, pp. 70–78; for more recent interpretations see J. Brundage, *Law, Sex, and Christian Society*, p. 218 and J. Laudage, *Priesterbild und Reformpapsttum im 11. Jahrhundert* (Cologne/Vienna, 1984), pp. 84–9 with further literature.

[9] According to the synod no woman could serve as housekeeper to a bishop, priest or cleric of any kind except for his mother, his sister, his aunt, or someone beyond all suspicion. For the text see *Conciliorum oecumenicorum decreta* J. Aberigo *et al.*, eds. (Bologna, 1973), p. 7.

[10] MGH Const. 1, p. 77 c. 2 in the imperial version. The reference to the *Codex iuris civilis* is misleading (cf. Novell. 123, c. 14 and p. 73, n. 1). The most likely precedent is c. 10 of the ninth council of Toledo (655), see B. Schimmelpfennig, "Zölibat und Lage der 'Priestersöhne' vom 11. bis 14. Jahrhundert," *Historische Zeitschrift* 227 (1978) 2–44, here pp. 11f., now reprinted in idem, *Papsttum und Heilige, Ausgewählte Aufsätze*, G. Kreuzer and S. Weiss, eds. (Neuried, 2005), pp. 133–176.

apparent why some historians are inclined to see the council of Pavia as an important step towards reform. This view, however, fails to take into account the main thrust of the legislation promulgated by both pope and emperor in 1022. Despite the rhetoric found in the first two canons—significant as a reminder of moral ideals—the issue in the main body of the remainder of the decrees was not so much the sexual probity of the clergy, but rather the great poverty into which the church had fallen despite her generous endowments by emperors and kings. The rich estates, patrimonies, and other goods of the church, lamented the canons of 1022, are acquired by "infamous fathers for infamous sons."[11] Such loss of property was to be prevented at all cost. The bulk of the legislation of 1022, therefore, spelled out in detail that sons and daughters of unfree clerics were to remain serfs forever. They were to belong to the church as chattel together with all their property.[12] In this period it is rare to find evidence for the practical effect of legislation like that of the council of Pavia, but the writer Adam of Bremen provided precisely such evidence for the sees of Hamburg and Goslar in Germany as we should have expected, given the imperial patronage at Pavia and the forceful and pious personality of Emperor Henry II (1002–1024).[13] The Bremen chronicler warmly praised Bishop Libentius of Hamburg for raising the income of his cathedral through the purchase of estates and the expulsion of the wives of canons from the city! As a result, Adam claimed, it was almost impossible to find a needy person. In other words, according to Adam the church of Hamburg could dispose of sufficient funds to assist the poor in the city once the unchaste cathedral canons had ceased to squander ecclesiastical income on their families. To sum up, pressing practical needs, the great poverty of the Roman church in particular, were the dominant themes at Pavia in 1022 and governed the measures of pope and emperor to limit the economic and social dislocations caused by married clergy and their support of their children. Despite the references to a general prohibition of marriage or concubinage for clerics in the records from Pavia, it should be noted that this theme is not developed in theological terms

---

[11] MGH Const. 1, p. 71, line 29ff.

[12] Schimmelpfennig, "Zölibat," (as in n.10) explains the surprising emphasis on unfree clergy as reflecting the status of priests at rural proprietary churches.

[13] Adam of Bremen, *Gesta Hammaburgensis ecclesiae pontificum*, 2nd ed., MGH Scriptores rerum germanicarum in usum scholarum (Hanover, 1876) 2.61, p. 82f with scholion 43. S. Weinfurter, *Heinrich II., Herrscher am Ende der Zeiten* (Regensburg, 1999), esp. pp. 158, 167, 248f.

in the main body of the decrees, nor is there more than an incidental reference to ritual purity.

The economic and social dislocations caused by married clergy had not disappeared fifty years later. A letter of Pope Gregory VII written in 1076 to William the Conqueror is an eloquent witness.[14] Gregory urged the king of England to expel Bishop Juhel from the see of Dol in Brittany. Juhel is said to have acquired the bishopric through simony and, moreover, "was not ashamed to enter openly into marriage", begetting children. Worse was to come. In the words of Gregory "he [Juhel] crowned a most frightful crime [his marriage]...by adding an abominable sacrilege. For by a monstrous outrage he married off the grown-up daughters of his illicit marriage, bestowing and alienating church lands and revenues by way of their dowries." There is no denying that at least in this particular case the alienation of ecclesiastical property appeared to Gregory VII as the worst offence the bishop of Dol had committed. The issue of ecclesiastical property was a constant in the papal struggle against simony and unchastity, the two issues that dominated the reform program in Rome beginning with Pope Leo IX (1049–1054) until the issue of investiture came to the fore in the 1070's. The hierarchy recognized that the prohibition of granting church property as benefices to married clergy was an even stronger inducement to errant clergy to abandon their wives than the threat of excommunication. The legislation of the Lateran council of 1059 that was reaffirmed in 1063 provides a clear example.[15] Its c. 3, in particular, forms the background to many of the pertinent references in the letters of Pope Gregory VII, but is also a significant illustration for the overall development in the second half of the 11th century concerning celibacy of clergy. The relevant section of the encyclical of Pope Nicholas II reads as follows in translation:

> Let no one hear the mass of a priest whom he knows with certainty to keep a concubine or a stealthily brought-in woman. For this reason the holy synod has decreed the following under threat of excommunication, saying: Whoever among priests, deacons, subdeacons publicly married a

[14] H. E. J. Cowdrey, ed. and trans., *The Epistolae vagantes of Pope Gregory VII* (Oxford, 1972), no. 16, p. 44f.

[15] A critical edition of the papal encyclicals ublicizing the decrees of the council of 1059 is by R. Schieffer, *Die Entstehung des päpstlichen Investiturverbots für den deutschen König*, MGH Schriften 28 (Stuttgart, 1981) pp. 208–225; see also D. Jasper, *Das Papstwahldekret von 1059* (Sigmaringen, 1986).

> concubine after the constitution regarding the chastity of the clergy which had been issued by the most holy Pope Leo, our predecessor of blessed memory, or did not dismiss one he had married earlier, shall not sing the mass, nor read the Gospels or the Epistles, as we declare and enjoin on behalf of the omnipotent God and on the authority of the blessed Apostles Peter and Paul; nor shall he remain in the choir room (*presbiterio*) for the divine offices with those who were obedient to the aforementioned constitution. Neither shall he obtain a benefice (*partem*) from the church until we have made a judicial decision regarding him, God willing.[16]

The prohibition to unchaste priests and lower clergy to serve at the altar and read the Scriptures as well as the startling innovation of a boycott of the mass by the populace speak a new language on the part of the papacy and the assembly. Unchaste clergy are to be deprived of their benefices and their cases were originally to be judged by the pope. Gone in the decree of 1059 are all references to unfree clerics and to the exile and/or enslavement of their wives.[17] A permanent deposition, however, was left up to ecclesiastical adjudication. The realization that it did not suffice to repeat the simple prescription not to have a wife as the Carolingian *Admonitio synodalis* had demanded, came evidently to the fore in determined reforming circles of the mid-eleventh century. The assembly of 1059 focused on realistic goals that presumably could be attained by using ecclesiastical discipline alone.

Especially noted should be the reference in the text to the "constitution regarding the chastity of the clergy which had been issued by the most holy Pope Leo, our predecessor of blessed memory". No such text has been preserved verbatim, but contemporaries were aware of legislation against married clergy at several of Leo's numerous synods. Most explicit is Peter Damian in a letter to Bishop Cunibert of Turin, and his testimony regarding papal legislation against married clergy has always been accepted at face value.[18] The letter is datable to 1064

[16] Schieffer (as in n.15), pp. 218–221. The encyclical which publicized several decisions of the council of 1059 is registered in Ph. Jaffé – W. Loewenfeld, *Regesta pontificum romanorum* with two versions sent by Pope Nicholas II (JL 4405/4406) and one for Pope Alexander II (JL 4501). Schieffer's edition shows that the later repromulgation omitted only the reference to papal adjudication but is otherwise little changed.

[17] The concept appears once again at the council of Melfi of 1089 held by Pope Urban II. See the edition of R. Somerville, *Pope Urban II, The collection Britannica and the Council of Melfi (1089)*, (Oxford, 1996) c. 12, p. 256.

[18] *Die Briefe des Petrus Damiani*, ed. K. Reindel (MGH, Die Briefe der deutschen Kaiserzeit IV, part 1–4, Munich, 1983–1993), letter # 112, part 3, pp. 258–288; see also J. J. Ryan, *Saint Peter Damiani and His Canonical Sources* (Toronto, 1956), pp. 101f.

according to Kurt Reindel, its editor. In the present context three segments of this letter in particular are relevant, one perhaps reflecting the boycott of 1059, another indicating Leo IX as originator of the boycott, and a third attributed to Pope Stephen IX.[19] As far as Leo IX is concerned, the fragments reveal first of all that this pontiff prohibited clerical marriage, a decree that was subsequently expanded by Stephen IX. Secondly, we learn that Leo decreed in a full synod that all Roman women who associated with clerics should become serfs of the Lateran. The third reference in Damian's letter is especially relevant. It preserves a prescription of Pope Stephen IX to expel unchaste clergy from the community of canons—this would presumably entail a loss of their benefice—and the choir room "so that they might desert their women and make amends through penance." This separation implies naturally the prohibition to celebrate mass or assist at the altar, precisely as demanded in 1059 by Pope Nicholas II and the council. Pope and assembly, therefore, simply reinforced legislation of the pontiff's predecessor, Stephen IX.

The expulsion of unchaste clergy—bishops were not mentioned and the expulsion at times might have been temporary—was not the only significant point of the legislation in 1059. Even more prominent was the mass boycott required in the opening sentences of c. 3 as quoted above: "Let no one hear the mass of a priest whom he knows with certainty to have a concubine..." This issue, too, was taken up in the letter of Peter Damian to Bishop Cunibert of Turin. Damian had participated in the 1059 council. He was perhaps the most ardent fighter at the time against lax morality, especially against all imaginable vices linked with sexual activity.[20] The implications of a mass boycott by the laity were certainly revolutionary, for a ninth-century forgery widely known and used in the 11th century, the canonical collection known as the Pseudo-Isidorian Decretals, had strictly prohibited in passage

Damian's letter has been translated by O. J. Blum in: Peter Damian, *Letters*, trans. Owen J. Blum, 7 vols. (Washington D.C., 1989–2005), here vol. 5 (1998), pp. 258–285.

[19] For details see this author's "Pope Gregory VII and the Prohibition of Nicolaitism," in: *Medieval Purity and Piety*, ed. M. Frassetto (New York/London, 1998) pp. 239–267, here p. 258, n. 30f.

[20] *Briefe* (as in n. 18 above), # 112; G. Fornasari, "S. Pier Damiani e lo 'sciopero liturgico,'" *Studi Medievali*, ser. 3, vol. 27 (1976), 815–32, here 817–19 and Ryan, *Canonical Sources*, item #182, p. 95; J. Boswell, *Christianity, Social Tolerance and Homosexuality: Gay People in Western Europe from the Beginning of the Christian Era to the XIVth Century* (Chicago, 1980), pp. 210–13; Brundage, *Sex, Law*, pp. 212ff.

after passage the accusation of any cleric by any layman.[21] And here, in 1059, a Roman council demanded from the laity to boycott unchaste priests. In positive terms this meant that the council asked the laity to judge the moral quality of the clergy.

The inspiration for the demand that the laity should boycott the masses of impure priests and bishops was probably not an earlier papal-conciliar decision but, rather, the events in Milan. In 1059 Pope Nicholas II had dispatched Peter Damian and Anselm of Lucca—the later Alexander II who repromulgated the 1059 decrees—as legates to the proud and independent city that was roiled by serious political, social, and religious unrest.[22] The *magistri* of the church could not be silent when the common crowd complained loudly and shamelessly about married clergy, Peter Damian had written to the pope prior to his setting out. He, Peter, did not see the point of "suppressing in the synod what is publicly proclaimed."[23] The Milanese faction heading the agitation, eventually known as the Pataria, had inconspicuous beginnings. Its first leader, the deacon Ariald of Carimate, who began to preach against immorality among the clergy in the countryside around Milan in the early 1050's, was a complete failure at first, a laughing stock for the higher clergy. Only with the assistance of Landulf Cotta, a notary of the Ambrosian church and a fiery preacher in his own right, could Ariald eventually create a faction in Milan that was strong enough to prevail against the leading powers of the day. Landulf and Ariald concluded a compact under oath that "they would not permit

---

[21] P. Landau, "Die Anklagemöglichkeit Untergeordneter vom Dictatus Papae zum Dekret Gratians," in: *Ministerium iustitiae: Festschrift für Beribert Heinemann*, eds. A. Gabriels and H. J. F. Reinhardt (Essen 1985), pp. 373–83 and W. Hartmann, "*Discipulus non est super magistrum* (Matth. 10.24)," in: *Papsttum, Kirche und Recht im Mittelalter*, ed. H. Mordek (Tübingen, 1991), pp. 187–200. It should be noted that the council of 1059 itself emphasized elsewhere (c. 10) that laymen were not allowed to judge or expel clerics. This statement was not transmitted in the later legislation discussed above. C. 10 of the council of 1059 is found in MGH Const. 1 (see n. 8 above), under no. 384, p. 548.

[22] H. E. J. Cowdrey, "The Papacy, the Patarenes and the Church of Milan," *Transactions of the Royal Historical Society*, 5th series 18 (1968), 25–48; reprinted in idem, *Popes, Monks and Crusaders* (London, 1984) as no. V. C. Violante, *La Pataria Milanese e la riforma ecclesiastica, I: Le premesse (1045–1057)* (Rome, 1955). Especially valuable as source is Peter Damian's report to Archdeacon Hildebrand (later Pope Gregory VII) in letter no.65 = *Briefe*, part 2, pp. 228–47.

[23] Damian, letter no. 61 = *Briefe*, part 2, here p. 208. Cf. R. I. Moore, "Family, Community and Cult on the Eve of the Gregorian Reform," *Transactions of the Royal Historical Society*, 5th series 30 (1980) 46–69, here pp. 50f. M. Blöcker, "Volkszorn im frühen Mittelalter," *Francia* 13 (1985) 113–49.

any priests and levites (deacons), to have wives from this day on."[24] It is often forgotten, however, that the Pataria not only attacked unchastity among clergy but condemned first of all the *luxuria* of the Milanese clergy. *Luxuria* is Peter Damian's favorite term to castigate the sinful lives of the clergy. What is condemned root and branch is an entire lifestyle as Ariald made clear. Ariald's vita, composed in 1075 by Andrea of Strumi, his disciple, faithfully recorded the essential themes of Ariald's first sermons:

> See, Christ says: "Learn from me because I am gentle and of humble spirit"; and again he says of Himself: "The Son of Man does not have a place to lay His head"; and again: "Blessed are the poor in spirit, for the kingdom of heaven is theirs." But in contrast to this, as you see, your priests [of the city of Milan] consider themselves richer because of earthly things, more exalted by building towers and houses, prouder because of honors, more beautiful because of soft and luxurious clothing: they are considered more blessed. And they, as you know, marry wives in public like laymen, just as accursed laymen imitate their fornication.[25]

The message of Ariald and Landulf caught on in Milan like wildfire. Important in the present context is that the agitation of the Patarenes was originally directed exclusively against the wives and concubines of priests and deacons. No one was to attend the masses of married clergy urged the Pataria. In vain did the higher clergy try to calm the situation and undermine the authority of Landulf and Ariald. On May 10, 1057, the usual solemn procession took place in the piazza in front of the cathedral of Milan in commemoration of the translation of St. Nazaro. Ariald addressed the crowd of his supporters. Thereupon the entire crowd with Ariald at its head invaded the cathedral and expelled unworthy priests by force. They were in the choir celebrating mass. On this day a momentous step from boycott to violence had been taken. Ariald and his supporters then went on to create a formulary

---

[24] See the references in n. 22 above; Violante, *Pataria*, p. 186.

[25] Andrea of Strumi, *Vita sancti Arialdi*, ed. F. Baethgen (MGH Scriptores 302, 1942–50) c. 19, p. 1063 or c. 10, p. 1055; Violante, *Pataria*, p. 182. G. Miccoli, "Per la storia della Pataria Milanese," in *Chiesa Gregoriana* (Florence, 1966), pp. 101–60, here p. 104f. for the characteristics of Andrea's account. For the technical meaning of *stuprum* see Brundage, *Sex, Law*, p. 29.

(*phytacium*) *de castitate servanda* that the clergy was forced to sign under threat of death.[26]

The influence of these events on the canons of 1059 is beyond doubt. It is equally certain that Gregory VII, the most important pope of the eleventh-century reform, was fully aware of them and in the beginning strongly approved of the Patarene movement. Other issues, simony and the question of the investitures of bishops and abbots by monarchs, dominated his reign, however.[27] As Cowdrey noted, except for the year 1075 and except with regard to Germany, Gregory did officially very little to enforce the papal regulations concerning celibacy. The eminent scholar described therefore as "excessive" the common historical opinion that "ascribed to Gregory VII an epoch-making role in demanding and enforcing the chastity of the clergy and in thereby establishing in the Latin church the closest possible association between priesthood and celibacy".[28] It should be emphasized, though, that in the course of Gregory's pontificate his attitude shifted, not so much because other issues were more important to the pope, but because as I would like to suggest he recognized the dangers of popular attacks on the ecclesiastical hierarchy—after all, not many years later anti-clericalism and heresy sprang from the same roots. For many reasons chastity of the clergy had to be enforced, not, however, by popular fiat, nor by the papacy, but rather by papal spokesmen, especially bishops. Gregory cannot have failed to be aware of the outrage expressed by many clerics who were literally up in arms about the prohibition of marriage and unchastity for ecclesiastics, in part at least because of the by now familiar linkage with popular boycotts.[29] Such boycotts were mentioned among the chief accusations against Pope Gregory VII raised by German bishops at the imperial Diet of Worms in late 1076 and constituted one of the reasons for the withdrawal of obedience from Gregory by German and Italian prelates. "...The entire administra-

---

[26] Most valuable among the voluminous historiography for these events are the works of C. Violante, *Pataria*, pp. 182–186, and H. Keller, "Pataria und Stadtverfassung, Stadtgemeinde und Reform: Mailand im 'Investiturstreit'", in: *Investiturstreit und Reichsverfassung*, ed. J. Fleckenstein (Sigmaringen, 1973), pp. 321–50.

[27] In general see H. E. J. Cowdrey, *Pope Gregory VII* (Oxford, 1998) and U.-R. Blumenthal, *Gregor VII* (Darmstadt, 2001).

[28] Cowdrey, "Gregory VII and Chastity" (as in n. 7 above), p. 280, but see p. 290f.

[29] A. L. Barstow, *Married Priests and the Reforming Papacy: The Eleventh-Century Debates* (New York/Toronto, 1982); E. Frauenknecht, *Die Verteidigung der Priesterehe in der Reformzeit*, MGH Studien und Texte 16 (Hanover, 1997).

tion of ecclesiastical affairs," wrote the imperial bishops in 1076, "has been attributed by you [Gregory VII] to popular furor...whereas you have, in as far as you could, deprived bishops of all power which by the grace of the Holy Spirit had been conveyed upon them."[30]

Gregory's own attitude in support of celibacy was, however, clearly expressed in the first years of his pontificate. Letters were sent out immediately after the Roman Lenten synod of 1075 to Archbishop Siegfried of Mainz and others like Bishop Burchard of Halberstadt in order to publicize the conciliar decisions. In a relevant section, following upon a decree against the heresy of simony, Gregory wrote:

> ...Those who are guilty of the crime of fornication should not celebrate masses or serve at the altar in lesser orders. Furthermore, we state that if these people ignore our rulings, or rather those of the holy fathers, the faithful should in no way receive their ministrations, so that whoever is not corrected for the love of God and the dignity of office might come to his senses by the shame of the world and the reproach of the faithful.[31]

A similar letter to Patriarch Sigehard of Aquileia is valuable because it contains the most detailed version of the 1075 decree against marriage of clergy. It includes the specific declaration that clergy who disobeyed the conciliar injunctions were not only to be excluded from service at the altar but also were not allowed to hold a benefice.[32] Just prior to the council Gregory had written to dukes Rudolf of Suabia and Bertulf of Carinthia, instructing them to have earlier decrees such as those of Pope Leo IX observed by the clergy—"even by force if necessary—", providing yet another link between Gregory VII and the decrees of 1059.[33] But already this early letter from January 1075 reveals that Gregory was fully conscious of the ambiguities of lay intervention, even if this intervention was carried out by dukes whom Gregory regarded

[30] *Die Briefe Heinrichs IV*, ed. C. Erdmann, MGH Deutsches Mittelalter, Kritische Studientexte 1 (Leipzig, 1937), Anhang A, p. 66, lines 20–25.

[31] JL 4931 published and translated by H. E. J. Cowdrey, *The Epistolae vagantes of Pope Gregory VII* (Oxford, 1972), no. 6, pp. 14–18 with the "Additional Note" regarding the dating of this set of letters. I accept Cowdrey's dating of the letters to 1075 despite Ch. Schneider, *Prophetisches Sacerdotium und heilsgeschichtliches Regnum im Dialog 1073–1077* (Münster, 1972), p. 79 n. 252 and p. 118 n. 365.

[32] This letter is found in the official register of Pope Gregory VII, critically edited by E. Caspar, *Das Register Gregors VII* (MGH Epistolae selectae II, vols. 1–2, Leipzig, 1920–21, 3rd repr. Berlin/Dublin/Zürich, 1967), here book 2, no. 62: p. 217. Gregory's register has been translated in its entirety by H. E. J. Cowdrey, *The Register of Pope Gregory VII 1073–1085* (Oxford/New York, 2002); see p. 156 for letter 2.62.

[33] *Das Register Gregors*, book 2, no. 45, pp. 182–185; trans. Cowdrey p. 135.

in this instance as the highest level of civil government. As Gregory explained to them, the dukes were to respond to critics of their use of physical coercion against clergy by a simple reference to "the obedience enjoined upon them" by the pope.[34]

Nonetheless, like Nicholas II and the council of 1059, Gregory VII remained willing to use the laity in order to enforce papal decrees if necessary. The possibility of a papal appeal to the populace enshrined as clause 24 of the *dictatus papae*, permitting accusations of clerics by 'subjects', was legally significant, because it enabled the papacy to intervene unilaterally whenever necessary or desirable.[35] Gregory took the initiative in this manner in the case of Bishop Otto of Constance. This bishop was one of the recipients of the letters sent out after the Lenten synod of 1075. In obedience to the papal request he, like several of his colleagues, held a local synod to repromulgate the Roman decrees at Constance. But the hostility of the lower clergy to the decree against nicolaitism was so great that the bishop had to abandon the promulgation of the relevant segment—interpreted by his critics as an abandonment of c. 3 of the council of Nicaea. Indeed, he had to go so far as to allow his clerics to take wives. Gregory's response was harsh:

> O the impudence! O the unparalleled insolence! That a bishop should despise the decrees of the apostolic see, should set at naught the precepts of the holy fathers, and in truth should impose upon his subjects from his lofty place and from his Episcopal chair things contrary to these precepts and opposed to the Christian faith.[36]

Appearances notwithstanding, in the letter Gregory unbent sufficiently to cite specific authorities in addition to the generic "precepts of the apostolic see," that is, the decrees of the February synod of 1075. In addition to a reference to St. Paul (1Cor. 5:11), Gregory referred to Pope Leo I and to Pope Gregory the Great. Gregory VII appears to have been profoundly convinced that in the last analysis nothing was needed except a reference to papal decisions whenever taken. It was pure graciousness when he condescended to cite anything else as a precedent. In his conclusion he ordered Bishop Otto of Constance to

---

[34] See n. 33.

[35] The *dictatus papae* is found in Gregory's register, book 2, no. 55a, here p. 207. The most recent translation of the famous documents is included in Cowdrey, *The Register*, pp. 149f.

[36] Cowdrey, *Epistolae vagantes*, no. 9, here p. 21 in Cowdrey's translation.

attend the next Lenten synod (February 1076). Without awaiting the results of this admonition, Gregory also wrote directly to the people of Constance. Moving beyond the essentially passive boycott of certain masses, enjoined in 1059 as well as by the Lenten synod of 1075 as we have seen, the pontiff in this letter freed the clergy and laity of Constance from obedience to the bishop and annulled all oaths of fealty to the bishop, "as long as he is a rebel against God and the apostolic see."[37] The Lenten council of 1076 suspended Otto, and finally, in 1080, he was deposed and excommunicated with other royal supporters. Bishop Altmann of Passau, a firm supporter of Gregory VII and like him a regular canon, was able to install a papal candidate as bishop of Constance, without, however, putting an end to the struggles over the bishopric which became a center of opposition to the Salian rulers.

Popular response to the papal decrees created strains elsewhere as well, for example in Salzburg, Erfurt, Mainz, Passau, or Thérouanne and Cambrai.[38] Detailed discussions would lead far beyond the present topic, but the situation in Thérouanne and Cambrai deserves some attention, because the events in northern France reflect very much a local and therefore different perspective. At Thérouanne, in defense against the popular boycott, Bishop Hubert apparently instructed his cathedral clergy to refuse baptism and burial to opponents of married clergy. Earlier, before Hubert's election to the bishopric in ca. 1079, Gregory had written to Countess Adela of Flanders, asking her to forbid clergy who refused to abandon their wives or concubines to celebrate mass. She was also asked to expel them from the choir of the cathedral and to deprive them of their benefices until they showed the fruit of penitence. She should replace them with chaste priests "from wherever she could find them." In particular she was not to listen to Archdeacon Hubert—the later bishop—who had fallen into heresy due to his incorrect contentions. This letter is dated November 10, 1076.[39] It is strikingly different in tone from a second letter sent at the same time to Count Robert, Adela's son. Here the pope requested merely that Robert should not obey bishops who themselves did not obey the Apostolic See—very much the same argument as found in the letter to Constance discussed earlier. There is nonetheless a certain shift in

[37] Cowdrey, *Epistolae vagantes*, no. 10, pp. 22–27.
[38] See Barstow, *Married Priests* and Frauenknecht, *Priesterehe*.
[39] *Briefe Gregors VII*, book 4, no. 10; trans. Cowdrey, *The Register*, p. 219f.

emphasis. Instead of calling for the use of force as he did in the letter to Adela or to the German dukes, Gregory demanded from Robert only a withdrawal of obedience in a letter that overall is completely pastoral in tone.[40] This trend became stronger in the course of Gregory's pontificate. Perhaps the fierce accusations levied against his reliance upon the laity by the German bishops assembled at Worms in December 1076 had not entirely missed their aim and reconfirmed hesitations that had been present even in 1059. As late as March 1077 Gregory repeated the injunctions proclaimed at the Lenten synod of 1075, including the call of a boycott of the masses celebrated by unchaste priests. At the great Roman synod celebrated in November 1078, however, the decree enjoining celibacy (c. 12) was exclusively addressed to bishops.[41] Bishops would be suspended if they did not use their disciplinary powers against unchaste priests, deacons, or subdeacons because of bribery. Interestingly it is only in this form that Gregory's measures on behalf of celibacy found an echo in contemporary canonical collections. By November 1078 the pontiff had indeed moved away from the reliance on the populace to enforce obedience to papal decrees upon an unwilling clergy. Resistance perhaps was too strong. The case of Ramirdus illustrates the point. The relatively early success of the Pataria in Milan could not necessarily be duplicated elsewhere. Ramirdus was burned alive in Cambrai, simply because "he dared to say that simonists and priests guilty of fornication were not allowed to celebrate mass and that their sacraments were not to be received."[42]

The papacy was clearly confronted with an uphill battle. The entrenched custom of clerical marriage was not easily eradicated, especially in the face of a skillful defense, ranging from references to the married clergy of the Old Testament as well as to the Eastern church, to the council of Nicaea and its supposed consideration of Paphnutius, to the New Testament itself. Heralds of the papal primacy like Bernold of Constance had an important role to play in the face of a determined opposition. If it has been said that Gregory VII was particularly influential, then this is certainly correct in one sense. No

[40] *Briefe Gregors VII*, book 4.11, trans. Cowdrey, *The Register*, p. 220f.

[41] *Briefe Gregors VII*, book 6, 5b, pp. 400–406, here p. 405f.; trans. Cowdrey, *The Register*, p. 285.

[42] *Briefe Gregors VII*, book 4, no. 20, p. 328, lines 22ff., trans. Cowdrey, *The Register*, pp. 230–232, here p. 231f. See R. I. Moore, *The Origins of European Dissent* (London, 1977), pp. 35–41 and 62f.

pope before him so consistently and systematically sought to enforce obedience to papal decrees. In respect to married clergy it must be added, however, that the final legislation promulgated by Pope Innocent II at the Second Lateran Council of 1139, to be taken up in Gratian's *Decretum*, owes nothing original to Pope Gregory VII for whom the legislation of 1059 had served as a constant guide.[43]

[43] *Conciliorum Oecumenicorum Decreta*, J. Alberigo *et al.*, eds. (Bologna, 1973), p. 198, c. 7.

AN ARAB CHRISTIAN PHILOSOPHICAL DEFENSE OF RELIGIOUS CELIBACY AGAINST ITS ISLAMIC CONDEMNATION: YAHYĀ IBN ʿADĪ

Thérèse-Anne Druart

When speaking of philosophy in Islamic lands during the Middle Ages, one often forgets that it gathered people from different religions working together in the pursuit of knowledge and wisdom. In his 1986 *Humanism in the Renaissance of Islam* Joel L. Kraemer has admirably shown that such was the case in tenth Century Baghdad.[1] Yet religious as well as cultural differences existed and could not be put under the rug. In this paper I wish to examine how an Arab Christian theologian and philosopher, Yahyā ibn ʿAdī, tries to tackle such deep religious and cultural differences. From apostolic times Christians valued celibacy and soon felt drawn to separate themselves from the world to live as hermits or monks. By the time Muhammad emigrated from Mecca to Medina in 622, the deserts of the East were peopled with Christian hermits and monks. Islam, on the other hand, objected to monasticism, celibacy, and the eremitical life from its inception. In popular Islamic culture, celibacy be it religious or by default, so to speak, is still regarded as the mother of all vices. Yahyā addresses this deep religious and cultural clash almost exclusively in philosophical terms, thereby emptying celibacy of its religious meaning.

Before presenting Yahyā's treatment of this topic, let us first examine the origin of Islam's objection to celibacy and monasticism. We can thereby more profitably consider Yahyā's defense of monastic celibacy and appreciate his need to couch it in philosophical terms.

According to the *Qurʾān*, which the Muslims consider uncreated, the origin of monasticism cannot be found in the will of God or in any form of divine inspiration. Rather, it arose from a mistaken invention of well-meaning, but deluded Christians. Sura 57:27 puts it:

---

[1] Joel L. Kraemer, *Philosophy in the Renaissance of Islam: Abū Sulaymān al-Sijistānī and His Circle* and *Humanism in the Renaissance of Islam: The Cultural Revival During the Buyid Age.* (Leiden, 1986). See also, Thérèse-Anne Druart, "Philosophy in Islam," in *The Cambridge Companion to Medieval Philosophy*, ed. A. S. McGrade (Cambridge, 2003), pp. 97–120.

> Then We made our messengers to follow in their footsteps, and We made Jesus son of Mary to follow, and We gave him the Gospel. And We put compassion and mercy in the hearts of those who followed him. And (as for) monkery [sic], they innovated it—We did not prescribe it to them—only to seek Allāh's pleasure, but they did not observe it with its due observance...." [I have used a contemporary English translation by a Muslim].[2]

Given the *Qur'ān's* assertion that monasticism constitutes a misguided Christian initiative, it is not surprising to find a tradition (*hadīth*) of the prophet Muhammad bluntly stating: "There is no monkery in Islam."

Furthermore, since priests are permitted to marry in the Oriental Churches, Muslims came to associate celibacy with monasticism and withdrawal from the world, an association they did not regard in positive terms. The famous Ibn Taymiyya himself, who died in 1328, issued the "fatwa," or Islamic judgment, about monks that would later serve as the theological foundation for the 1996 killing of the Trappist monks in Tibhirine in Algeria. In this "fatwa" he quotes the *Qur'ān* and this famous tradition. Our topic, then, is not one of mere interest for the medievalist; it is perennial in scope.

Yahyā was born in 893 in Iraq in Takrit, an important Christian center, well known for its remarkable library. As a young man, he moved to Baghdad, the intellectual Center of the time, where he spent the remainder of his life until his death in 974. He was a layman, married, with at least one son, earning his family's livelihood as a scribe, translator of philosophical texts from Syriac into Arabic, and probably also as a book dealer.[3] Already at that time the inculturation of Christians was such that they no longer spoke Syriac, but rather Arabic, and were writing theological texts in Arabic. Yahyā penned numerous theological treatises in Arabic for his Syrian Orthodox or Jacobite community or against the members of the Church of the East, i.e., the Nestorians, or to defend Christian views against the Muslims. In Islamic circles he was known as "al-Mantiqī" i.e., the logician. In fact, he studied philosophy with the famous al-Fārābī (870–950), a Muslim of sort, and was one

---

[2] *The Holy Qur'ān*: Arabic Text with English Translation and Commentary by Maulana Muhammad Ali, new ed. (Ohio, 2002). In fact the *Qur'ān* in the early chapters presents a fairly positive view of monks, but later chapters are more negative.

[3] Cf. Sidney H. Griffith in his introduction to Yahyā ibn ʿAdī, *The Reformation of Morals*: *A parallel Arabic-English Edition, Translation, and Introduction*, Eastern Christian Texts, 1 (Provo, 2002), pp. xiii–xxviii.

of the leading members of the Aristotelian School in Baghdad. One of his more popular ethical treatises, *The Reformation of Morals*, was very influential among both Muslims and Christians and helped him to attract numerous disciples from various religious persuasions.

As both the *Qur'ān* and the "hadith" condemn monasticism in no uncertain terms and are, by extension, opposed to a person's remaining unmarried and childless, Yahyā could not ground his arguments in these sources. The *Qur'ān* does speak of Jesus as a great prophet, however, and acknowledges that God entrusted him with a "book", the Gospel. We might expect Yahyā to refer to this book. That he does not do so stems, no doubt, from the fact that the *Qur'ān* regards Christian Scriptures as having been altered to the point of making claims that contradict what Jesus actually said or did. Examples include the claim that God is a Trinity of persons, and that Jesus is the Son of God, who died on the cross and rose again. As Muslims do not recognize the canonical gospel text as Christians have it, Yahyā cannot argue on these grounds either. He is left with philosophy, by default, as the common language of discourse.

Regarding the circumstances that led Yahyā to write this work,[4] we know nothing. One part of this text is a letter supposedly written by a Muslim in 964. Obviously, this work is intended for a Muslim audience with some philosophical education. Its structure is rather complex, beginning with a treatment of the opinions of various sages on the renunciation of offspring. The context makes it clear that, for Yahyā, "having offspring" signifies not merely procreation as such, but also the task of raising children and caring for a family. Yahyā presents four arguments articulating the Muslim's view that when Christians renounce

[4] This work can be found in Arabic and a French translation as *Traité sur la continence de Yahyā ibn 'Adī*, ed. Vincent Mistrih, O.F.M., Studia Orientalia Christiana, Collectanea, 16 (Cairo, 1981). The text is divided into paragraphs with continuous numbering, to which I refer. The edition is based on two versions of the text; the complete version is found solely in Ms. 370 of the Copt Orthodox Patriarchate in Cairo, and the abbreviated version in two Rome, Biblioteca Apostolica Ms Vat. Ar. (Mss) 134 and 115. "Continence" is not a good translation of the title. In his *The Works of Yahyā ibn 'Adī: An Analytical Inventory* (Wiesbaden, 1977), Gerhard Endress describes it as "A discussion of arguments for and against celibacy," p. 120. Griffith, in his translation of *The Reformation of Morals*, speaks of "the so-called Treatise on Continence" (p. xliv). I have chosen to render it more literally as the *Giving Up of Having Offspring*. Griffith is preparing a translation *cum* edition for the Eastern Christian Texts Series, cf. "Yahyā b. 'Adī's Colloquy *On Sexual Abstinence and the Philosophical Life*," in *Arabic Theology, Arabic Philosophy. From the Many to the One: Essays in Celebration of Richard M. Frank*, ed. James E. Montgomery, Orientalia Lovaniensia Analecta (Leuven, 2006/7), pp. 299–333.

having offspring they thereby oppose God, become his enemies, and are odious to Him. Yahyā refutes these arguments, showing that they are bad syllogisms, based on a false or partially false premise. He then presents his own arguments in favor of the Christian position. There follows a letter supposedly written by one of Yahyā's close Muslim friends, to a third mutual friend. Its author claims that in this treatise Yahyā misunderstood some of his views, a claim to which Yahyā replies, by refuting his arguments, before concluding his own letter with three questions. The friend answers them in a letter dated Monday, tenth night of Muharram of the year H353, i.e., 964, only to be refuted again by Yahyā who, not surprisingly, has the last word.

It is unlikely that this collection of texts constitutes a real correspondence. Quite often, Arabic philosophical treatises are presented in this manner, as a letter in response to a friend's question, the apparent "correspondence" being a rhetorical ploy aimed at making the text more lively and attractive to its audience. Let us leave this question aside, however, in order to focus on the arguments.

Though the work openly defends a Christian conception against criticisms from Muslims and contains numerous brief prayers for Yahyā's friends, its argumentation is almost exclusively philosophical and its theological or religious passages likewise manifest heavy philosophical leanings.

From the outset, Yahyā claims that the four arguments depicting the renunciation of offspring as an abomination all rest on a flawed basic premise. They assume that this renunciation is the ultimate end of Christianity; they view it as a universal requirement, whereas it is only one of the means to attain Christianity's true aim. Our author presents this true aim in philosophic language: it is happiness, described as focusing on the acquisition of true sciences and divine wisdom. The expression "divine wisdom" may mean knowledge of God, in a religious sense, or metaphysics, or both. In fact, Yahyā seems to blend both meanings and to deliberately shift from one to the other.

Interestingly, we must wait until the final exchange before we find any allusion to Muhammad and his companions or to Christ and his apostles. But even here, philosophical analysis remains in the forefront. For instance, Yahyā's dear but anonymous Muslim friend asks that we imagine two young men of good and balanced character, keen intelligence, and excellent health. If, he argues, one of these young men were to remain celibate and solitary, locked in the pursuit of knowledge, he would lead an impossible life and, therefore, in fact regress, while the other, despite the practical needs to care for his wife and children, would thrive (nn. 91–93). Yahyā's Muslim friend presents several historical examples in support of this claim, beginning with philosophers and ending with prophets. Socrates, Plato, and Aristotle, he notes, the three greatest philosophers, each lived in cities, had friends and disciples, and died leaving an estate, wives, children, and slaves. The prophets did so, as well. Even Christ—though he was an exception in a sense, which remains unstated, because of a bad patch in the manuscript—lived for the most part with his disciples. He did not order them to give up their house, wives, and children; nor did he prevent them from marrying. The friend makes the same argument for just kings, such as Alexander the Great, as well as for Muhammad and his companions, who also died living estates, wives, and children. These latter two examples also served as governors of a nation subject to human or divine laws, within which philosophic ends and activities were allowed to flourish (nn. 94–97). We should take note here of Muhammad's inclusion in a treatment of just kings.

Especially striking in Yahyā's reply to the foregoing is the pride of place he gives to philosophers over the prophets and even Christ. Following a long-standing tradition confusing Socrates and Diogenes,[5] he denies that Socrates led an ordinary life, claiming instead that he lived in solitude in a cistern. Yahyā casts the fact of Socrates' marriage in utilitarian terms; it was merely a means for Socrates to restrain his temper through regular exercises in toleration of his wife's crustiness (nn. 125–26). Similarly, Yahyā argues, the other philosophers and just kings who married and produced offspring did so for one of the six valid reasons, each of which fosters closeness to God and thereby shows that procreation may be virtuous in some circumstances. Stated succinctly, he lists these reasons as follows. One may, in procreating, aim at the birth of 1. a prophet; 2. a just king; 3. a pious priest; 4. a learned scholar; or 5. one may procreate as cure for diseases stemming from lack of sexual activity, or finally 6. as prevention of those same diseases which, if contracted, would inhibit true scholarship (n. 59). According

[5] The philosopher-physician al-Rāzī (ca. 864–925 or 932, the Latin Alrazes) deals with this same tradition in his *Philosophic Life*, in which Socrates has been said to have lived in a jar in the desert: Arabic in *Abi Bakr Mohammadi Filii Zachariae Raghensis (Razis), Opera Philosophica Fragmentaque Quae Supersunt*, ed. Paul Kraus (Cairo, 1939), p. 99; English translation in "The Book of the Philosophic Life," by al-Rāzī, trans. Charles E. Butterworth, *Interpretation*, (20/3) (1993), 227.

to Yahyā, if Aristotle fathered a daughter, it was probably as a cure of, or prevention against, one such disease (n. 127). The same may be said for the prophets. As for Christ, he showed that renunciation of procreation is not necessarily a violation against temperance. Muslim thinkers had often employed Aristotle's conception of virtue as a mean between two extremes to argue that temperance, the virtue concerned with the appetites of food, drink, and sex, requires that one be moderate in the domain of sex, neither indulging too much, nor abstaining altogether. These thinkers decried complete abstinence as one of the extremes that should be avoided (n. 129). They also followed Aristotle in claiming that as God the creator does nothing in vain, the vegetative faculty, which includes the reproductive organs, must be used in moderation and not simply discarded (n. 1). Yahyā replies that Christ gave up procreation and ordered his friends to do so as well. Christ also practiced voluntary poverty and sent his disciples on journeys without even provision for two days (n. 129). Taking up the notion that virtue is a mean and the argument that temperance therefore necessitates some degree of sexual activity, Yahyā dismisses it on the grounds that not every virtue is a mean. He cites as examples the faculties of seeing and hearing, wherein virtue is constituted, not by moderate, but rather by the maximal use of these faculties. Yahyā considers that the core of the problem is a syllogistic mistake: the quantifier of the premise that virtue is a mean is not universal as the adversary believes, but rather particular.

The only other religious argument concerns hermits, though the term is not used. Muslims claim that a perfectly solitary life in the desert is not properly human, but rather characteristic of wild animals. Yahyā, on the other hand, asserts that the quality of such a life can only be understood by those who have experienced it. Genuine hermits, he asserts, possess such intellectual acumen as to reach divine illumination, a fact which prompts Yahyā to liken them to those in Plato's cave who broke free from their chains and went to the light, only to be seen as mad by their former fellow prisoners still enchained in the cave of ignorance (n. 124).

As philosophy is the only common language between Yahyā and the Muslims, it is not surprising that Yahyā and his adversaries use philosophical arguments. Yahyā's basic strategy is to claim that the aim of Christianity is happiness, expressed as the attainment of true sciences and divine wisdom. He is careful never to explain what he means by divine wisdom, leaving his readers with the impression that the Christian life leads to the highest scholarship rather than to union with God or holiness. This conception of happiness allows him to argue that renouncing procreation is an excellent means for such an aim, but that this means is not suited for all. There are those who find this renunciation fairly easy and enjoy the freedom it offers them to consecrate more time to scholarship. These need simply to take proper care of their health (n. 104), through a simple and sound diet (n. 120). In such a case, the celibate life offers fewer distractions. But for some people complete sexual abstinence would lead to illness, which in turn would adversely affect their life of scholarship. Thus, he argues, should the celibate life represent more of a hindrance than a help to scholarly life, it would be better to marry. Celibacy, in short, is not the best path for every Christian. Marriage and procreation are seen as virtues when offspring are desired for one of Yahyā's six reasons listed earlier, i.e., aiming at the procreation of prophets, just kings, pious priests, and excellent scholars, or at the cure or prevention of diseases caused by a lack of a sex life.

The potential for marriage to impinge the scholarly life is an old and pervasive theme in philosophy. Abelard presents the same kind of arguments, for instance, in his *Historia Calamitatum*, when he describes Heloise's efforts to convince him not to marry her. Let us recall here that Yahyā himself *was* married; he had at least one son, and was a busy and respected scholar who earned his family's livelihood as a scribe and translator. If Yahyā wrote this treatise at the request of his church, the hierarchy made a smart move in entrusting the defense of monastic celibacy to an active and respected married man. His arguments had a particular force since, as a husband, father, and respected scholar, no self-serving motive would prompt him to praise the virtues of celibate life. He also comments, while referring to scholars leading an ordinary life, that private means allow one to buy useful books and to study with great masters. His own profession put him in contact with many books and scholars.

In his argument, Yahyā must also counter one of the fears Muslims harbor about celibacy, namely that it could lead to the extinction of the human species. He does so on several fronts. First, recalling that for some people marriage is preferable to celibacy as a context for the pursuit of happiness and scholarship, he claims that some people will always reproduce themselves. Furthermore, human sperm will always have the capacity to produce people with "procreative" leanings, thereby further assuring the perpetuity of the species. Though his argument is not as clear as one might wish, it seems based on the Neoplatonic principle of plenitude, with its assumption that eventually all possibles must be realized (n. 14). Second, even if *per impossibile* all people would become celibate scholars, God, if He so wished, could simply bypass the necessity of procreation and directly create more human beings, as He did in the case of Adam (n. 18). Third, the adversary's argument assumes that an increase of good is always a good, but Yaḥyā notes that such a premise is only partially true. For instance, almsgiving is good, but if one increases its amount to those less worthy of it than others, then the increased donation cannot be said to be good. In this case, one ought to diminish the amount given to the less worthy mendicant in order to be more generous to the more worthy. This type of decrease in almsgiving would not be an evil, but rather a good, since the amount of money will be more worthily distributed. Finally, Yaḥyā counters the view that an increase in the number of human beings leads to greater economic prosperity with the assertion that, in fact, the greater the population, the more frequent wars would arise as an attempt to control the size of the same limited resources.

Yaḥyā was famous as a logician and he enjoys showing that his adversaries' arguments are invalid because one of their premises is couched in universal rather than particular terms, i.e., quantified by an "all," instead of a "some." It makes the adversary appear as if he did not know even the most elementary logic.

There is no doubting Yaḥyā's wisdom in using a language that his adversary could accept and he does argue skillfully. Yet, some of his own arguments are rather weak and the implied equation of religious celibacy with a desire to better one's scholarship undermines the very meaning of celibacy. Maybe Yaḥyā thought it would be impossible to explain the true meaning of the celibate life to Muslims and so decided not to try.

In his brief analysis of this text Griffith claims that "one notices immediately [its] openly religious dimension."[6] For my part, I think that Yaḥyā's zeal for logic obfuscates the religious dimension. One wonders, for instance, why a Christian in a defense of celibacy would say the following, which I quote in Griffith's own translation:

[6] *The Reformation of Morals*, p. xlv.

> I think that Aristotle, Plato, and Socrates were the most excellent in terms of making choices, the most perfect in conduct, and more successful than any of the other practitioners of philosophy and religion[7] (n. 96).

Griffith suggests that Yahyā follows "the Ancient Christian penchant for equating monasticism with the practice of the philosophy of Christ." This may well be true, but, as Yahyā's Muslim audience was generally unaware of this penchant in Christianity and of its meaning, we may well suspect that his arguments left them with a peculiar conception of celibacy and monasticism.

[7] *The Reformation of Morals. Ibid.*

DEPICTIONS OF CHASTITY: VIRTUE MADE VISIBLE

Susan L'Engle

In 1969 a daughter was born to Cher and Sonny Bono. They named her Chastity, an uncommon and burdensome name for a child to bear in this time and place. The negative resonance of this name still prevails, clearly articulated in a 1996 interview with Chastity Bono, where the reporter commented: "When she was born in 1969, Chastity Bono got stuck with that name forever.... 'Not that many people call me Chastity anyway,' she says. She prefers Chas. Hell, wouldn't you?"[1]

Today in the twenty-first century we all have personal takes on the meaning of the word chastity and its relevance to our individual lives, shaped by our upbringing and education and supplemented by input from various media. In the Middle Ages, however, chastity was an all-pervading and multivalent concept that regulated the lives of lay men and women, and clergy alike. The ideals of chastity were expressed verbally by churchmen, theologians, philosophers, poets, and heads of family—and recorded in sermons, Saints' Lives, advice manuals for rulers, courtesy books, and poems of courtly romance. For many of these texts, artists created images and compositions to illustrate and reinforce the verbal discourse, and it is these visual manifestations that will be analyzed and discussed in this project.

As a medievalist I am interested in the various ramifications of chastity within the strata of medieval society; as an art historian, I want to explore how the notion of chastity can be represented visually, and what circumstances provoke its illustration. My main source has been the manuscript illuminations to various texts, and these will be supplemented by comparable examples of art in monumental format. These images, besides their role as illustration or decoration, served also to moralize, support religious ideas, instruct or frighten the viewer, and sometimes even amuse. Function notwithstanding, as constructs of their time they must be seen as "loaded," reflecting the ideas and interests consciously or unconsciously upheld by the social environments in which

[1] Published in *OutSmart Magazine*, November, 1996.

they were created, and projecting messages that we may no longer be able to fully interpret.[2] While examining them we should bear in mind how they have most often been understood, and also how they may often have been misconstrued.

It is rarely possible to isolate the precise intention behind the creation of a particular image, or to decipher how it affected the cultural segments in which it was viewed. And as the same motif is repeated along the centuries, its resonance necessarily adjusts to the contemporary audience. Nanette Salomon brilliantly demonstrates this point as she charts the evolution of the pictorial composition known as the *Venus Pudica*, a depiction of a female nude who covers her genitals with one hand.[3] The pose, generally construed as "modest" or "chaste" has its earliest representation in Praxiteles's *Knidian Aphrodite*, created around 350 BC and known today in a Roman copy of the original.[4] In ancient Greek art it is regarded as the first monumental cult statue of a goddess to be represented entirely nude—and the first monumental female nude sculpture to be positioned with her hand over her pubic area. For Salomon, "Praxiteles's Aphrodite is in the condition of both complete nudity and self-conscious nakedness... that sexually defines the represented woman by her pubis, and... keeps her in a perpetual state of vulnerability.[5] This motif quickly became popular for representations of Venus and Aphrodite and generated a large number of imitations, with the additional gesture of covering the breasts.[6] An analysis of this pose must take into account how ancient Greeks differentiated male and female capacities for controlling physical desires: Men resisted physical and psychological attacks by their intelligence, while women were seen to be ruled by their emotions and were more inclined to indulge them. The poets envisioned women as sexually insatiable, feeling no need to

[2] On art and ideology, see especially Jonathan J. G. Alexander, "Iconography and Ideology: Uncovering Social Meanings in Western Medieval Christian Art," *Studies in Iconography* 15 (1993), 1–44, and "*Labeur* and *Paresse*: Ideological Representations of Medieval Peasant Labor," *Art Bulletin* 72 (1990), 436–452.

[3] See Nanette Salomon, "The Venus Pudica: Uncovering Art History's 'Hidden Agendas' and 'Pernicious Pedigrees,'" in *Generations & Geographies in the Visual Arts: Feminist Readings*, ed. Griselda Pollock (London/New York, 1996), pp. 69–87.

[4] Vatican City, Vatican Museum, Museo Pio Clementino; reproduced in Salomon, "The Venus Pudica," Figure 5.1.

[5] Salomon, pp. 70–72.

[6] See the Capitoline Aphrodite, reproduced in Salomon, cited above, n. 3, Figure 5.4 and the Medici Aphrodite, reproduced in R. R. R. Smith, *Hellenistic Sculpture* (London, 1991), fig. 100.

dominate their passions. Aristotle claimed that men kept themselves chaste through rational self-control and resistance to indulgence, while women must submit to authority and rely on outside control to maintain their chastity since they could not control themselves.[7] Viewed in this light, the "modest" gesture of Praxiteles's Aphrodite would appear to fulfill the dichotomous purpose of hiding her genitals while simultaneously directing attention to them, thus evoking woman's rampant physicality.

In the Christian period the "pudica" position was adopted for representations of Adam and Eve in their expulsion from Paradise, here not so much a display of modesty but rather to express shame and humiliation. In most medieval compositions—such as a scene from the thirteenth-century Morgan Library Picture Bible (fig. 1)—Adam also covers his genitals,[8] a gesture in a sense feminizing, since he assumes a pose hitherto confined to female representations. In Masaccio's dramatic *Expulsion from Paradise*, however, while Eve hides her genitals from the viewer, Adam covers his face to conceal his expression of shame.[9] We see the artist's conception, once again, of referencing the woman by her external sexual features, while the male is characterized by an inward, psychological response.

Somewhat later in the fifteenth century the *Venus pudica* was reintroduced into western European tradition with Botticelli's *Birth of Venus*, "the first monumental image since Roman times of the nude goddess in a pose derived from the classical statues of Venus."[10] Despite the similarity of pose, in contrast to the Greek prototype, the visual message transmitted by Botticelli's painting has shifted, reflecting at one level the contemporaneous Neo-Platonism of the Florentine Humanist Marsilio Ficino, presenting the goddess as an intellectual representation of beauty, rather than an example of erotic love. "Pudica" gestures

[7] Aristotle, *Politics*, 1260a20–4; 1277b20–4, cited in Anne Carson, "Putting Her in Her Place: Woman, Dirt, and Desire," in *Before Sexuality: The Construction of Erotic Experience in the Ancient Greek World*, eds. David M. Halpern, John J. Winkler, and Froma I. Zeitlin (Princeton, N.J., 1990), p. 142.

[8] In the Morgan Library composition the hand gesture supplements the fig leaf that is already in place.

[9] Florence, Santa Maria del Carmine, the Brancacci Chapel, painted in the early fifteenth century; illustrated in Ornella Casazza, *Masaccio and the Brancacci Chapel* (Florence, 1990), fig. 21.

[10] Cf. the well-known Janson, *History of Art* (New York, 1986), p. 432. *Birth of Venus* is housed at the Uffizi, Florence.

Figure 1 New York, The Pierpont Morgan Library and Museum, Ms M.638, fol. 2r, detail. The Morgan Library Picture Bible. Tempera and ink on parchment. With permission of the Pierpont Morgan Library.

were further rearranged in Titian's sixteenth-century *Venus of Urbino*,[11] imparting an ambiguous physicality to the motif: the goddess is now conceived as a languid, reclining figure, and her passive, drooping hand draws attention to while hiding the pubic area. Is she placidly proclaiming her chastity, or tantalizing the viewer? Dominating the foreground, this Venus projects into our own space, granting us a sense of vicarious participation in the scene and perhaps possession over her body. In the nineteenth century however Manet's figure of *Olympia* changed the energy of this pose.[12] In this composition *Olympia* sits upright and boldly seeks eye contact, the tension of her sharply attenuated fingers deliberately drawing attention to that which it hides, daring the viewer to respond. Ironically, the chief reason for the uproar over this painting's presence in the Salon of 1865 was not that it seemed overly sensuous, or provocative, but that the public thought it ugly, departing from the idealized female figure in the guise of goddess or nymph. Besides the lack of academic polish in Manet's painterly treatment, *Olympia* could be recognized as an ordinary Parisian woman, an everyday sight, whose nudity, so directly presented, offended the contemporary critical eye.[13] Much the same occurred in 1991 with the nude, pregnant figure of the actress Demi Moore as it appeared on the cover of *Vanity Fair*.[14] The photograph is a study in conflicting messages: the actress's modest gestures to cover herself direct attention to her ripe, bulging body and the body itself is the greatest advertisement of her lack of chastity. Over a hundred years later, this photograph was as offensive to American eyes as *Olympia* had been to Parisians, since in many states it had to be covered up on the newsstands, relying on the actress's decapitated gaze and the large MORE DEMI MOORE on the cover to attract the reader. As Madeline Caviness observed, "...the photograph is taken as a simulacrum of the real figure; the signifier is conflated with the signified and transgresses the boundaries that have been agreed for reality, as

---

[11] Uffizi, Florence.

[12] Paris, Musée du Louvre.

[13] See George Heard Hamilton, *Manet and His Critics* (New Haven/London, 1986), pp. 67–80, and Otto Friedrich, *Olympia: Paris in the Age of Manet* (New York, 1992), pp. 1–3.

[14] Cover, *Vanity Fair*, August, 1991; photograph by Annie Leibovitz; illustrated in Madeline H. Caviness, "Obscenity and Alterity: Images that Shock and Offend Us/Them, Now/Then?" in *Obscenity: Social Control and Artistic Creation in the European Middle Ages*, ed. Jan M. Ziolkowski (Leiden/Boston, 1998), pp. 155–75, fig. 17–17.

opposed to more lenient ones for 'art.' A pregnant nude Demi Moore cannot be allowed on the street, staring back at the voyeur."[15]

This initial visual excursion has sought to demonstrate the fluctuating artistic objectives, social receptions, and interpretations of images, over time and geographical space. As slippery as the interpretation of pictorial material can be, exegesis of the verbal presents its own contradictions and diversity of meanings. For example, "chastity" is not synonymous with "virginity," for chastity, unlike virginity, may be regained. Virginity is a physical condition, implying a body as yet innocent of sexual congress. The concept of chastity begins with a state of mind, or an attitude: it involves much more than sexual abstinence, and in fact abstinence is not always a condition of being chaste. "Continence," a word used generally in reference to self-restraint, was often assigned a specifically sexual context. Even up into the thirteenth century the terms *continentia* (continence), *castitas* (chastity), and *pudicitia* (purity) could be used interchangeably to denote the virtue concerned with sexual matters.[16]

In the Middle Ages, textual constructions of the chaste body developed from patristic accounts of chastity and virginity, prescribed for the life situations in which most women found themselves: virginity, marriage, and widowhood. These circumstances also distinguished the degrees of chastity to which women could aspire: the first and highest rank was held by virgins; the second level encompassed widows who abstained from a second marriage; and the third comprised married women faithful to their husbands.[17] Virginity was exalted for young girls, who were urged to preserve their sexual purity and modesty before marriage. For wives, the ideal of virginity was converted to that of chastity, which was considered the foundation for a woman's honor. Married chastity involved restricting one's sexual activity to one's husband, while observing the Church's proscriptions against having sexual relations on forbidden days.[18] Tertulian, though finding in virginity "the most perfect sanctity," since it had not known fornication, praised the chastity of the

---

[15] Caviness, "Obscenity and Alterity," pp. 159–60.

[16] Pierre J. Payer, *The Bridling of Desire: Views of Sex in the Later Middle Ages* (Toronto, 1993), pp. 154–55.

[17] Mary Louise Lord, "Dido as an Example of Chastity: The Influence of Example Literature," *Harvard Library Bulletin* 17 (1969), 22–44, 216–32, at p. 26.

[18] On compulsory periods of abstinence from sexual relations between married couples, see James Brundage, *Law, Sex, and Christian Society in Medieval Europe* (Chicago, 1987), pp. 155–64.

widow, since it was "sensible of the right it has sacrificed and knows what it has experienced."[19] St. Augustine believed that chastity was a gift from God, and while approving the institution of marriage, nevertheless contended that sexual relations that were not for the purpose of procreation were nothing but lust, and should be avoided.[20] For Aquinas chastity was most perfectly expressed by virginity. Conjugal chastity was praiseworthy since it abstained from illicit pleasures, and widowhood added something over and above common chastity but was not perfect because it did not achieve complete immunity from sexual pleasure.[21] In discussions of chastity, the virtues of humility, obedience, modesty, piety, and temperance are prescribed for virgins, widows, and wives,[22] and often these virtues were conflated in the term *chastity*.

Imaging Chastity

This section draws on the preceding definitions and concentrates on these questions: How does "chastity" look? What objects, attributes, postures, gestures, or metaphorical devices did artists use to describe it? It will be seen that the iconography of chastity was primarily inscribed upon, though not exclusive to, the female body, and the overwhelming majority of discourse on this topic was directed at the woman.

In the course of my research I found that the visualization of chastity was not easily conceived, though artists found many ways to depict the unchaste or the absence of chastity. In the twelfth century, for example, the carved image of *luxuria* appears on many portals and doorways, usually portraying a woman suffering in Hell; serpents biting the parts of her body through which she sinned in life. In one very graphic version the serpent emerges from the figure's vagina and chews at her breasts, a "penis-serpent," in Michael Camille's interpretation.[23] Besides

---

[19] Tertullian, "Ad Uxorem" ("To his Wife"), *Treatises on Marriage and Remarriage*, trans. William P. Le Saint, Ancient Christian Writers No. 13 (Westminster, Virginia, 1951), p. 21, quoted in Cindy L. Carlson and Angela Jane Weisl, eds., *Constructions of Widowhood and Virginity in the Middle Ages* (New York, 1999), p. 2.

[20] St. Augustine, *Soliloquiorum Libri Duo*, PL XXXII, cols. 878–80.

[21] Aquinas, *Summa theologica*, 2–2.152.3, ad 5; Payer, *The Bridling of Desire*, p. 159.

[22] Diane Bornstein, *The Lady in the Tower: Medieval Courtesy Literature for Women* (Hamden, Connecticut, 1983), p. 119.

[23] Toulouse, Musée des Augustines, discussed and illustrated in Michael Camille, "The Image and the Self: Unwriting Late Medieval Bodies," in *Framing Medieval Bodies*, Sarah Kay and Miri Rubin, eds. (Manchester, 1994), pp. 62–99, at pp. 79–80, fig. 21.

this unambiguous focus on erotic zones and genitalia, more subtle signs could convey the idea of impurity or transgression. The long hair deemed appropriate for women expressed varying social connotations according to its appearance.[24] A maiden wore her long hair loose and flowing, and as a rite of passage, put her hair up neatly, and covered it after marriage.[25] If a married woman appeared in public with her hair down this was seen to infringe social custom and denote inappropriate behavior, particularly sexual activity.[26] Thus is explained the need, in medieval civil courts, for rape victims to display torn clothes and disheveled hair as proof of sexual attack. Women with loose, straggly locks are depicted in numerous compositions that illustrate stories of rape and incest.[27] Particularly significant is a depiction of Saint Agnes being dragged away to a brothel by pimps who touch her body and tousle her hair into spikes, signifying the sexual aggression she suffered during her martyrdom.[28] Untidy hair was also used to identify women as prostitutes. In the Bible, for example, the prophet Hosea was instructed to take a prostitute for a wife and have children with her.[29] Bolognese thirteenth- and fourteenth-century illustrations for the book of Hosea, (fig. 2)

---

[24] As Bartlett observes, the contrast between cut hair and long hair "was used to mark status, ethnic identity, age, and sex." Robert Bartlett, "Symbolic Meanings of Hair in the Middle Ages," *Transactions of the Royal Historical Society*, 6th ser. 4 (1994), 43–60 at p. 44.

[25] See also Kim M. Phillips, "Maidenhood as the Perfect Age of Woman's Life," in *Young Medieval Women*, Katherine J. Lewis, *et al.*, eds. (New York, 1999), pp. 1–24 at pp. 8–9, on hair as contradictory signs of sexuality and chastity.

[26] "Unpinned, tumbling or disheveled, hair is infused with sexual power... Catholic nuns traditionally shaved their heads on becoming 'brides of Christ' and covered their hair with veils..." See Karen Stevenson, "Hairy Business: Organizing the Gendered Self," in *Contested Bodies*, Ruth Holliday and John Hassard, eds. (London/New York, 2001), pp. 137–152, at p. 140. See also Bartlett, "Symbolic Meanings" pp. 54–55. In addition, married women and widows traditionally expressed mourning by loosing and tearing at their hair (and faces) as can be observed in representations of the *Slaughter of the Innocents*, the *Crucifixion*, and the *Lamentation of Christ*; see illustrations in Mosche Barasch, *Gestures of Despair in Medieval and Early Renaissance Art* (New York, 1976), especially in Chapter 6, pp. 57–86.

[27] Among these the Biblical accounts of the Levite's wife, Tamar, and Potiphar's wife; discussed and illustrated in Diane Wolfthal, *Images of Rape: The "Heroic" Tradition and its Alternatives* (Cambridge, U.K., 1999), especially Chapter 2.

[28] Illustrated in the Saint Agnes Cycle in the Pamplona Bible, Augsburg, Universitätsbibliothek, Cod. I.2.4.15, fols 249r–249v; see Wolfthal, *Images of Rape*, pp. 43–44 and figs. 22–23.

[29] Hosea 1.2–3: "When the Lord first spoke through Hosea, the Lord said...Go, take to yourself a wife of harlotry and have children of harlotry, for the land commits great harlotry by forsaking the Lord. So he went and took Gomer the daughter of Diblaim, and she conceived and bore him a son."

Figure 2 Madrid, Biblioteca Nacional, Ms Vitr. 21–4, fol. 341r, detail. Bible, *Hosea and Gomer*. Tempera and ink on parchment. With permission of the Biblioteca Nacional.

generally depict the prophet seizing the wrist of his future bride Gomer, whose long, tangled hair indicates her social dishonor; Hosea's grip in turn implies force and sexual aggression.[30]

Sometimes a single attribute could have multiple meanings. Female virginity has its classic representation in the myth of the unicorn, a beast that supposedly could not be captured by force, but rather by trickery. A hunter would lead a female virgin to a spot frequented by the unicorn and leave her alone. The unicorn, then, sensing the maiden's purity, would approach, lay its head on her lap, and fall asleep, at which point the hunter would slay it. This popular theme was used to decorate objects such as mirror cases and was placed in miniatures and in the marginal decoration of countless books of hours, often associated with the Virgin Mary. The set of seven Unicorn Tapestries at The Cloisters in New York gives a detailed pictorial account of the pursuit and slaughter of this mythical beast. In the seventh tapestry the unicorn is shown once more alive and in captivity, symbolizing the resurrected Christ.[31]

From another perspective, the fifteenth-century Florentine *Fior di Virtù* utilizes the unicorn to illustrate the vice of intemperance, classifying it as an animal with such a taste for young maidens that whenever it sees one it goes to her and falls asleep in her arms, thus allowing its capture. In the woodcut that illustrates this account (fig. 3) human intemperance—defined as the gratification of all one's desires according to one's pleasure—is further represented by the naked lovers on the bed.[32]

Clothing could also function as a signifier of either virtue or immodesty. At mid-eleventh century, Guibert of Nogent, honoring the chastity his mother staunchly maintained throughout her husband's impotence during the first three years of marriage, noted, "how almost impossible it would be for women of the present time to keep such chastity as this... how wretchedly have modesty and honor in the state of virginity declined from that time to this our present age... So much does the extravagance of their dress depart from the old simplicity that in the enlargement of their sleeves, the tightness of their dresses, the distortion

[30] Madrid, Biblioteca Nacional, Ms Vitr. 21–4, fol. 341r. The seizing gesture as a visual indicator for rape is discussed in Wolfthal, *Images of Rape*, p. 41.

[31] New York, Metropolitan Museum of Art at The Cloisters, woven in Brussels, ca. 1500.

[32] See *The Florentine Fior di virtu of 1491. Translated into English by Nicholas Fersin [sic] with facsimiles of all the original wood cuts. Published for the Library of Congress* (Philadelphia, 1953), p. 90.

Figure 3 Reproduced from the facsimile of the Florentine *Fior di Virtù* of 1491, translated into English by Nicholas Fersin [sic] with facsimiles of all the original wood cuts. Published for the Library of Congress (Philadelphia, 1953), p. 90: *The Unicorn.*

of their shoes of Cordovan leather with their curling toes, they seem to proclaim that everywhere modesty is a castaway."[33] In this passage, Guibert remarkably pictorializes immodest behavior, associating it with the new fashion of wide sleeves and form-hugging dresses. Artists very appropriately used these modish garments to clothe their representations of Superbia in manuscripts of Prudentius's *Psychomachia*; as well as depictions of Salome dancing before Herod and the Apocalyptic Whore of Babylon in Biblical narratives: all female personages of adverse reputation. Beyond women, however, it was the adoption of this fashion by men that provoked the most criticism. Twelfth-century monastic chroniclers found greater signs of moral decline in the tight fitting clothing and long, fluttering trains of men "whose flowing locks and mincing gait completed a transvestite assault on the styles of a martial past."[34] A twelfth-century initial opening a French manuscript of St. Gregory's *Moralia in Job* aptly illustrates the chroniclers' plaint, exemplified by the costume worn by a dragon-slaying knight.[35] His close-fitting robe delineates his pectorals; a slit up the left side reveals a well-turned leg in colored hose. Tight at the upper arm, the sleeves of his robe widen and fall open at the wrist, revealing a striped tunic beneath. On his feet, as on the feet of his assistant below, narrow slippers end in sharp, drooping points, with absolutely no utility other than to attract attention. In yet another context—an unusual series of miniatures in a book of hours that utilizes the Seven Deadly Sins to illustrate the Seven Penitential Psalms—stylish attire is flaunted by the male personification of Lust (fig. 4) who also rides a goat, a symbol of ardent sexual desire.[36]

---

[33] C. C. Swinton Bland, revised, trans., John F. Benton, in *Self and Society in Medieval France: The Memoirs of Abbot Guibert of Nogent (1064?–c.1125)* (New York, 1979), p. 65.

[34] Diane Owen Hughes, "Regulating Women's Fashion," in *A History of Women: Silences of the Middle Ages*, ed. Cristiane Klapisch-Zuber (Cambridge, Massachusetts, 1992), pp. 136–58ff, at p. 137. Orderic Vitalis criticized men's adoption of long, pointed shoes, apparently originally designed by Fulk of Anjou to "hide the shape of his malformed feet and to conceal 'protuberances, which are commonly called bunions.'" Owen Hughes, above, citing Ordericus Vitalis, *Historiae Ecclesiasticae*, ed. Auguste Le Prévoste, 5 vols. (Paris, 1840–1855), vol. 3, p. 323.

[35] Dijon, Bibliothèque municipale, Ms 168, fol. 4r; illustrated in color in Jean Porcher, *Medieval French Miniatures* (New York, 1960), plate XII; the manuscript is described in Walter Cahn, *Romanesque Manuscripts: The Twelfth Century*, 2 vols. (London, 1996), vol. 1, fig. 140, and vol. 2, Catalogue no. 59, pp. 73–4.

[36] New York, Pierpont Morgan Library and Museum, Ms M.1001, fol. 98r; executed in Poitiers, France, ca. 1475, by Robinet Testard.

Figure 4 New York, The Pierpont Morgan Library and Museum, Ms M.1001, fol. 98r. Robinet Testard, *Lust*. Book of Hours. Tempera and ink on parchment. With permission of The Pierpont Morgan Library.

Attributes of Chastity

A common article of dress associated with chastity is the girdle or belt, which clasps the waist, holds garments closed, and guards the purity of its wearer.[37] In an illustration to Jean de Stavelot's texts on Saint Benedict the prophet Elias represents Benedict's vow of chastity and protection of his virginity. Flanked by flowering, thorny trees, with both hands the prophet grips the wide belt tightly fastened around his waist, as though to reinforce its power.[38] The text below reads: "Elias guarded his virginity like a flower among thorns; he who preserves his virginity will be crowned with gold." But the belt has further implications. Cinched tight, it represents chastity preserved, loosened, it suggests that the sexual organs are made available, implying either an invitation to sex, or the sexual violation of the wearer. A painting on a fifteenth-century jousting shield depicts a kneeling knight facing the ideal lady he has chosen as a symbolic shield to protect him in a forthcoming tournament.[39] The lady dangles the end of her golden belt before him. Belts and other articles of a woman's clothing were attributed with semi-magical protective power, but here the belt simultaneously suggests her sexual availability. Her fingering the belt may allude to future favors if he is successful in the joust.

The girdle plays a significant part in a number of illustrations to Causa 36 of Gratian's *Decretum*, which considers the seduction and ensuing rape of a young woman. Medieval artists portrayed rape by various devices, including the violent grabbing of the woman's wrist, improper touching of her breast, cupping her chin, seizing her from behind, as well as the actual forced intercourse where these gestures are also employed. In some *Decretum* images, however, defloration is conveyed by the loosening or removal of the woman's girdle.[40] In Causa 36 we are told that a young man invited a young girl to a clandestine banquet without the knowledge of her parents, and subsequently ravished her. The historiated initial F that opens this Causa in a late

---

[37] See especially François Garnier, *Le Langage de l'Image au Moyen Âge*: Grammaire des Gestes (Paris, 1989), pp. 169–74 and pp. 372–3.

[38] Chantilly, Musée Condé, Ms 1401, fol. 132v, executed between 1432 and 1437; illustrated in Garnier, *Le Langage* p. 373.

[39] See Michael Camille, *The Medieval Art of Love: Objects and Subjects of Desire* (New York, 1998), pp. 61–63, and illustrated in fig. 50.

[40] Commented on and illustrated in Garnier, *Le Langage* pp. 170–71 and illustrated in figures 236–38 and p. 323, color plate 29.

twelfth-century French manuscript[41] depicts the young woman standing at left, her seducer patting her breast with one hand and tugging at her girdle with the other. A thirteenth-century miniature portrays the two protagonists face-to-face: the young man reaches out with both hands to grasp the young woman, who suspends her belt and energetically thrusts it away from her attacker, attempting to preserve her virginity.[42] A final illustration to Causa 36, (fig. 5) features the belt itself being displayed by the young man in a court of law; his possession of this item constituting proof of the rape.[43]

In illustrations to allegorical narratives, personifications of chastity and virtue are usually embodied by female figures. The clothing worn by Virtue in a miniature illustrating a Flemish fifteenth-century copy of the *Discord of Fortune and Virtue* resembles a religious habit: a blue robe over a simple white shift, with head and neck covered by a white hood.[44] Weighty and serene, Virtue faces the viewer and exudes stability, contrasting with her companion Fortune's precarious nature, represented by her wheel and blindfold, tilting, fragile body, and stylish, frivolous clothing, the feminine equivalent of that worn by the figure of Lust in Figure 4.

Virtue's posture and attire directly reflect the precepts set down in courtesy books for women, which spelled out exactly how a gentlewoman was expected to look and behave.[45] In these guidebooks for manners and etiquette every woman, regardless of her rank, is told to be humble and obedient, and modest in dress and deportment. In a passage devoted to beauty in girls, one author asserts: "The four necessary virtues in young women are modesty, piety, chastity, and beauty. Beauty and chastity go together because beauty without chastity is

[41] Troyes, Bibliothèque municipale, Ms 60, fol. 209r; illustrated in Anthony Melnikas, *The Corpus of the Miniatures in the Manuscripts of Decretum Gratiani*, 3 vols. (Rome, 1975), vol. 3, p. 1150, fig. 7.

[42] Autun, Bibliothèque municipale, Ms 80, fol. 259v; illustrated in Garnier, *Le Langage* p. 323, color plate 29.

[43] Laon, Bibliothèque municipale, Ms 372, fol. 257r, illustrated in Garnier, *Le Langage* fig. 238, and Baltimore, Walters Art Museum, Ms W.135, fol. 333r (fig. 5).

[44] Brussels, Bibliothèque royale, Ms 9510, fol. 11r; Cf. Martin le Franc, *L'estrif de Fortune et Vertu*; the miniature is illustrated in *Medieval Mastery: Book Illumination from Charlemagne to Charles the Bold 800–1475*, exh. cat. (Leuven, 2002), p. 294, Catalogue no. 76.

[45] See especially Bornstein, *The Lady in the Tower*.

Figure 5 Baltimore, The Walters Art Museum, Ms W.135, fol. 333r, detail. Gratian, *Decretum*; Causa 36. Tempera and ink on parchment. With permission of The Walters Art Museum.

like adorning a pig with precious jewels."[46] Robert of Blois advised in his *Chastoiement des dames*, written in the third quarter of the thirteenth century, that women should be courteous and temperate in all things, should not show anger or quarrel, should walk in grace and dignity with the gaze directly forward, and expose only face, throat, and hands.[47] The physical aspects of this advice are emphasized in many fifteenth- and sixteenth-century portraits of noblewomen such as the *Portrait of a Lady* in the National Gallery, London, where the sitter's dress covers her up to the clavicle and down to the wrists of her carefully clasped hands; her head is veiled to the eyebrows, and her calm, composed gaze is directed, unfocused, slightly to the left in line with the position of her body.[48] It was important to avoid eye contact in a public place, as a Parisian husband instructed his fifteen-year-old wife, around 1394: "...when you go to a town or to church...keep your head straight, your eyelids decently lowered and motionless, and your gaze eight feet directly in front of you and on the ground without looking around at any man or woman to the right or left, or looking up, or shifting your gaze unsteadily from place to place, or laughing, or stopping to talk to anyone in the street."[49] Gianozzo had similar advice for his wife in Alberti's *Della Famiglia*: "Chastity has always been worth more to anyone than beauty. A beautiful face is to be praised, but wayward eyes cover it with disgrace, make it blush from shame or turn pale from grief or anger. A graceful body is charming, but one immodest gesture, one unchaste act will soon defile it."[50] Directed to women, in Renaissance discourse these ideas can be seen as "both an idealized and overdetermined state of feminine virtue and as a site for the exercise of misogynistic assumptions about women's limited capacity for sexual restraint."[51]

---

[46] Niccolò Vito di Gozze, *Governo della famiglia, di M. Nicolò Vito di Gozze, gentil'huomo etc.* (Venice, Aldo [Manuzio], 1589), pp. 35–36.

[47] See Bornstein, *The Lady in the Tower*, pp. 59–60.

[48] Executed by the workshop of Rogier van der Weyden around 1460; illustrated in Jill Dunkerton, *et al.*, eds., *Giotto to Dürer: Early Renaissance Painting in the National Gallery* (New York/London, 1991), opposite p. 290.

[49] *A Medieval Home Companion: Housekeeping in the Fourteenth Century*, ed., trans. Tania Bayard (New York, 1991), p. 37.

[50] Leone Battista Alberti, *The Albertis of Florence: Leon Battista Alberti's Della Famiglia*, introduction, trans. Guido A. Guarino (Lewisburg, New York, 1971), p. 221.

[51] Cristelle L. Baskins, "*Il Trionfo della Pudicizia*: Menacing Virgins in Italian Renaissance Domestic Painting," in Kathleen Coyne Kelly and Marina Leslie, eds.,

Modesty and impropriety are wonderfully contrasted in a miniature illustrating Book 2 of Valerius Maximus's *Memorable Deeds and Sayings of the Romans* (fig. 6), which discusses the dangers of drinking wine and is especially critical of intemperance in women.[52] The artist has opposed the excessive behavior of the lower classes with the more reserved conduct of higher society. In the foreground rude figures in working-class dress enjoy their drink: one bleary-eyed fellow raises a hand and declaims; a serving woman lifts a bowl high and fiddles under her gown as though preparing to expose herself; a drunken man on the floor appears to be arranging a tryst with a woman on the bench. In counterpoint, the pale gentlewoman at the nobles' table in the background is frozen in obedience to correct chaste behavior: she is properly covered, exposing the minimum of flesh, her eyes are lowered decorously and she abstains from wine.

Chastity Exemplified

For the encouragement of female chastity, the Church provided examples of chaste women as role models: Susanna, for conjugal fidelity, Anna for faithful widowhood, and most important, the Virgin Mary for virginity.[53] In the fourteenth century Paolo da Certaldo counseled young virgins to "live according to the example of the Holy Virgin Mary, the first and foremost virgin of virginity, queen and mirror of all other virginities."[54] Her perfect and decorous behavior was exalted in sermons, hymns, and devotional literature. Above all, Mary represented the highest grade of chastity, for, though she conceived and gave birth to a son, apparently neither circumstance served to rupture

---

Menacing Virgins. Representing Virginity in the Middle Ages and Renaissance (Newark, New Jersey, 1999), pp. 117–31 at p. 118.

[52] Los Angeles, J. Paul Getty Museum, Ms 43r: The Temperate and the Intemperate.

[53] Lord, "Dido as an Example," p. 27. Susanna's story is told in an apocryphal addition to the book of Daniel. For an analysis of images of the parable of Susanna and the Elders in the context of patristic literature, see Kathryn A. Smith, "Inventing Marital Chastity: the Iconography of Susanna and the Elders in Early Christian Art," *Oxford Art Journal* 16 (1993), 3–24. Anna's exemplary behavior is described in Luke 2.36–37: "She lived with her husband seven years from her virginity and as a widow till she was eighty four. She did not depart from the temple, worshiping with fasting and prayer night and day."

[54] Paolo da Certaldo, *Libro di buoni costumi*, ed. Alfredo Schaffini (Florence, 1945), pp. 170–71.

Figure 6 Los Angeles, The J. Paul Getty Museum, Ms 43r/91.MS.81 recto. Master of the Dresden Prayer Book, *The Temperature and the Intemperate; Valerius Maximus, Faits et dits mémorables des romains*. Tempera and ink on parchment; 175 × 194 mm. With permission of the J. Paul Getty Museum.

her hymen, and she remained perpetually virgin. Representations of the *Annunciation* demonstrate the proper behavior and posture for a young woman accosted by a stranger in her private quarters, who proposes she receive a child into her womb by supernatural intervention: fear, awe, humility, and finally, resignation and obedience.[55] And too, impregnation took place through entirely chaste methods. According to Luke, the angel Gabriel told the young woman: "The Holy Spirit will come upon you and the power of the Most High will overshadow you."[56] Artists interpreted this somewhat enigmatic description by various pictorial devices. In many *Annunciation* scenes we see the hands of God the Father launch the Dove of the Holy Spirit down a beam of light directed towards the Virgin, at times targeting her chest; in other instances her womb.[57] The early Church fathers claimed that chastity was maintained through bypassing the Virgin's sexual organs and penetrating her through the ear, *ad aurem*,[58] the so-called "telephone" *Annunciation*, represented by the Dove coasting directly into that organ on a ray of light, or by the actual figure of the baby Jesus riding the same beam.[59] Fra Filippo Lippi contrived a far more erotic conception scene in his delicate Annunciation panel at the National Gallery, London.[60] Here, as the kneeling Gabriel faces the seated Virgin in a garden, the fluttering Dove hovers in space at the Virgin's midsection and ejects golden droplets, like celestial sperm, towards a small slit in the Virgin's garments that spits out its own golden spray, suggesting, as Leo Steinberg observed, that fecundation took place by light, and that

---

[55] See examples in David M. Robb, "The Iconography of the Annunciation in the Fourteenth and Fifteenth Centuries," *Art Bulletin* 18 (1936), 480–526.

[56] Luke 1:35.

[57] See examples in Robb, "The Iconography" figs. 9, 13, 16, 17, 18–22, and Leo Steinberg, "'How Shall This Be?' Reflections on Filippo Lippi's *Annunciation* in London, Part I," *Artibus et Historiae* 16 (1987), 25–44, figs. 4, 6, 12.

[58] For summary of early discussions on this method see Steinberg, "How Shall This Be?" pp. 26–31.

[59] A particularly engaging representation featuring both the nude baby Jesus carrying a cross and the Dove, in transit towards Mary's ear, is found on a panel in the amazing altarpiece executed by Meister Bertram von Minden at the Kunsthalle in Hamburg, beautifully illustrated in *Goldgrund und Himmelslicht: Die Kunst des Mittelalters in Hamburg*, exh. cat. (Hamburg, 1999), pp. 103, 106.

[60] London, National Gallery, NG 666, painted by Fra Filippo Lippi, ca. 1448–50. The full painting is illustrated in color in Steinberg, "How Shall This Be," fig. 15 and Dunkerton, *et al., Giotto to Dürer*, pp. 274–75, cat. no. 23.

at this site the Second and Third Persons of the Trinity are flashing light signals at each other.[61]

The Virgin's labor and childbirth was also chaste and took place without pain or undue fuss, as Saint Bonaventure described in his *Meditations on the Life of Christ*: "At midnight on Sunday, when the hour of birth came, the Virgin rose and stood erect against a column that was there... Then the Son of the eternal God came out of the womb of the mother without a murmur or lesion, in a moment; as He had been in the womb so He was now outside, on the hay at His mother's feet." This account is precisely illustrated in a fourteenth-century manuscript copy of this text (Paris, Bibliothèque nationale de France, Ms ital. 115, fol. 19r), complete even to the curious column that has somehow materialized against a wall of the rude cave in which the birth takes place.[62] The newborn child lies at the Virgin's feet. Not a hair is ruffled on her head nor a fold of her gown disturbed; nobody, not even Joseph, would have had an improper glimpse of her undergarments or nether regions. One would imagine that the expectant mother, reading this devotional passage, would pray to the Virgin for a safe delivery and hope that her own experience would be as swift and painless.

Marital Chastity

Normal human women of course could not aspire to giving birth and still remaining virgin, but they could resolve to be chaste in their marriages. What did chastity in marriage mean? The idea of conjugal chastity did not require that husband and wife should abstain from sex altogether, but that their carnal encounters take place during the legitimate times prescribed by the Church, and they be faithful to each other, rejecting any sex outside the marriage. Alcuin points out in *De virtutibus et vitiis liber*, addressed to a count, that chastity is equivalent to the angelic life.[63] He makes it clear that chastity is chiefly a monastic virtue and that normal men could not hope to be angels any more

---

61 Steinberg, pp. 35–38; this detail is illustrated in figs. 16 and 17.

62 See *Meditations on the Life of Christ, an Illustrated Manuscript of the Fourteenth Century*, Isa Ragusa and Rosalie B. Green, eds. (Princeton, 1961), where the text is translated and illustrated on pages 32–3, and Claude Dalbanne, "Un manuscrit italien des 'Meditationes Vitae Christi' à la Bibliothèque nationale," in *Les Trésors des bibliothèques de France* (Paris, 1929), pp. 51–60, pl. XXVII.

63 *PL* 101, 18:626.

than they could be saints. Instead of urging his patron to renounce sex, Alcuin instead reminds the count that legitimately married couples should engage in intercourse only at the proper times.[64]

Nevertheless, devotional literature presents numerous tales of married couples who chose abstinence over intercourse. Saint Cecilia, a third century Roman, enjoyed great popularity in the Middle Ages primarily for the late fifth-century Legend that presented her as a young Christian patrician who was obliged to marry a pagan called Valerian. Cecilia had already vowed her virginity to God and refused to consummate the marriage. She converted Valerian to Christianity on their wedding night, telling him that an angel would kill him if he tried to make love to her. Cecilia sent him to Pope Urban to be baptized and on his return home, the angel appeared and crowned them with wreaths of lilies and roses—well known symbols of chastity and martyrdom—to commemorate their commitment to chastity. According to the legend the wreaths will always keep their fragrance, and will only be visible to those who are chaste. A miniature in the *Meditation Picture Book of Madame Marie*, made for a thirteenth-century noblewoman, depicts the celebration of Cecilia and Valerian's chaste love thus: the seated, haloed figures, clad royally in fur-lined cloaks, turn towards each other as an angel flies down from heaven and thrusts a crown of red and white flowers towards Cecilia, who reaches out to her spouse and hands him a similar wreath.[65] What would the owner of this devotional manuscript feel when she gazed at this image? Should she aspire to marital chastity?—and would she desire a flowered crown?

Other pictorial examples promoting conjugal chastity are found in monumental format. In a late fourteenth-century Florentine panel the kneeling figures of Prince Henry of Hungary and his wife make a vow of marital continence before the crucified figure of Christ, observed at far left by the king of Hungary.[66] To emphasize the purity of this

[64] Phyllis G. Jestice, "Why Celibacy? Odo of Cluny and the Development of a New Sexual Morality," in *Medieval Purity and Piety: Essays on Medieval Clerical Celibacy and Religious Reform*, ed. Michael Frassetto (New York/London, 1998), pp. 81–115 at p. 85. On marital chastity see also Donald Weinstein and Rudolph M. Bell, *Saints and Society. The Two Worlds of Western Christendom, 1000–1700* (Chicago/London, 1982), chapter 3, especially pp. 74–97.

[65] Paris, Bibliothèque nationale, Ms nouv. acq. fr. 16251, fol. 98r, illustrated and described in *Medieval Mastery*, pp. 214–15, cat. no. 44.

[66] Florence, St. Martin of Mensola, predella panel; reproduced in Weinstein and Bell, *Saints and Society*, p. 77, fig. 11.

vow the two are depicted with golden halos, implying that this is an act worthy of sainthood. In another fourteenth-century altarpiece the blessed Umiltà, a thirteenth-century matron of Faenza, convinces her husband to convert to a life of chastity.[67] Although she had wished for a humble life as a young girl, she dutifully accepted marriage and motherhood for nine years, until she contracted a serious illness. Upon recovery Umiltà suddenly resolved to follow her childhood desires, and retired to a cell to live an ascetic life, while her husband sought a monastery to do the same. We are not informed what became of the many children. In the painting the couple is seated on a low chest outside the bedchamber; Umiltà, her body chastely covered and her head draped in a veil, holds a book in one hand and gestures persuasively to her seemingly hesitant husband with the other. The husband's reluctance is understandable, for the vow of celibacy among noblemen and women was not to be taken lightly. Members of the noble families had the obligation to marry: to produce children to continue the family name, increase the financial patrimony, and maintain its prestige. Young men and women who aspired to live saintly lives often had to yield to social pressures, since "Chastity ran counter to every expectation of noble behavior, and because the behavior of highborn people was a matter of lively interest and scrutiny, a nobleman who lived in continence with his lawful wife was a subject of wonder."[68]

Defending Chastity

Outside of marriage, women were enjoined to remain chaste. Although maidens could not aspire to having their virginity preserved supernaturally like the Virgin Mary, they were encouraged to keep it by the examples of female saints who defended their purity against fearsome trials.[69] These "menaced virgins" are described and pictured in the biographies of saints, a category of literature whose idealized narratives

[67] Reproduced and described in ibid., p. 92, fig. 13.

[68] Ibid., p. 76. For case studies of women who maintained their virginity throughout marriage, see Dyan Elliott, *Spiritual Marriage. Sexual Abstinence in Medieval Wedlock* (Princeton, New Jersey, 1993), especially chapter six: "Virgin Wives," pp. 266–301.

[69] Cynthia Hahn suggests that in the face of women's well-known sexual insatiability, "women who controlled that desire became heroic models of sexual abstinence for both genders during the Middle Ages." See Cynthia Hahn, *Portrayed on the Heart: Narrative Effect in Pictorial Lives of Saints from the Tenth through the Thirteenth Century* (Berkeley, 2001), p. 91.

served as models for Christian behavior. In this type of story a pagan either attempts to rape a consecrated virgin himself, or sends her to a brothel to be raped, but the deed is never committed because a miracle intervenes. As Coyne Kelly demonstrates, "In stories of circumvented rape, the consecrated virgin may lose her limbs or her life, but never her virginity. *Virginity* always outlasts the *virgin*."[70] Chastity or virginity is represented by the tortures these saints suffered in its defense, and the torture and its resistance become a visual metonym. One well-known example is Agatha, a third-century Christian virgin, sought in marriage by a Roman consul. Rejected, he first attempted to corrupt her by sending her to a brothel, and when this failed, he sent her to prison, where torturers twisted and pinched her breasts before cutting them off (fig. 7).[71] This episode of Agatha's martyrdom is illustrated in a variety of texts, most commonly at the Suffrages section in books of hours, or in choir books, at the site of Agatha's feast day. In Figure 7, exceptionally, the historiated initial S opens Bartolo of Sassoferrato's commentary on Book 45 of Justinian's *Digest*, which deals with verbal contracts.[72] Here in the upper register Agatha's breasts are cruelly gripped by giant pincers; in the lower the saint is viewed in prison behind bars, her breasts torn and bleeding. Much the same persecution was directed to Agnes, another Roman martyr, who was ordered to sacrifice to Vesta or be sent to a brothel. Upon refusing she was stripped naked, and suddenly her hair miraculously grew long enough to cover her entire body, a visible sign of modesty and chastity preserved. As she entered

---

[70] Kathleen Coyne Kelly, "Useful Virgins in Medieval Hagiography," in *Constructions of Widowhood and Virginity in the Middle Ages*, Cindy L. Carlson and Angela Jane Weisl, eds. (New York, 1999), pp. 135–64, at p. 137. On sainthood in various historical and cultural contexts, see Renate Blumenfeld-Kosinski and Timea Szell, eds., *Images of Sainthood in Medieval Europe* (Ithaca/London, 1991), and *Chaste Passions: Medieval English Virgin Martyr Legends*, ed. and trans. Karen A. Winstead (Ithaca/London, 2000).

[71] Madrid, Biblioteca Nacional, Ms 197, fol. 128r. On Saint Agatha, see Magdalena Elizabeth Carrasco, "An Early Illustrated Manuscript of the Passion of St. Agatha (Paris, Bibliothèque Nationale, Ms fonds lat. 5594)," *Gesta* 24 (1985), 19–32; and especially Martha Easton, "Saint Agatha and the Sanctification of Sexual Violence," *Studies in Iconography* 16 (1994), 83–118, with extensive bibliography at footnote 4.

[72] Saint Agatha serves as a patron saint of wet-nurses, bell-founders, and jewelers, and is invoked against diseases of the breast as well as fire and earthquakes. Since the opening passage of the first section of this manuscript was illustrated with an image of the Virgin and Child, it seems likely that at this location, the second major text division, the figure of the highly venerated Saint Agatha is used, like that of the Virgin, to validate the text it precedes.

Figure 7 Madrid, Biblioteca Nacional, Ms 197 fol. 128r, detail. Niccolò di Giacomo da Bologna, *Saint Agatha*, Bartholomaeus de Saxoferrato *In primam et secundam digesti novi partem commentaria*. Tempera and ink on parchment. With permission of the Biblioteca Nacional.

the brothel an angel threw a mantle of light around her, terrifying all those who would approach, and preventing her violation.[73]

From another standpoint, further examples of what Ilse E. Friesen has called "the hairy holy women" demonstrate the fluctuating cultural implications of the body hair of female saints.[74] If virginity and purity had not been maintained, repentance and acts of penitence were also valued behavior. Mary Magdalene, whose luxuriant tresses anointed the feet of Christ, according to apocryphal legend later retired to the desert to spend thirty years as a penitent, going without food and clothing. Her story was paralleled by and merged with that of the sixth-century courtesan Mary of Egypt, who also repented of her life of sin and spent forty years as a hermit in the desert. Both women were reputedly clothed only by the long hair from their heads, although artists sometimes portrayed them covered with a pelt of body hair. Their nakedness presents conflicting messages: while on the one hand it symbolizes a return to the original state of prelapsarian innocence and humility, on the other it reminds the viewer of their sexuality and the sin of lust for which they were atoning.[75] In the thirteenth century, however, both women were taken up as role models for men and women who aspired to the ascetic life, and promoted by the mendicant orders as symbols of penitence. Mary Magdalene's embellished *vita* created by the Dominican Jacobus de Voragine in his *Legenda aurea* provided many suggestions of scenes in which artists could represent her. In this account, although she lived without food and water in the desert, she subsided on spiritual fare: angels carried her to heaven seven times a day at the canonical hours where she was sustained by the music of heavenly choirs (fig. 8).[76] This miraculous episode is depicted in Figure 8, where two pairs of angels suspend the beatific figure of Mary Magdalen, covered with

[73] For a more detailed account of the story of St. Agnes and a list of female virgin martyrs submitted to some form of sexual assault, see Robert Mills, "Can the Virgin Martyr Speak?" in *Medieval Virginities*, Anke Bernau, *et al.*, eds. (Toronto/Buffalo, 2003), pp. 187–213, at pp. 189–91.

[74] See Ilse E. Friesen, "Saints as Helpers in Dying: The Hairy Holy Women Mary Magdalene, Mary of Egypt, and Wilgefortis in the Iconography of the Late Middle Ages," in *Death and Dying in the Middle Ages*, Edelgard E. DuBruck and Barbara I. Gusick, eds. (New York, 2001), pp. 239–256.

[75] See Susan Haskins, *Mary Magdalen: Myth and Metaphor* (New York, 1993), pp. 230–32.

[76] Described in *The Golden Legend of Jacobus de Voragine* (New York, 1969), pp. 355–64 at pp. 360–61.

Figure 8 Cambridge, The Fitzwilliam Museum, Ms 201, fol. 27.2. Single leaf cutting, *Saint Mary Magdalen* Tempera and ink on vellum. Reproduction by permission of the Fitzwilliam Museum, Cambridge.

a shimmering robe of hair, an attractive advertisement for the benefits to be reaped by penitence.

Returning to the defense of chastity, other women mutilated themselves or summoned a physical deformity to escape rape, a strategy aimed at destroying their physical attractiveness and making them repulsive to men. In 870 Ebba the Younger, abbess of Scotland's Coldingham Abbey, together with her nuns, cut off her nose and lips to disgust and repel the Danish invaders.[77] In another legend, Wilgefortis, supposedly the daughter of a pagan king of Portugal, took a vow of chastity, and was then against her will betrothed to a pagan king of Sicily. She prayed to become transformed into the likeness of Christ, and, miraculously, grew a mustache and beard (fig. 9).[78] Her husband-to-be cancelled the engagement, and the maiden's father was so incensed that he ordered her crucified.[79] Saint Lucy, a fourth-century virgin and martyr, allegedly suffered numerous tortures in defense of her virginity. Among them, she was reputed to have had her eyes torn out and subsequently restored, and is usually depicted carrying her eyes on a plate or dish.[80] The canonical story was taken up in the Florentine *Fior di Virtù* and slightly, modernized, characterizing the saint as a beautiful nun with whom a rich nobleman fell in love.[81] In this account the nobleman, unsuccessful in wooing her, went one day in a passion to the convent and dragged her out. When the nun asked why she was chosen, the nobleman replied: "Because of thy eyes that are so beautiful." She then responded: "Since my eyes give you so much pleasure I have decided to satisfy your desire," and went away, ostensibly to

---

[77] Her story is related by Matthew Paris, see *Rerum Britannicarum Medii Aevi Scriptores*, Matthaei Parisiensis, *Chronica Majora*, pp. 391–92. On St. Ebba and other women who mutilated themselves in defense of virginity, see Jane Tibbets Schulenberg, "The Heroics of Virginity: Brides of Christ and Sacrificial Mutilation," in *Women in the Middle Ages and the Renaissance*, ed. Mary Beth Rose (Syracuse, 1986), pp. 29–72. On Margaret, a thirteenth-century princess who also threatened to cut off her nose and lips to preserve her virginity, see Weinstein and Bell, *Saints and Society*, p. 88.

[78] Baltimore, Walters Art Museum, Ms W.170, fol. 174v.

[79] On Wilgefortis, see Kathleen Coyne Kelly, *Performing Virginity and Testing Chastity in the Middle Ages* (London/New York, 2000), pp. 52–53, Elizabeth Nightlinger, "The Female *Imitatio Christi* and Medieval Popular Religion: The Case of St. Wilgefortis," *Feminea medievalia* 1 (1993), 291–328, and Ilse E. Friesen, *The Female Crucifix: Images of St. Wilgefortis since the Middle Ages* (Waterloo, Ontario, Canada, 2001), and "Saints as Helpers in Dying," in *Death and Dying in the Middle Ages*, pp. 244–45.

[80] For a summary of her story and further bibliography, see David Hugh Farmer, *The Oxford Dictionary of Saints*, 3rd ed. (Oxford/New York, 1992), pp. 304–305.

[81] See *The Florentine Fior di virtu of 1491*, p. 102.

Figure 9 Baltimore, The Walters Art Museum, Ms W.170, fol. 174v, detail. Gold Scrolls Group, *Saint Wilgefortis*, Book of Hours, use of Rome. With permission of the Walters Art Museum.

fetch her belongings from her cell. There the nun clawed out her own eyes, then called for the nobleman and said: "Since you are so in love with my eyes, here, take them and be satisfied." In the illustration that accompanies the story (fig. 10) the nobleman, aghast, raises his arms in horror as the gentle nun presents him with her extracted orbs, that lie on a platter like two grapes. The tale concludes with a moral: "The nun saved her innocence, preferring to lose her eyes rather than her soul, just as Christ teaches in the Gospels,"[82] and it is interesting here that "soul" is used as a metaphor for bodily purity.

Male personages also worked to safeguard their chastity/virginity. A frequently illustrated example is the Old Testament story of Joseph who flees the sexual advances of Potiphar's wife, inverting the conventional theme of the male aggressor.[83] This unnamed woman snatches Joseph's cloak in her effort to seduce him, and later accuses him of rape after he has escaped.[84] Staged in her bedchamber, many representations depict her as the epitome of lust, often with parts of her body bared. In the sixth-century Vienna Genesis, one of the earliest examples, she leans forward from the edge of a golden bed, dressed in a transparent gown, and seizes a trailing end of Joseph's purple robe.[85] In some examples she is pictured entirely nude, sitting up in bed and lunging towards the fleeing Joseph.[86] Joseph, on the other hand, is consistently portrayed as horrified and resisting, poised in urgent flight.

For men the preservation of chastity was less concerned with physical violation than with the resistance of temptation. In religious literature a standard *topos* is the story of the celibate male assaulted by lewd

---

[82] Cf. *The Florentine Fior di Virtu*, p. 103.

[83] Genesis 39: 6–7. See the important, detailed analysis and discussion of this story and its illustrations in the Middle Ages and beyond in Wolfthal, *Images of Rape*, pp. 44–45, 161–179.

[84] As Barbara J. Essex comments, "every man's nightmare—the woman who cries rape when none occurred," in *Bad Girls of the Bible: Exploring Women of Questionable Virtue* (Cleveland, Ohio, 1999), p. 39.

[85] Vienna, Österreichische Nationalbibliothek, Cod. Theol. gr. 31, pict. 33; illustrated in Kurt Weitzmann, *Late Antique and Early Christian Book Illumination* (New York, 1977), p. 83, pl. 26.

[86] Two examples are a fifteenth-century painting in Munich (Munich, Alte Pinakothek, Master of the Joseph Sequence, *Joseph and Potiphar's* Wife), illustrated in Wolfthal, *Images of Rape*, fig. 100 and a sixteenth-century miniature in a prayer book, painted by the Master of the David Scenes in the Grimani Breviary (Copenhagen, Royal Library, Ms Gl. Kgl. Saml. 1605, 4°, fol. 26r), illustrated in *Illuminating the Renaissance: The Triumph of Flemish Manuscript Painting in Europe*, Thomas Kren and Scot McKendrick, eds. (Los Angeles, 2003), p. 439, fig. 136a.

Figure 10 Reproduced from the facsimile of the Florentine *Fior de Virtù* of 1491, translated into English by Nicholas Fersin [sic] with facsimiles of all the original wood cuts. Published for the Library of Congress (Philadelphia, 1953), p. 102: *Saint Lucy*.

women, provoking a scene of spiritual heroism. As Louisa Enright notes, "Potiphar's wife comes on the scene to show that Joseph can surmount being tested by a temptress, a common motif in the classic hero quest..."[87] Although temptations of the celibate often come from supernatural cause, the stories of resistance to sexual seduction are more down-to-earth. The encounter with a woman was vividly human, and successful resistance was a personal victory over the flesh. John Arnold identifies four methods through which male chastity is successfully defended in narrative situations: 1) by means of bodily chastisement; 2) by force of will; 3) through a moment of revelation such as a dream or a vision; and last, 4) by divine intervention.[88] The first two are given visual equivalents in a miniature that illustrates the suffrage of Saint Anthony Abbot in the Hours of Henry VIII, written and illuminated around 1500 (fig. 11).[89] Born in Egypt (ca. 251–356) Anthony Abbot, devoted to the hermit's life, lived for twenty years in an abandoned tomb, where the devil tempted him in various forms. In Figure 11 we see the devil as a comely, horned woman, beckoning to Anthony from the entrance to his tomb. Repudiating the invitation with a glare, Anthony prepares to discipline his body and escape the temptress by entering the fire.

Forced Chastity

In illustrations to legal texts, particularly of canon law, we encounter a great body of iconographical material. The last ten cases in Gratian's *Decretum* deal with sex and marriage, and considerations of conjugal relationships. Here artists defined pictorially a variety of chastity-related situations, utilizing aspects of physical appearance, dress, and body language that had visual relevance in contemporary society. Gratian's discussions of marriage and sex revolve around what he termed the conjugal debt, the right and duty of husband and wife to provide each

[87] Louisa Enright, "Let's Stop Using the Bible to Buttress Misogynist Views," *Daughters of Sarah* 19 (1993), 36–38 at p. 37.

[88] See John H. Arnold, "The Labour of Continence: Masculinity and Clerical Virginity," in *Medieval Virginities*, Anke Bernau, et al., eds. (Toronto/Buffalo, 2003), pp. 102–118 at pp. 104–108.

[89] New York, Pierpont Morgan Library and Museum, Ms H.8, fol. 183v. For a description of this manuscript see Roger S. Wieck, William M. Voelkle, and K. Michelle Hearne, *The Hours of Henry VIII: A Renaissance Masterpiece by Jean Poyet* (New York, 2000), where the suffrage of St. Anthony Abbot is illustrated and discussed on pp. 158–59.

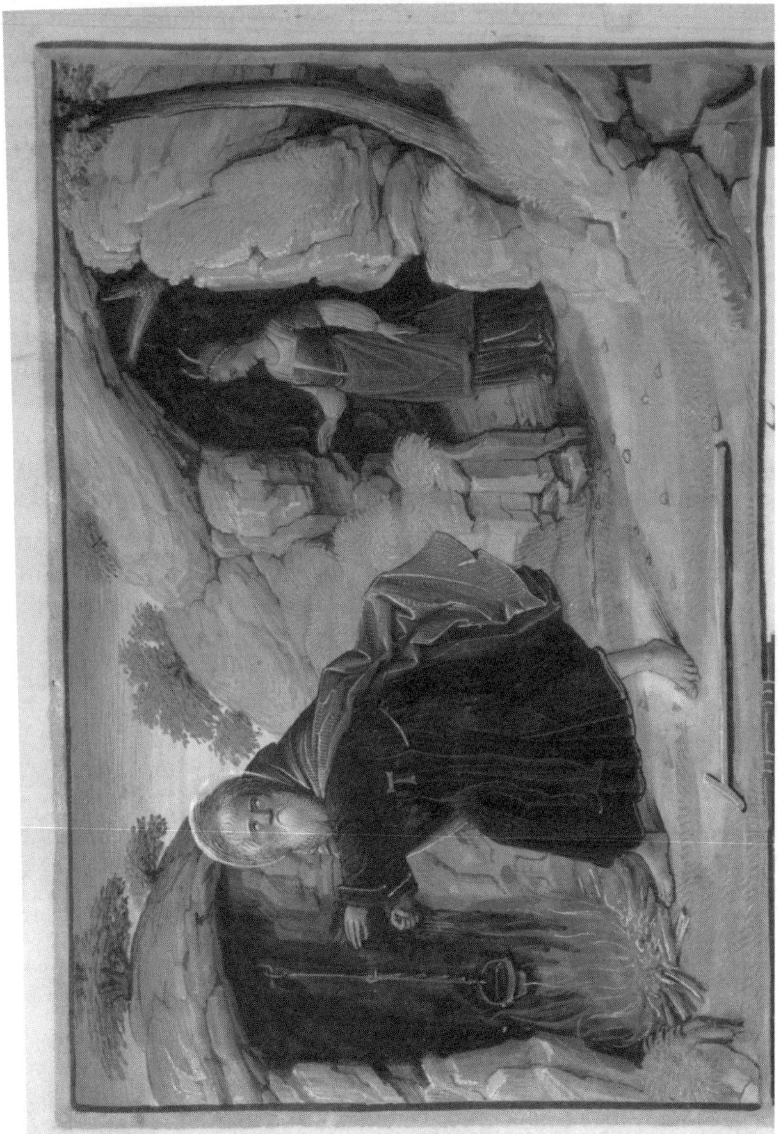

Figure 11 New York, The Pierpont Morgan Library, Ms H.8 fol. 183v, detail. Jean Poyet, *Saint Anthony Abbot*, The Hours of Henry VIII. Tempera and ink on parchment. With permission of The Pierpont Morgan Library.

other with sexual intercourse upon request.[90] Sexual obligations might be suspended during Lent and other seasons of penance, but spouses were required to fulfill the marital debt at all other times.

Conjugal duty could only be dispensed with by mutual consent. If one spouse was temporarily or permanently prevented from fulfilling it—stemming from a natural cause, such as frigidity or impotence; from castration; or from the effects of sorcery—this would automatically force chastity on both. Castration, beyond taking place for medical reasons, was a punishment assigned to selected crimes, including rape and sodomy, the most celebrated instance being the unfortunate Abélard, emasculated by his wife's guardian.[91] One artist's representation of this process is found in the lower margin of a thirteenth-century copy of the *Coutumes de Toulouse* (Paris, Bibliothèque nationale de France, Ms latin 9178, fol. 32v, dated 1296) (fig. 12).[92] As the text does not deal with punishments, the grounds for this particular castration can only be conjectured. A prisoner stands hunched at center, guarded by armed soldiers, one of whom pulls up the prisoner's chemise and hides his head, exposing his body to public humiliation and making accessible his private parts. The surgeon, standing behind, wields a knife and pulls at a cord tied to the victim's testicles to isolate them and to stem the bleeding after excision.[93] Although it has been argued that after his castration, Abélard would still have been able to maintain a physical relationship with Heloise, this incident impelled both to take up the monastic life and remain chaste for the rest of their days.[94]

[90] On marital sex, and the conjugal debt, see Elizabeth Makowski, "The Conjugal Debt and Medieval Canon Law," *Journal of Medieval History* 3 (1977), 99–114; Brundage, *Law, Sex, and Christian Society*, pp. 241–2.

[91] According to his own account, the mutilation was administered to him in his sleep so he suffered little pain.

[92] Paris, Bibliothèque nationale, Ms fonds lat. 9187, fol. 32v, dated 1296. For a full description of this manuscript and its marginal illustrations, see Susan L'Engle, "Justice in the Margins: Punishment in Medieval Toulouse," *Viator* 33 (2002), 133–65.

[93] For another interpretation of the presence of the cord as a method of castration in itself, see Emmanuel Le Roy Ladurie, "The Aiguillette: Castration by Magic," in Emmanuel Le Roy Ladurie, *The Mind and Method of the Historian* (Chicago, 1981), pp. 84–96 at p. 93.

[94] For conjectures and arguments about the extent of Abélard's castration, see Yves Ferroul, "Abélard's Blissful Castration," in Jeffrey Jerome Cohen and Bonnie Wheeler, eds., *Becoming Male in the Middle Ages* (New York/London, 1997), pp. 129–49, and Jacqueline Murray, "Mystical Castration: Some Reflections on Peter Abelard, Hugh of Lincoln, and Sexual Control," in Jacqueline Murray, ed., *Conflicted Identities and Multiple Masculinities: Men in the Medieval West* (New York/London, 1999), pp. 73–91.

Figure 12 Paris, Bibliothèque nationale, Ms fonds lat. 9187, fol. 32v, detail. Castration scene, *Coutumes de Toulouse*. Ink and wash on parchment. With permission of the Paris, Bibliothèque nationale de France.

A situation examined by Gratian in Causa 33 of the *Decretum* considers chastity imposed for another reason: a husband's temporary impotence attributed to sorcery. The opening passage reports that in this case the wife, unhappy with conjugal abstinence, sought out another man and committed adultery with him, and was later legally separated from the first husband and officially united with the second man. According to the church courts, if the husband's continuing impotence was satisfactorily proved, the woman could be granted a divorce and the chance to remarry if she declared that she wanted to have children (*volo esse mater et filios procreare*).[95] Many illuminators represented the wife's liberation from her forced chastity by the successful coitus of the new couple, and an especially narrative pictorial sequence in a fourteenth-century French or English copy of the *Decretum* (fig. 13) sums up the whole case.[96] In this quadripartite miniature, at upper left the wife accuses her husband of impotence in the Church court; at upper right she has successful coitus with another man; at lower right the first couple is formally separated by the judge, and at lower left the new couple is wed.[97] It would seem that to the Church, in a particularly humane

[95] Gratian, *Decretum*, C.33 q, 1 c. 2; Gregorius IX, *Decretales*, 4.15.1. The decretalists considered impotence or frigidity an obstruction to matrimony, although less justified for terminating an already consummated union.

[96] Cambridge, Fitzwilliam Museum, Ms 262, fol. 86v.

[97] I must stress that this is my own reading of this narrative sequence, which has previously elicited a number of conflicting interpretations. James Brundage noted that the illuminator seemed to have placed the images in the wrong order, and proposed the following sequence: "In the bottom left panel a couple exchange marital consent in the presence of a priest. The episode at upper right shows them attempting unsuccessfully to consummate their union. At the upper left the wife complains to a bishop about her husband's incapacity; and in the lower right panel the bishop symbolically annuls the marriage by disjoining the couple's hands." See Brundage, *Law, Sex, and Christian Society*, caption to Plate 13. Michael Camille however felt that the illuminator had purposely paired the images in the upper and lower registers, alleging that "the wife's explanation of her spouse's incapacity and its demonstration go together above, and the symbolic coming together of hands at the wedding below is contrasted with their separation." See Michael Camille, "Manuscript Illumination and the Art of Copulation," in *Constructing Medieval Sexuality*, Karma Lochrie, Peggy McCracken, and James A. Schultz, eds. (Minneapolis, 1997), pp. 58–90 at pp. 71–73. At the 12th International Congress of Medieval Canon Law held at The Catholic University of America, Washington, D.C., August 1–7, 2004, Frederik Pedersen, for whose important insights and suggestions I am very grateful, questioned my interpretation, arguing that the normal order in which medieval images should be read was from right to left, bottom to top. My colleague Robert Gibbs in his description of the composition sided with the interpretation given by Melnikas in his *Corpus*, *The Corpus of the Miniatures in the Manuscripts of Decretum Gratiani* (n. 41 above) where he affirms that the lower register depicts the second marriage on the left, and at right, the bishop rejoining the adulterous woman with her first

Figure 13 Cambridge, Fitzwilliam Museum, Ms 262, fol. 86v, detail. Gratian, *Decretum*, Causa 33. Tempera and ink on parchment. Reproduction by permission of the Fitzwilliam Museum, Cambridge.

ruling, when forced chastity occurred in a marriage both spouses were not necessarily obligated to remain chaste.

Conclusions

Various visual examples have been offered in response to the question, "How does chastity or unchastity look." Many of them express the notion that sexuality and the naked body are socially shameful or inappropriate, and, particularly for women, must be camouflaged by clothing and an attitude of submission—even in our own time. Although the observance of chastity and modesty has often been equated with spiritual purity, pictorial representations overwhelmingly define it with physical components. At the same time, the visual articulation of chastity can be expressed metaphorically, and its essence conveyed by gesture, posture, and material attributes.

Depictions of modesty and chastity have been created throughout the history of humankind, directed to a diversity of viewers. In the Middle Ages and Renaissance, the period that most examples discussed in this paper have addressed, chastity was a precious commodity and seen worthy of being defended, by conscious actions or by passive noncompliance, often in the face of great adversity. With what have we replaced this notion today?

---

husband. See Susan L'Engle and Robert Gibbs, *Illuminating the Law: Legal Manuscripts in Cambridge Collections* (Turnhout, 2001), pp. 148–50; Melnikas, vol. 3, p. 1031. I have based my own interpretation first, on the order in which Gratian presents the case at the beginning of Causa 33: "Quidam vir maleficiis inpeditus uxori suae debitum reddere non poterat. Alius interim clanculo eam corrupit; a viro suo separata corruptori suo publice nubit," and second on the illuminator's cues for identifying the woman's first and second partners. Most reproductions of this composition have been in black and white, which obscures the identification of individual characters. The illuminator of Fitzwilliam Museum Ms 262, however, very carefully assigned different colors to the costumes of the first and second husbands: the first wears a lavender robe, and the second is clad in brown. It becomes clear then that the only sequence that makes sense, in line with Gratian's description of the case, is: upper register, left: Husband 1 in lavender is accused by his wife before the bishop; upper register right: Boyfriend 2 in brown is shown in coitus with the wife; lower register right: the bishop wrenches apart the hands of the wife and Husband 1, in lavender, as Boyfriend 2 observes obtusely at left; and finally, lower register left: a cleric joins the hands of the wife and Boyfriend/husband 2, in brown. The illuminator may have created an anomalous order, but his color-coding signals how he intended it to be read. In addition, the body language of the protagonists is carefully differentiated in the individual ceremonies of joining and separating hands by the bishop.

Illustrations

Figure 1. New York, The Pierpont Morgan Library and Museum, Ms M.638, fol. 2r, detail. The Morgan Library Picture Bible. Tempera and ink on parchment. With permission of the Pierpont Morgan Library.

Figure 2. Madrid, Biblioteca Nacional, Ms Vitr. 21–4, fol. 341r, detail. Bible, *Hosea and Gomer*. Tempera and ink on parchment. With permission of the Biblioteca Nacional.

Figure 3. Reproduced from the facsimile of the Florentine *Fior di Virtù* of 1491, translated into English by Nicholas Fersin [sic] with facsimiles of all the original wood cuts. Published for the Library of Congress (Philadelphia, 1953), p. 90: *The Unicorn*.

Figure 4. New York, The Pierpont Morgan Library and Museum, Ms M.1001, fol. 98r. Robinet Testard, *Lust*. Book of Hours. Tempera and ink on parchment. With permission of The Pierpont Morgan Library.

Figure 5. Baltimore, The Walters Art Museum, Ms W.135, fol. 333r, detail. Gratian, *Decretum*; Causa 36. Tempera and ink on parchment. With permission of The Walters Art Museum.

Figure 6. Los Angeles, The J. Paul Getty Museum, Ms 43r/91.MS.81 recto. Master of the Dresden Prayer Book, *The Temperature and the Intemperate; Valerius Maximus, Faits et dits mémorables des romains*. Tempera and ink on parchment; 175 × 194 mm. With permission of the J. Paul Getty Museum.

Figure 7. Madrid, Biblioteca Nacional, Ms 197 fol. 128r, detail. Niccolò di Giacomo da Bologna, *Saint Agatha*, Bartholomaeus de Saxoferrato *In primam et secundam digesti novi partem commentaria*. Tempera and ink on parchment. With permission of the Biblioteca Nacional.

Figure 8. Cambridge, The Fitzwilliam Museum, Ms 201, fol. 27.2. Single leaf cutting, *Saint Mary Magdalen* Tempera and ink on vellum. Reproduction by permission of the Fitzwilliam Museum, Cambridge.

Figure 9. Baltimore, The Walters Art Museum, Ms W.170, fol. 174v, detail. Gold Scrolls Group, *Saint Wilgefortis*, Book of Hours, use of Rome. With permission of the Walters Art Museum.

Figure 10. Reproduced from the facsimile of the Florentine *Fior de Virtù* of 1491, translated into English by Nicholas Fersin [sic] with facsimiles of all the original wood cuts. Published for the Library of Congress (Philadelphia, 1953), p. 102: *Saint Lucy*.

Figure 11. New York, The Pierpont Morgan Library, Ms H.8 fol. 183v, detail. Jean Poyet, *Saint Anthony Abbot*, The Hours of Henry VIII. Tempera and ink on parchment. With permission of The Pierpont Morgan Library.

Figure 12. Paris, Bibliothèque nationale, Ms fonds lat. 9187, fol. 32v, detail. Castration scene, *Coutumes de Toulouse*. Ink and wash on parchment. With permission of the Paris, Bibliothèque nationale de France.

Figure 13. Cambridge, Fitzwilliam Museum, Ms 262, fol. 86v, detail. Gratian, *Decretum*, Causa 33. Tempera and ink on parchment. Reproduction by permission of the Fitzwilliam Museum, Cambridge.

WHAT MAKES A MARRIAGE: CONSENT OR CONSUMMATION IN TWELFTH-CENTURY GERMAN LITERATURE

Claudia Bornholdt

According to his early chroniclers and hagiographers, the Northumbrian king and martyr saint Oswald (d. 642) was a married man and the father of at least one son.[1] In twelfth-century Germany, however, when Oswald's life was recorded in the German vernacular and in the shape and form of the then popular rhymed verse epics, various details concerning the saint's life and especially concerning his marriage and death had been significantly changed. The German epic *Der Münchner Oswald* unfolds as follows:

Oswald, the orphaned, and twenty-four year-old king of England prays to God expressing his desire to marry a virtuous woman if God deems this appropriate.[2] God sends his response in a dream, informing Oswald that he supports and encourages his wish to find a queen because Oswald needs to secure an heir for his kingdom and a companion for himself. Since Oswald cannot think of a suitable bride himself, an angel appears before him advising him to seek his bride-to-be in a foreign, heathen country and to convert her to Christianity. Later, while at council with his advisors, the pilgrim Warnmunt appears at the meeting and clarifies the words of the angel. He recommends to Oswald the beautiful heathen princess Pamige. She secretly believes in God, but she is also very well guarded by her father, Aron, who has killed all of her previous wooers. Oswald dispatches a messenger (a talking raven) to ask the heathen king for his daughter's hand in marriage. The proposal is rejected and the messenger is incarcerated,

[1] The oldest written version of the legend of St. Oswald is contained in the Venerable Bede's *Historia ecclesiastica gentis anglorum* from 731 (Bertram Colgrave and R. A. B. Mynors, eds., *Bede's Ecclesiastical History of the English People* [Oxford, 1969]). For a recent discussion of the transmission of the legend see Marianne E. Kalinke, *St. Oswald of Northumbria: Continental Metamorphoses. With an Edition and Translation of "Ósvalds saga" and "Van sunte Oswaldo deme konninghe"* (Tempe, AZ, 2005), pp. 1–9.

[2] *Der Münchner Oswald. Mit einem Anhang: die ostschwäbische Prosabearbeitung des 15. Jahrhunderts*, ed. Michael Curschmann, ATB 76 (Tübingen, 1974).

but he eventually manages to escape after he has obtained the girl's consent to marriage. Now Oswald and a large Christian army sail to the heathen country and, by means of much deceit and cunning and through heavenly intervention, Oswald and Pamige can flee together. The escape party is pursued by Aron and his army. Oswald defeats them in battle and, assisted by a variety of miracles, converts them to Christianity. Upon their return to England, Oswald marries Pamige. At the wedding feast God appears in the guise of a pilgrim. He tests Oswald's faith and orders that the newlyweds should not consummate their marriage; a stipulation to which both spouses agree:

> [God:] "You are not supposed to engage in any sin with your wife! [...] Listen, here is how you can resist sin: you must have water in front of your bed; whenever your manhood overcomes you, jump into the water. Your wife must do the same." [...] Saint Oswald, the mighty lord, served God in a praiseworthy manner; he and the queen, who also wanted to be God's handmaiden, began to lovingly lie next to each other, yet they abstained from worldly love: whenever worldly desire overcame them, they each jumped into the water."[3]

The German narrative of St. Oswald belongs to a group of pre-courtly German epics commonly referred to as minstrel epics (*Spielmannsepen*) because scholars considered them to be compositions of lay minstrels or jongleurs. The entire group is comprised of a total of only five works, which most likely were composed some time in the second half of the twelfth century, and which are the earliest indigenous German narratives that have largely worldly themes and topics.[4] Four of these works—*Der Münchner Oswald, Orendel, König Rother*, and *Salman und Morolf*—are bridal-

[3] "'du solt aber chainer sunden mit der frauen pflegen!/ .../ merk, wie du den sunden solt widerstan:/ wasser soltu vor deinem pet han;/ wann dich dein manhait wil betwingen,/ so soltu in daz wasser springen./ also tuo auch deu frau dein,'/.../ sand Oswalt der furst reich/ dienet got gar wirdikleich,/ er und deu kunigin:/ die wolt auch gotes dienerin sein./ si begunden liebleich pei einander ligen,/ aber weltleicher lieb si sich gar verzigen:/ wenn si der werlt fręud betwang,/ ietweders in daz wasser sprang" (*Der Münchner Oswald*, verses 3510, 3515–19, 3527–3534).

[4] These early vernacular epics are only preceded by German adaptations of the French *Alexander* and the *Chanson de Roland*, by the *Kaiserchronik*, the first vernacular German chronicle, which dates to around 1150, as well as by several shorter vernacular religious and historical texts, among them *Das Lob Salomons* (The Praise of Solomon); *Diu Hochzeit* (The Wedding), an allegorical reading of the Song of Songs; the *Annolied* and the *Ezzolied*, both religious narratives, the first, a praise of the life and deeds of the bishops of Cologne and the second, a hymn of God's creation and salvation.

quest tales that relate the hero's quest for a bride he has to obtain in a foreign country against her father's will.[5]

These German stories about the kings Oswald, Orendel, Rother, and Solomon do not only stand at the rise of vernacular fiction in Germany, they are also the earliest representatives of vernacular bridal-quest narrative in the German-speaking area, and they share one peculiarity: they all address the idea of marital chastity. This article will focus on the representation of marriage in the German bridal-quest epics. I will outline how the idea of marriage and especially that of chaste marriage appears in the works and then suggest possible reasons that may explain the predominance of the chastity motif in twelfth-century Germany.

As I have argued in a previous study, bridal-quest narratives were known in the Germanic world at least from the late sixth century on.[6] The earliest example can be found in Gregory of Tours' *Historia Francorum* (ca. 575–590) and its seventh and eighth-century continuations.[7] Bridal-quest narratives also occur in thirteenth and fourteenth-century Scandinavia, in the ninth or tenth-century Latin *Waltharius* poem, and in the German so-called minstrel epics. All of these Germanic bridal-quest narratives share a characteristic plot, in which a nobleman, urged by his councilors, sets out on a quest to attain a suitable wife and to sire an heir and successor to the crown. To accomplish his quest, the wooer travels to a foreign country, sometimes first sending messengers and proxy-wooers. He employs various means to elope with his future wife who is generally well protected by her father. The hero often defeats a pursuing army before he finally returns to his home country where the wedding takes place.

Two of the four twelfth-century German bridal-quest narratives, however, contain a surprising variation of this paradigm because they end with the newlywed couple's resolve to observe perpetual marital

---

[5] In *Salman und Morolf* the plot is reversed. Here King Solomon has to twice win his wife Salme back from her heathen abductors. Walter Haug appropriately referred to the content of the epic as a bridal quest with reversed premises in "Brautwerbung im Zerrspiegel: Salman und Morolf," in *Sammlung—Deutung—Wertung. Mélanges de littérature médiévale et de linguistique allemande offerts à Wolfgang Spiewok*, ed. Danielle Buschinger (Stuttgart, 1988), pp. 179–88.

[6] Claudia Bornholdt, *Engaging Moments: The Origins of Medieval Bridal-Quest Narrative*, Ergänzungsbände zum Reallexikon der germanischen Altertumskunde 46 (Berlin/New York, 2005).

[7] The *Chronica Fredegarii* (completed ca. 642) and the *Liber historiae Francorum* (727).

chastity. Those works are the aforementioned *Münchner Oswald* and the epic *Orendel*, which relates the story of Orendel, the unmarried son of the king in Trier. Like Oswald, the young Orendel expresses his wish to marry. He is advised by his councilors to go and win the Christian queen of Jerusalem. He does so, and after many battles and great suffering, Orendel eventually returns home to Trier with his bride-to-be and the relic of the Seamless Garment of Christ which he had obtained in the Holy Land. He transfers the relic to the cathedral in Trier where it is still located today, and he marries his bride. However, just like Oswald, Orendel and his wife never consummate their marriage:

> After they had sat there and were done drinking and eating and the Grey Cloak [Orendel] was supposed to go to sleep with lady Bride in his chambers, then, as he stepped toward the bed, an angel appeared before him and spoke: "Listen, King Orendel, God and His mother have sent me to you, so that you do not engage in any kind of [physical] love with Bride, your lady, for the course of nine years. Truly, that is God's command." As soon as he heard these words, the praiseworthy hero got up and went, as ordered, to the place where he knew that his good sword was lying (he swore oaths; the sword was inside a golden sheath). Truly, he placed that sword between himself and the maiden. His lady Bride asked him whether it was customary in his country that when a woman was married to a man, they had to have a sword between them. Then the Grey Cloak spoke:
>
> "Not at all, lady! The voice of God commanded that we shall not enjoy any kind of love from today on for nine years: truly, that was ordered by God." Then the noble maiden spoke: "Lord, now put your sword back into its sheath!" Lady Bride spoke in the following manner: "I can easily remain without a man for ten years!"[8]

---

[8] "Dô si alsô gesâzen/ und getrunken unde gâzen/ und der Grâwe Roc solt gân slâfen/ mit frouwen Brîden in die kemenâte,/ dô er an daz bet getrat,/ ein engel im under die ougen sach,/ er sprach: 'hoerstu, künig Orendel,/ mich hât got und sîne muoter zuo dir gesendet,/ daz du keiner slahte minne/ mit frouwen Brîden solt gewinnen/ bis von hiut über niun jâr,/ daz gebiut dir got, daz ist wâr.'/ Als er die rede dô vernam,/ ûf stuond der degen lobesan,/ er gieng alsô gerihte,/ dâ er sîn guot swert wüste,/ [er swuor bî tiuren eiden,/ ez stecket in einer guldenen scheiden]./ Daz legt er in ganzen trouwen/ zwischen sich und die jungfrouwen./ Frouw Brîde frâget in der mêre,/ ob ez in sînem lande site wêre,/ welhe frouwe neme einen man,/ daz si ein swert zwischen in müesten hân./ Dô sprach der Grâwe Roc:/ 'Nein ez, frouwe, daz weiz got!/ uns enbiutet die gotes stimme,/ vil edele küniginne,/ daz wir keiner slahte minne/ mit einander sollen gewinnnen,/ wan von hiut über niun jâr:/ daz enbiutet uns got, daz ist wâr.'/ Dô sprach daz edel megetîn:/ 'Hêre, nun stôz dîn swert wider în!'/ Alsô sprach frouwe Brîde:/ 'zehen jâr mag ich wol ân ein man belîben'" (*Orendel*, ed. Heinz Steinger [Halle/Saale, 1935], verses 1779–1814). The scene repeats itself

The endings to the bridal quests of Oswald and Orendel are puzzling, to say the least. They undermine the very logic of the tales, since the sole purpose of the hero's quest and his willingness to accept and tolerate the hardships involved in completing it was to obtain a wife and to father an heir for his kingdom. One possible explanation for these inconsistent and illogical endings could lie in the overall dominant religious content of the works or in the hagiographic and historical transmission of the subject matter. As pointed out before, however, the historical St. Oswald most likely was not a virgin. Bede relates in 731 AD that Oswald was the godfather to the pagan king Cynegisl, whose daughter he subsequently married, and that Oswald's son, Oethelwald inherited the throne of Deira after his father's death.[9] In the early eleventh century, when Oswald's relics had reached the continent, the Benedictine monk Drogo (d. 1084) composed a life of Saint Oswald which largely relied on Bede's account.[10] In accordance with Bede, Drogo states that Oswald was married to a pagan king's daughter. New to Drogo's version is that Oswald's marriage to the pagan princess is for the first time placed in the context of the conversion motif; an idea that resurfaces in the German epic. At the time the cult of St. Oswald reached Germany—probably at the same time as the first relics of the saint reached southern Germany in the year 1071, accompanied by a version of Drogo's *Vita Oswaldi*—Oswald was not a virgin.[11] In Bede's and Drogo's as well as later Latin *vitae* of St. Oswald, the king dies a martyr's death and there is no mention of a bridal quest or his chaste marriage. St. Oswald's virginity and marital chastity is a later, exclusively German introduction to the life of the saint, meaning that Oswald's chaste marriage at the end of *Der Münchner Oswald* cannot be explained as a loan from the historical or the hagiographic tradition.

Likewise, Orendel's chaste marriage lacks historical or hagiographic sources. Actually, the account of Orendel does not seem to have any sources at all nor any known parallel transmission. Orendel seems to

in slight variation when Orendel and Bride retire to their chambers after their first nine years of abstinence are over (*Orendel*, verses 2844 ff.), and then again at the very end of the epic (vv. 3864 ff.).

[9] Bede, iii.7 and iii.23. See iii.24 for an additional reference to Oswald's son.

[10] See Kalinke, pp. 3–6, for a detailed discussion of the spread of the legend of St. Oswald on the continent. Drogo's *Vita Oswaldi* is edited in *Acta Sanctorum*. Augusti, II, 5–12. Aug. 5: "De S. Oswaldo rege ac mart.," pp. 83–103.

[11] See Kalinke, *St. Oswald*, pp. 5–6.

be solely a fictional character that most likely was created in order to tell the story of the Seamless Garment of Christ on the occasion of the translation of the relic to the newly-remodeled cathedral of Trier in the year 1196.[12] Since the bridal-quest paradigm seems to have been especially productive in twelfth-century Germany, we can speculate that Orendel's or rather the relic's story was composed according to that paradigm in order to appeal to the contemporary audience. There is, however, no apparent reason why the author of the story broke with narrative convention and ended the story with the protagonists' marital chastity.

While the fictional accounts of Orendel's and Oswald's life abound in legendary elements—both heroes are assisted in their quests by various miracles and heavenly interventions and Oswald is a canonized saint—their endings remain an oddity. If they were indeed composed to spread the *vita* of St. Oswald and the details surrounding the acquisition of Trier's sacred relic to a larger, vernacular audience, and if these accounts were indeed clad into the shape of bridal-quest narratives in order to make them more accessible and interesting for the contemporary audience, it nevertheless remains to be asked why the very purpose of the heroes' quests, namely to secure progeny and royal succession, was replaced with the motif of marital chastity. The question becomes even more interesting considering that previous to these German compositions neither Oswald nor Orendel were associated with the virgin state or with marital chastity.

Put differently: Why was the story of Oswald, his quest for and conversion of a pagan princess not told in the same way in the German vernacular as Bede, Drogo, and others had done before? If the answer to this question should be that the author consciously chose a more contemporary and seemingly fashionable narrative paradigm, namely that of bridal-quest narrative, why did he transmute St. Oswald's marriage into a virgin marriage? And, on a similar note, why was the legend surrounding the Seamless Garment of Christ not composed as a conventional hagiographic story, as a legend, *passio, vita*, as a crusading tale or an adventure story, but instead as a bridal-quest narrative that, against all conventions and the logic of the narrative, concluded in a chaste marriage?

---

[12] See Uwe Meves, *Studien zu König Rother, Herzog Ernst, Grauer Rock/Orendel* (Frankfurt am Main/Bern, 1976), pp. 227–42.

Possible answers to these questions are easier to obtain with respect to the romance of St. Oswald because the German author somehow had to accommodate the fact that his bridal-quest protagonist was a canonized saint. The historical King Oswald had died on the battlefield and was venerated as a martyr saint; the fictional king in the German bridal-quest narrative, however, had to survive the battle against his future father-in-law and the latter's heathen army in order to successfully complete his quest, win his bride, and christianize his enemy. Consequently, he could not die a martyr saint and instead was transformed into a confessor saint. Together with the miracles that occurred during his bridal quest, Oswald's marital chastity helped to underpin his saintly state, regardless of the consequences this change had for the inherent logic of the narrative. At least this new ending allowed the author to tell the story of Oswald's bridal quest to the end. This admittedly rather speculative explanation for the odd ending of *Der Münchner Oswald* does not apply to *Orendel* however, because Orendel is not a historically attested figure. He is neither a canonized saint nor is he presented as a saint in the epic itself so that there are neither text-internal nor external reasons to emphasize the idea of marital chastity in Orendel's bridal-quest story.

To gain a more comprehensive picture, I will now briefly discuss the other two German twelfth-century narratives that address the issue of marital chastity, albeit more indirectly than *Orendel* and *Der Münchner Oswald*. In *König Rother*, arguably the oldest of the four bridal-quest epics, King Rother's quest for the daughter of the king of Constantinople is closely connected with issues of succession to the royal house of the Carolingians and thus deeply embedded in worldly matters of kingship and royal legacy.[13] Although Rother's elaborate quest—which he has to repeat once more after his wife is abducted back home to her father's country—results in a consummated marriage and the fathering of a son, this progeny is special because it is explicitly sanctified by God: *do wart die vrowe lossam/swanger einis kindis,/einis* <u>*seligin*</u> *barnis* ("Then his wife became pregnant with child, a <u>holy</u> child").[14] King Rother, it seems,

[13] See Christa Ortmann and Hedda Ragotzky, "Brautwerbung, Reichsherrschaft und staufische Politik. Zur politischen Bestimmungsfähigkeit literarischer Strukturmuster am Beispiel des 'König Rother,'" *Zeitschrift für deutsche Philologie* 112 (1993), 321–43; and Ferdinand Urbanek, *Kaiser, Grafen und Mäzene im 'König Rother'* (Berlin, 1976).

[14] *König Rother*, ed. Theodor Frings and Joachim Kuhnt, 3rd ed. (Halle/Saale, 1968), verses 2943–45. My emphasis.

consummates his marriage not to satisfy any sexual desire or out of selfish motives but for the larger good of his kingdom and for the entire Christian world, because he sired Pippin, the heir to the Holy Roman Empire and ancestor of the line of the Carolingians. But even though the story of King Rother does not close with the protagonist's virginal marriage, it nevertheless closes with the idea of marital chastity because both Rother and his wife turn away from the world and take up the *vita religiosa* by entering monasteries immediately after the knighting of their son and the transfer of the crown:

> [Berchter, Rother's advisor, is speaking:] "We shall become monks, my dear lord; we must help our wretched souls: this life is only temporary!" Upon that the good king said that he would gladly do that. Rother took his exceptionally praiseworthy wife by her hand and told her of his intention. The good woman spoke: "That is the best advice Berchter has ever given! Now follow us, noble king, it will not cause us any disadvantage!"[15]

Besides the announcement of the conception and birth of Rother's son, there is no mention of any other children or of any other spousal intimacy in the entire work. We can therefore carefully conclude that Rother's marriage, though not virginal, is deliberately depicted as a marriage initially spent in sexual moderation which was later transformed into a chaste marriage.

The fourth twelfth-century German bridal-quest narrative, the epic *Salman und Morolf*, approaches the issue of marital intimacy from a quite different angle. The epic opens with the information that King Solomon, who is named and modeled after the biblical King Solomon, had abducted his wife Salme from her heathen father, converted her to Christianity and had made her queen of Jerusalem.[16] Instead of being concerned with the king's bridal quest, as is the case in the other German stories, the plot in *Salman und Morolf* revolves around the queen's two elopements with two heathen kings and the adventures experienced by Morolf, the king's brother, in his attempts to recover her. The epic

[15] "'wir munichin uns, trut herre min,/ wir sulin der armin sele wegen:/ diz ist ein unstade leven!'/ do sprach der koninc gote,/ daz her dat gerne date./ Rother bi der hant nam/ die vrowen also lossam/ unde sagete ir sin gemote./ da sprach die vrowe gote:/ 'iz ist der bezziste rat/ den Berker getan hat!/ nu volge uns, koninc edele,/ iz ne kumit uns nicht ubele!'" (*König Rother*, verses 5172–8514).

[16] I will refer to the protagonist as Solomon, except where I quote the title of the work.

ends with Salme's death at the hands of Morolf, and Solomon's second marriage to the formerly heathen princess Affer.[17]

Interpretations of *Salman und Morolf* tend to focus on Salme's adulterous behavior and on Morolf's astuteness in winning her back. Scholars read the narrative as a warning against unfaithful wives, and they consider the work a prime example of medieval misogyny, in which the deceitfulness of the evil woman is presented as a warning for the (male) audience.[18] According to these interpretations, the work demonstrates that only sly and cunning men, such as Salman's brother Morolf, are able to deal with such women and restore order to the world.[19]

---

[17] The epic is included in the group of bridal-quest epics because it contains two bridal quests (the two heathen wooers' quests for Salme). Moreover, as Walther Haug has shown, the entire plot of the epic is told as a bridal-quest story with altered or reversed premises. Here, the paradigm is used to tell Morolf's efforts in winning back the eloped queen. See Haug, "Brautwerbung im Zerrspiegel," pp. 179–188.

[18] The most important studies to *Salman und Morolf* are Sabine Griese, *Salomon und Markolf. Ein literarischer Komplex im Mittelalter und in der frühen Neuzeit* (Tübingen, 1999), esp. pp. 77–137; Hans-Joachim Böckenholt, "Untersuchungen zum Bild der Frau in den mittelhochdeutschen Spielmannsdichtungen" (Ph.D. diss., Universität Münster, 1971), pp. 84–141; and the respective chapters in Michael Curschmann, *Der Münchener Oswald und die deutsche spielmännische Epik. Mit einem Exkurs zur Kultgeschichte und Dichtungstradition* (München, 1964) and *Spielmannsepik. Wege und Ergebnisse der Forschung von 1907–1963* (Stuttgart, 1968). See also Lydia Miklautsch, "Salman und Morolf—Thema und Variation," in *Ir sult sprechen willekomen: Grenzenlose Mediävistik: Festschrift für Helmut Birkhahn zum 60. Geburtstag*, Christa Tuczay, Ulrike Hirhager, and Karin Lichtblau, eds. (Bern, 1998), pp. 284–306.

[19] Since minstrels are explicitly mentioned in the epic and especially since Morolf encompasses many of the characteristics generally assigned to this social group, nineteenth-century scholars concluded that a minstrel was responsible for the work's composition and, by extension, also for the composition of the other so-called minstrel epics (hence the name!). Today, however, scholars agree that while minstrels may have distributed and performed the works, they most likely did not compose them. The extant written versions are believed to be the work of educated and literate clerics. The idea of traveling minstrels who were responsible for spreading tales circulating among the people (*Naturpoesie*) ultimately derives from Jacob Grimm's "Vorrede," in Jacob Grimm, *Ueber den altdeutschen Meistergesang* (Göttingen, 1811), repr. in *Spielmannsepik*, ed. Walter Johannes Schröder (Darmstadt, 1977), pp. 1–7. Various nineteenth-century scholars picked up this idea and expanded it, arguing that minstrels were not only responsible for the distribution but also for the composition of the works. See, for example, Friedrich Vogt, *Leben und Dichten der deutschen Spielleute im Mittelalter. Vortrag gehalten im wissenschaftlichen Verein zu Greifswald am 29. November 1875* (Halle, 1876), repr. in *Spielmannsepik*, pp. 18–48, and Paul Piper, "Allgemeines über die Spielmannsdichtung," in Piper, *Die Spielmannsdichtung. Erster Teil: Die reine Spielmannsdichtung* (Berlin/Stuttgart, 1887), repr. in *Spielmannsepik*, pp. 49–71. For a summary of the present scholarly view see Norbert H. Ott, "Spielmannsdichtung: II. Deutsche Literatur," in *Lexikon des Mittelalters*, vol. 7 (München, 2002), cols. 2115–2116.

In conjunction with the prevalence of the chastity motif in the other pre-courtly German bridal-quest epics, I would like to suggest turning the focus away from Salme's adulterous behavior or Morolf's cunningness in winning her back. If we instead look more closely at the depiction of King Solomon, the epic of *Salman und Morolf* can be read as an *exemplum*, which promotes the idea of marital chastity by way of exhibiting the negative consequences uncontrolled physical love have on the king's *ratio* and royal virtues as well as on his ability to govern. I argue that *Salman und Morolf*, similar to the other German bridal-quest epics, promotes the idea that marital intercourse should solely serve the purpose of procreation and not the satisfaction of sexual desire or passion. The biblical king Solomon was the perfect figure for such a didactic purpose. Especially in the medieval German reception, Solomon was regarded as the epitome of the wise and just ruler and a model of the *rex pacificus*. He occupied a central position in the *translatio imperii*. That special role within the line of the German monarchy finds its symbolic representation in the fact that Solomon features in central position on the crown of the Ottonian emperors. Not surprisingly, references to Solomon's legendary wisdom and rule abound in German medieval literature. Just as widespread, however, are allusions to Solomon's other legendary quality: his love for women that ultimately caused his fall from grace.

Significantly, *Salman und Morolf* is the only German twelfth-century bridal-quest epic that explicitly mentions a couple's intimacy: The tale tells us this: King Solomon loved his wife. He experienced all the pleasures with her when he lay in her snow-white arms in the bedroom. This made the king very happy. Later suffering and agony arose for the sake of this beautiful woman; many a proud knight had to lose his life.[20]

The allusion to future distress brought about by or rather for the queen is only one of many such references in the text. In this particular instance, however, the interdependence of love and suffering and here explicitly of physical love and suffering is most apparent. Throughout the romance, the narrator's comments stress the king's inappropriate behavior, that is, his fixation on his wife which distracts him from his

---

[20] "Also kundet uns diß lieht:/ kunig Salmon was sin frauwe liep./ gantzer freuden er mit ir pflag,/ da er in der kemenaten/ an iren sne wißen armen lag./ Des was der kunig wol gemeit/ sich huop da leit und arbeitt:/ umb das vil wonder schone wip/ must manig stolczer ritter/ verlieren sinen werden lip" (*Salman und Morolf*, ed. Alfred Karnein [Tübingen, 1979], stanzas 19–20).

royal duties and virtues. His sexual desire results in his losing control over his best-known qualities: his wisdom and good judgment. Solomon becomes an *exemplum* of the negative consequences of uncontrolled love and sexual desire; he is rendered as a typical *Minnesklave* (slave of love) or *Frauensklave* (slave of women).[21]

There are many examples in medieval German literature and poetry where King Solomon is included in lists of biblical and literary *exempla* of *Minnesklaven* or *Frauensklaven*, often together with Aristotle, King David, Samson, or Absalom. Especially in later medieval German literature, stanzas referring to famous slaves of love (*Minnesklaven*) are included in Arthurian romances and poetry to warn of the dangers of love in general. The so-called *Frauensklaven* stanzas serve a similar purpose only that they warn men more distinctly of the dangers of female temptation and slyness.[22]

The portrayal of King Solomon as a slave of love in *Salman und Morolf* is, as I argue in more detail in another place, the key to the interpretation of the whole epic as a didactic *exemplum* that warns of the negative consequences of carnal love.[23] The epic depicts in great detail how Solomon's sensual love for his wife causes him to lose his wisdom and *ratio* and hence his ability to act as a responsible and honorable king. Solomon's enthrallment to his corporeal desires, brought about

---

[21] This is expressed most clearly in stanza 155: "'Were ich also wise als du, kunig Salmon,/ und were also schone als Abselon/ und sunge als wol als Horant,/ mochte ich min frauwe nit betzwingen,/ ich hette ein laster an der hant.'" ("If I were as wise as you, King Solomon, and as beautiful as Absalon, and if I could sing as beautifully as Horant—if I were not able to control my wife, I had suffered dishonor [or: incurred a vice].").

[22] Examples of the *Minnesklave* in thirteenth to fifteenth-century German literature and art are collected in Friedrich Maurer, "Der Topos von den 'Minnesklaven'. Zur Geschichte einer thematischen Gemeinschaft zwischen bildender Kunst und Dichtung im Mittelalter," *Deutsche Vierteljahresschrift für Literaturwissenschaft und Geistesgeschichte* 27 (1953), 182–206. A more thorough distinction between *Minnesklaven* and *Frauensklaven* is provided by Rüdiger Schnell, *'Causa Amoris.' Liebeskonzeption und Liebesdarstellung in der mittelalterlichen Literatur* (Bern/München, 1985). See also Norbert H. Ott, "Minne oder *amor carnalis*? Zur Funktion der Minnesklaven-Darstellung in mittelalterlicher Kunst," in *Liebe in der deutschen Literatur des Mittelalters. St. Andrews-Colloquium 1985*, Jeffrey Ashcroft, Dietrich Huschenbett, and William Henry Jackson, eds. (Tübingen, 1987), pp. 107–125; and Heimo Reinitzer, "Über Beispielfiguren im *Erec*," *Deutsche Vierteljahresschrift für Literaturwissenschaft und Geistesgeschichte* 50 (1976), 597–639.

[23] Claudia Bornholdt, "'in was ze schouwen also not': *Salman und Morolf* bildlich erzählt," in *Visualisierungsstrategien in mittelalterlichen Bildern und Texten*, Horst Wenzel, C. Stephen Jaeger et al., eds. (Berlin, 2006), pp. 226–247.

by the extraordinary beauty of his wife, comes to an end only after she has been killed by his brother.

The epic closes with the information that Solomon lived happily for 33 years with his second wife, Affer, his *werde minne* (his "appropriate and noble love"), who, unlike Salme, had voluntarily converted to Christianity and who, unlike Salme, had consented to marrying Solomon.[24] Her consent is important because it makes Solomon's second marriage an *unio cordis* rather than an *unio carnis* like his first marriage. Solomon and Affer's consensual marriage corroborates the marriage traditions prevailing in twelfth-century Germany which basically followed the distinction Hugh of St. Victor made in his *De beatae Mariae virginitate*, where he states that *Matrimonium non facit coitus, sed consensus.*[25]

The continuation of *Salman und Morolf*, which is extant in an imprint from Straßburg, supports my reading of the epic as a didactic text that *ex negativo* advocates marital chastity. According to this continuation, Solomon and Affer have two sons, but they nonetheless live in sexual moderation, and, like King Rother and his wife, they spend the later years of their lives in marital chastity. The narrator of the continuation describes in detail the great love shared by Solomon and his second wife: "They loved each other dearly; they lived together in friendship and in moderation, just as two good spouses are supposed to do."[26] This comment clearly refers to the couple's moderation in all aspects of life, including their sexual intimacy. This comment also stands in harsh contrast to Solomon's first marriage which he consummated often and for pleasure's sake only. That first marriage had to fail because it was solely founded on Solomon's corporeal desires. Enticed by Salme's beauty, Solomon abducted her, forcefully converted her to Christianity, and then married her without her or her father's consent. Solomon's passion and unrestrained physical love continued to shape that marriage

[24] *Salman und Morolf*, stanza 783, 5.

[25] Hugh of St. Victor, *De beatae Mariae virginitate*, in *PL* 176.857–876; here 858. See also Reinitzer, "Beispielfiguren," p. 613, n. 62; Penny S. Gold, "The Marriage of Mary and Joseph in the Twelfth-Century Ideology of Marriage," in *Sexual Practices and the Medieval Church*, Vern L. Bullough and James Brundage, eds. (Buffalo, 1982), pp. 102–117; and the respective chapters in James A. Brundage, *Law, Sex, and Christian Society in Medieval Europe* (Chicago/London, 1987).

[26] "Ir beder liebe die was grosz/ Sy liebetent einand' vnd lebetent früntich in aller mosz/ Als dan zwey liebi ee\ lüte söllen leben" (Continuation of *Salman und Morolf*, Straßburg Ms, p. 259, verses 13–15).

causing Solomon to become a fool and to be unfit to fulfill his royal duties. He corrects all those mistakes in his second marriage in which sexual intercourse seems to serve the sole purpose of procreation.

To sum up the findings: Germany's earliest indigenous vernacular narratives with largely secular themes are bridal quests or reversals of bridal quests that end with a discussion of the protagonists' marriage or, more precisely, with the appropriate degree of marital intimacy in a marriage. The two most religiously-colored narratives, *Der Münchner Oswald* and *Orendel*, converge in perpetual marital chastity. The quest in *König Rother*, the epic with the strongest imperial emphasis, is the only one to observe the inherent logic of the bridal-quest paradigm as it results in a consummated marriage and the fathering of an heir. Here, however, consummation is explicitly sanctified because it serves the particular purpose of ensuring the future of the Holy Roman Empire. *Salman und Morolf* finally, with its reversed and at times parodied bridal quests, stands in the tradition of narratives about the literary *exempla* figure of the slave of love (*Minnesklave*). That epic can be read as an expansive version of that literary *topos*, presenting the twelfth-century audience with a warning about the destructive consequences of sensual love; it warns of *armor carnalis* and *unio carnis* and instead advocates marital consensuality and moderation (that is, *unio consensus*).

How can we explain the obvious focus on consensual marriage and marital chastity in these works at a time when the majority of vernacular literature is rich with secular adventures and fantastic creatures, as in *Herzog Ernst* and the *Alexander* epics; gory battles and crusading themes, as in the *Rolandslied*; or religious and historical themes, such as in the *Kaiserchronik*, *Annolied*, and other short religious narratives? Most importantly, how can we account for the prevalence of the idea of marital chastity in stories told according to a narrative paradigm whose very plot motivation and inherent logic is the establishment of royal progeny?

The least trouble in attempting to answer these questions is certainly caused by the *moniage* in *König Rother*, as additional examples for it are easily found in contemporary non-bridal-quest literature, such as the French and German cycles of Guillaume and Willehalm.[27] The

[27] Compare Guillaume in the Old French *Moniage Guillaume* (second half of twelfth century) and Willehalm and Kyburg in Ulrich von Türheim's Middle High German *Rennewart* (1240/1250). A possibly earlier and thus contemporary example to *König*

perpetual marital chastity of the protagonists in *Der Münchner Oswald* and *Orendel* on the other hand, is unique to the literary tradition of the twelfth century. It does, however, have likely models in contemporary historical and hagiographic writings and story telling.[28] As Marianne Kalinke has proposed in a recent study, the most immediate source for the German romance of Oswald seems to have been the virginal marriage of the German Emperor Henry II and his wife Cunegund of Luxembourg.[29] I would like to extend that idea and suggest that the hagiographic and literary tradition revolving around Germany's first royal saint was in fact responsible for the recurrence of the motif of marital chastity in all of the twelfth-century German epics I have discussed so far.

The marriage of Henry II of Germany and Cunegund of Luxembourg remained childless and their lack of progeny was quickly seen as the consequence of the couple's deliberate renunciation of all sexual union. Reports of Henry and Cunegund's chaste marriage began immediately after the emperor's death in 1024, first in laments and a few decades later also in historical sources.[30] Already in the late eleventh century, oral legends surrounding the marriage of the couple seem to have formed, whereas efforts to "officially" canonize Henry II did not commence until the 1140s, when his *vita* was composed by a Bamberg deacon called Adalbert and eventually presented to the Pope

---

Rother is Heime's *moniage* in the Old Norse *Þiðreks saga* which was based on German sources that may well date to the second half of the twelfth century.

[28] A well-known early occurrence of the idea of marital chastity in a semi-literary/historical context is the story of the chaste lovers related by Gregory of Tours in his *History of the Franks* (*Historia Francorum*) and also in his *Book of Miracles* (*Liber in Gloria Confessorum*, 31). In this story the spouses, upon the woman's urging, swear a vow of chastity on their wedding night (Gregory of Tours, *Historiarum Libri Decem*, ed. Bruno Krusch, 2 vols., 7th rev. ed. Rudolf Buchner, trans. W. Giesebrecht [Darmstadt, 1988], I:47).

[29] Marianne Kalinke, *St. Oswald*, see n. 1 above. Kalinke's position opposes that of Ingrid Bennewitz, who argued for a reversed direction of influence in "Kaiserin und Braut Gottes. Literarische Entwürfe weiblicher Heiligkeit," *Historischer Verein Bamberg*, Bericht 137 (2001), 133–148. The following discussion of Henry and Cunegund and the sources transmitting their legend(s) is strongly indebted to two lectures held by Marianne Kalinke: "Henry and Cunegund and the Issue of Consensuality in Marriage" (Lecture in Göttingen, 2002) and "Historiography, Hagiography, and the Rise of Vernacular Fiction" (Lecture sponsored by the Center of Advanced Studies at University of Illinois at Urbana-Champaign, September 8, 2003).

[30] Compare Renate Klauser, *Der Heinrichs- und Kunigundenkult im mittelalterlichen Bistum Bamberg* (Bamberg, 1957), pp. 31–33. The first historical accounts to address the couple's chastity are Frutolf of Michelsberg's (d. 1103) *Chronicon Universale* or *Weltchronik* and Leo of Ostia's chronicle of the monastery of Montecassino (1060).

in 1145. One year later, Pope Eugene III proclaimed in the bull of Henry's canonization that Henry "had preserved chastity until the end of his life" (*integritatem castimoniae usque in finem vitae conservavit*).[31]

In the last decades of the twelfth century, a monk from Bamberg composed the *Vitae Heinrici Additamentum*, probably in connection with the increased veneration of empress Cunegund, who was canonized in 1200. The *Additamentum* consists of three new chapters to the emperor's legend that are exclusively devoted to the idea of his chaste marriage. The first of these chapters elaborates on the events leading to the couple's marriage and it adds a detailed bridal-chamber scene as well as extensive praise of marital chastity.[32] Shortly afterwards, in the early thirteenth century, Ebernand of Erfurt composed the first vernacular legend of Henry and Cunegund, entitled *Kaiser und Kaiserin*.[33]

In both the Latin *Additamentum* and the German verse legend of Henry and Cunegund the couple consensually and simultaneously makes a vow of chastity on their wedding night. Ebernand of Erfurt summarizes their motivation as follows: "Thusly true love was in both their minds. She (true love) was such a master that, wherever she began to burn, people do not want to give in to corporeal love."[34] The bedroom-scene in *Kaiser und Kaiserin* peaks in a ceremonial act during which Henry and Cunegund swear their love and perpetual marital chastity to each other:

He took both of her white hands in his and spoke: "My Lady and wife, I will promise you one thing and you shall promise the same to me, namely that we will live chastely and give ourselves to God here

---

31 The papal bull is reprinted in Philipp Jaffé, *Monumenta Bambergensia*, Bibliotheca rerum Germanicarum 5 (Berlin, 1869), pp. 331–332 and in MGH, Scriptorum IV (1841), p. 813b.

32 *Vitae S. Heinrici additamenta und Vita S. Cunegundis*, ed. Georg Waitz. MGH SS IV (Hanover, 1841), pp. 816–828.

33 Ebernand von Erfurt, *Heinrich und Kunegunde*, ed. by Reinhold Bechstein, Bibliothek der gesammten deutschen National-Literatur von der ältesten bis auf die neuere Zeit 39 (Quedlinburg/Leipzig, 1860).

34 "sus was die wâre minne/ in ir beider sinne;/ die was solch meisterinne, dô sie begunde brinne,/ sint woldens niht beginne/ der vleischlîchen minne" (*Kaiser und Kaiserin*, verses 925–930). Henry's promise to protect Cunegund against potential future harm is referring to the consequences their vow of perpetual chastity has for the future of the kingdom and potentially also for Cunegund's future as his wife. Since a king was expected to produce offspring it was not uncommon that in cases where the queen remained without child, the retainers urged the king to dispose of the seemingly barren wife or to sire a son with a mistress. Henry's words seem to incorporate that possibility for they assure Cunegund that he will remain chaste and that he will uphold their chaste marriage under all circumstances.

and now; I will always hold you as an honorable empress and, truly, I will not let you be subjected to the slightest bit of harm."[35]

In Ebernand von Erfurt's vernacular written legend as well as in his sources—the Latin *Additamentum* and oral legends circulating in southern Germany—Henry and Cunegund are said to have observed marital chastity until their death, just as Oswald and his wife in the Bavarian bridal-quest romance *Der Münchner Oswald* and the protagonist in the Trier narrative of *Orendel*. And even though in the latter two accounts the spousal vow of chastity is made by heavenly decree, they share so many motifs with the legend of Henry and Cunegund that some sort of interdependence and direct literary borrowings must be assumed to have existed. Kalinke has shown this in light of the legend and epic of Oswald.[36] In that case the connection of the two works is more readily established than in other works because both Henry and Oswald are historical kings and canonized saints. There is good reason to believe that a no longer extant earlier German legend of St. Oswald had borrowed the chastity motif from the legend of Henry II and Cunegund, most likely from earlier oral versions that circulated in Bavaria since around the turn of the twelfth century.[37] The author of *Der Münchner Oswald* included that motif in his story of St. Oswald, regardless of the fact that closing a bridal-quest narrative with a chaste marriage would cause him to violate the narrative paradigm and the logic of the story. It is also quite possible that the a-historical, entirely fictitious narrative of Orendel and the virgin marriage of its protagonists were influenced by or maybe even directly modeled after the legend of Henry, the lost German legend of Oswald, or the German romance of Oswald.[38]

---

[35] "er nam ir hande wîze/ beide in die sîne,/ er sprach: 'vrouwe mîne,/ ein dinc wil ich geloben dir,/ gelobe ouch dû daz selbe mir,/ daz wir kûschlîche leben/ unt uns got alhier begeben;/ ich wil dich halden immermêr/ als eine keiserinne hêr,/ des wil ich letzen dich fur wâr/ gewaldes niht als umbe ein hâr:'" (*Kaiser und Kaiserin*, verses 940–950).

[36] Kalinke, *St. Oswald*, see n. 1 above.

[37] As Kalinke convincingly argues, the Old Norse legend of St. Oswald was most likely based on such a lost German legend, which, among other motifs, delivered the chastity motif (Kalinke, *St. Oswald*, see note 1 above).

[38] Another possible influence on both *Der Münchner Oswald* and *Orendel* is the German legend of St. Alexius. In the so-called *Alexius A*, the motif of perpetual marital chastity is greatly amplified and the entire legend closely resembles the legend of Henry and Cunegund. I am discussing this connection as well as the two legends in greater detail in a forthcoming monograph.

Moreover, the description of Henry and Cunegund's love in the *Additamentum* closely resembles that of Solomon and his second wife, Affer, in the Salzburg continuation of *Salman und Morolf*. In the former we are told that Henry and Cunegund had "one heart and one soul, and they were two only in flesh but one in spirit."[39] In his vernacular rendering of the *vita*, Ebernand of Erfurt reinforces this idea and expands it. He adds that the love they shared was so deep that people wondered how they managed to remain chaste. According to Ebernand, the spouses enjoyed each other's company so much that they spent every minute of the day and of the night together:

> The queen and her good husband, whatever one of them did first, the other one did right afterwards; both were eager to do good things. He loved her as dearly as he loved his own life. No man will ever be able to love his wife more dearly. Whenever the pure, mighty lord, had to ride away from her, which happened frequently for the sake of the kingdom, he always informed her about his departure and task. Also, he never returned home so fast that he would not first go and see her: one rarely saw him not do that. She obeyed to his wishes both in public and in private. They were very intimate, they did not sleep separately. Truly, that may surprise you that they spent their time in such a manner and nevertheless remained chaste! God himself protected both of them.[40]

As a comparison, in the Straßburg continuation of *Salman und Morolf*, the narrator also explains that Solomon and Affer shared a deep love and friendship:

> She faithfully honored her marriage. She was at all times willing to serve God. She lived without hate or anger. She loved Solomon immeasurably. He found no piece of mind and no rest when he could not be with her at all times. Truly, you shall know this, Solomon was also always on the queen's mind. They loved each other dearly; they lived together in friendship and in moderation, just as two good spouses are supposed to do.[41]

---

39 "cor unum et anima una, et erant duo non tam in carne una quam in uno spiritu" (*Vitae S. Heinrici additamenta und Vita S. Cunegundis*, p. 819, a).

40 "die kunegîn und ir guoter man,/ swes ir ein vor began,/ daz tet ze stunt der ander nâch;/ in waz ze guoten dingen gâch./ er hielt sie liep sô sîn lîp,/ ez endorfte nieman sîn wîp/ gehalden minniclîcher./ der reine hêre rîcher,/ swan er iergen von ir reit,/ alse dicke ez sich getreit,/ ze schaffen umbe des rîches nôt,/ vil guotlîch er ir enpôt,/ swaz er ze tuone hâte;/ er enkam ouch nie sô drâte/ wider geriten, ern sêhes an:/ daz sach man in vil selden lân./ uberlût unt stillen/ kunde sie sîns willen/ harte wol gevâren./ heimelîch sie wâren,/ si ensliefen niht in sundern./ wol mac ûch des wundern,/ daz sie die zît alsô vertriben/ unde kûsche dannoch bliben./ dô hâte got der guote/ sie beide in sîner huote" (*Salman und Morolf*, verses 1169–1194).

41 "Ir ee hielte sy mit gantzer stetikeit/ Got zů dienen was sy bereit zů aller zyt/ Sy

Both the marriage of Henry and Cunegund and that of Solomon and Affer are described as ideal marriages and they serve as models for the audience/readership. Both marriages were entered freely and by spousal consent and both are characterized by love and respect. Henry and Cunegund had chosen to remain virgins whereas Solomon and Affer chose to consummate their marriage, but only to procreate and ensure royal succession.

At this point we can summarize the findings regarding the representation of marriage in the twelfth and early thirteenth-century German literary and legendary works I have looked at: St. Henry's, St. Oswald's and Orendel's marriages are unconsummated, virginal (or celibate) marriages to which both spouses agreed simultaneously during their wedding night. Solomon's second marriage and Rother's marriage are marriages that were consummated solely for the purpose of securing progeny and royal succession. Otherwise the spouses live in friendship and they seem to observe sexual moderation. They entirely refrain from sexual intercourse in their more mature years. The negative consequences of passionate, corporeal marital love (or *concupiscentia*) are vividly depicted in the narration of Solomon's first marriage in *Salman und Morolf*. As we have seen, the idea of marriage and questions of the appropriate spousal interaction in a marriage are central aspects of the first indigenous vernacular German verse narratives. As I will now briefly outline below, the very same topics also shaped the contemporary theological debate in Germany and the Western Christian world in general.

The twelfth century was characterized by a continued debate regarding the practice of marriage, clerical celibacy, gender roles, sexuality, and marital chastity; issues that prevailed since the days of the Early Church fathers and that became particularly prominent in connection with the Gregorian reform and the first and second Lateran Councils in 1123 and in 1139. One major issue in the theological debate of the twelfth century was the question of the essence of marriage, leading to the distinction of physical and spiritual marriage, and the rationalization of consent marriages that did not require to be validated by consumma-

lebede one has vnd nyt/ Sy liebete salomon usz der mossen fast/ Er hette weder růge nach rast/ Wanne er nit alle zyt bie ir was/ Für wol sollent ir wissen das/ Ir beder liebe die was grosz/ Sy liebetent einand' vnd lebetent früntich in aller mosz/ Als dan zwey liebi ee\ lüte söllen leben." (Continuation of *Salman und Morolf*, Straßburg Ms, p. 259, verses 4–15).

tion. Unlike Gratian, who regarded sexual intercourse a necessity of a complete marriage, Peter Lombard and Hugh of St. Victor considered the partners' consent as the sole requirement for the formation of the marital bond.[42] This latter definition began to dominate canon law in the second half of the twelfth century and it eventually resulted in Pope Alexander III (d. 1181) issuing marriage decrees in which spousal consent became the sole criterion for a Christian marriage. It was thus finally established in the twelfth-century that, in accordance with the custom in Roman Law, a marriage was considered legally binding if it was entered by *consensus* and *maritalis affectio*, that is by consent between the partners and by the mutual intent of both partners. *Coitus* or *concubitus*, the consummation of the marriage, was not required for the union to be legally binding.

That definition of marriage also allowed for the inclusion of the unconsummated marriage of the Virgin Mary and Joseph in canon law and hence put an end to the debate regarding the essence of marriage that had shaped previous centuries. Additionally, the definition also included all those lay people who entered into marriage but had chosen to remain virginal. Consequently, spiritual or chaste marriages that were entered by spousal consent but remained unconsummated became a viable option for all those who wanted or had to remain in the world but were concerned about their corporeal purity. Hugh of St. Victor explicitly referred to those instances in which a couple decides to refrain from sexual union in his *De sacramentis*. In accordance with Augustine he defined marriage as an association between a man and

---

[42] Hugh of St. Victor (1096–1141) developed his definition of marriage in his two treatises *De beatae Mariae virginitate* (*PL* 176.857–876) and *De sacramentis christianae fidei* (*PL* 176.173–618). Hugh addresses the issue of carnal union referred to in scripture as "two in one flesh" by positing two sacraments in marriage. The first is the sacrament of Christ and the Church, that is, a corporeal union that requires the consummation of the marriage. The second and greater sacrament is the union of God and the soul which does not require consummation. Peter Lombard (1100–1160/4) described marriage as one sacrament with two aspects: a spiritual and a physical one, that is, will and nature. He considered Mary and Joseph's marriage, which was purely spiritual, just as perfect as a physically consummated marriage, if not more holy as it was free from carnal acts. Compare Peter Lombard, *Libri IV Sententiarum*, studio et cura PP. Collegii S. Bonaventurae, 2nd ed., 2 vols. (Quaracchi, 1916), esp. p. 26. Informative overviews of the twelfth-century developments in the marriage debate can be found in Margaret McGlynn and Richard J. Moll, "Chaste Marriage in the Middle Ages: 'It were to hire a greet merite,'" in *Handbook of Medieval Sexuality*, James Brundage and Vern Bullough, eds. (1996), pp. 103–122, and in Penny S. Gold, "The Marriage of Mary and Joseph, pp. 102–117 (see n. 25 above).

a woman consecrated by a compact of mutual agreement that neither will leave that association.[43] The couple's consent to such an association makes a marriage and if the couple jointly consents to a carnal union, that contract is considered binding, meaning that both spouses are constrained to consummate their union. If, however, the couple consensually agrees to refrain from sexual intercourse and instead mutually vows continence, that vow is considered binding as well. In other words, a couple had the freedom to decide at the time of their marriage whether their consent to marriage included *coitus* or not.[44] The same emphasis on the consensual vow of the spouses was required when couples who had already consummated their marriage wanted to enter religious orders or transfer their marriage into a chaste marriage. Thus, the choice to live in marital chastity had been facilitated by the firm establishment of consent marriages in the twelfth century which had made chaste marriage a viable option before the law. As Hugh of St. Victor and Augustine before him had clearly stated, couples were free to choose whether or not they were to consummate their union, as long as the decision was made freely and simultaneously by both spouses at the moment of their marriage.

Evidence for an increasing movement toward perpetual conjugal chastity in the high Middle Ages can be found in various saints' lives, accounts of virgin kings, and in profane literature from England and France.[45] The German bridal-quest epics must be included in this list of profane examples of that practice as well. As the previous discussion has shown, the couples in these German works closely observe the marriage conventions established in the twelfth century: the spouses consent to the marriage and, if they choose to refrain from sexual

---

[43] See Gold, "The Marriage," p. 109.

[44] Gold, "The Marriage, p. 109; McGlynn and Moll, "Chaste Marriage," p. 108.

[45] For examples and a more in-depth discussion compare John Bugge, *Virginitas: An Essay in the History of a Medieval Ideal* (The Hague, 1975); Peter Brown, *The Body and Society: Men, Women, and Sexual Renunciation in Early Christianity* (New York, 1988); Dyan Elliott, *Spiritual Marriage: Sexual Abstinence in Medieval Wedlock* (Princeton, 1993); John W. Baldwin, *The Language of Sex: Five Voices from Northern France around 1200* (Chicago/London, 1994); Robert Folz, *Les saints rois du Moyen Âge en Occident (VIe–XIIIe siècles)*, Subsidia Hagiographica 68 (Brussels, 1984); Gábor Klaniczay, *Holy Rulers and Blessed Princesses: Dynastic Cults in Medieval Central Europe*, trans. Éva Pálmai (Cambridge, U.K., 2002); originally published as *Az uralkodók szentsége a középkorban: Magyar dinasztikus szentkultuszok és európai modellek* (Budapest, 2000); André Vauchez, *Sainthood in the Later Middle Ages*, trans. Jean Birrell (Cambridge, U.K., 1997); originally published as *La sainteté en Occident aux derniers siècles du moyen âge. D'après les procès de canonisation et les documents hagiographiques* (Rome, 1981); and Brundage, *Law, Sex, and Christian Society*, see n. 25 above.

intercourse, they simultaneously and consensually make their promise of chastity. This is most evident in the Latin and German legends of Henry II of Germany. In *Der Münchner Oswald* and *Orendel*, the couples act on the urging of God and an angel respectively, but it is nevertheless emphasized that both spouses simultaneously and freely give their consent to the observance of perpetual marital chastity. Likewise, King Rother and his wife as well as King Solomon and Affer jointly decide to transform their marriage into a chaste marriage in the later years of their lives. Their marriages serve as examples of a marital intimacy that was free of lust and controlled by the will, just as Augustine had prescribed. Moreover, they exemplify Augustine's idea that couples who adopted a chaste lifestyle after having passed the reproductive age, would strengthen their marital bond.[46] That idea is nicely reflected in Solomon's second marriage as described in the continuation to *Salman und Morolf* but also in *König Rother*. Both works depict ideal lay marriages in which marital intercourse serves the purpose of procreation alone. As soon as the couples have secured their line and passed on the crown to their heirs, they entirely abstain from all marital union. In other words, as soon as the kings in these works have fulfilled their secular duties, they turn away from the world and devote the last years of their lives to their spiritual well-being. A counter example is given in Solomon's first marriage in *Salman und Morolf*. It demonstrates the negative consequences brought about by *concupiscentia*. Solomon gives in to corporeal pleasures and he loses control over his will and his ability to reign.

As I have argued earlier, Henry's II and St. Oswald's chaste marriages in the vernacular German writings are easily explained on the grounds of their sainthood for both were venerated as confessor saints. They are representatives of the large group of saints who preserved their virginity.[47] According to Weinstein and Bell, the large number of virginal saints in the Middle Ages went hand in hand with a decrease in the number of martyr saints and an increase in the number of confessor saints; a development that also encompassed the growing number of royal saints in Western culture. Especially for the sovereign but also for highborn men and male heirs in general however, the social pressure

46 McGlynn and Moll, "Chaste Marriage, p. 104.

47 Donald Weinstein and Rudolph M. Bell, *Saints and Society: The Two Worlds of Western Christendom, 1000–1700* (Chicago, 1982), p. 74.

to procreate was enormous. They were expected to produce heirs to continue their lines and ensure their succession. But even though their vows of chastity "ran counter to every expectation of noble behavior," the eleventh and twelfth centuries saw a significant rise in the number of royal saints.[48] Not all of these royal saints remained unmarried. Forced by social and family pressure, they often gave in to marriage. For many of them, such as for Henry II of Germany, their virginal marriage became a significant reason for their canonization. Similarly, many young women and especially young men agreed to marry out of social pressure, without, however, necessarily consummating their marriages. Accounts of such forced marriages that remained chaste can be found especially in hagiographic and historical sources.

As this discussion has demonstrated, in the twelfth century, the idea of chaste or virginal marriage also penetrated the newly established vernacular literary tradition. Especially in twelfth-century Germany, the idea of marital chastity runs like a thread through the earliest vernacular fictional writings. The German epics I have discussed stand at the very beginning of the vernacular literary tradition in Germany and thus at the transition from oral to written narrative, from historiography to fiction, and, most importantly in our context, from religious to secular themes. These epics are informed reflections of the marriage debate of the twelfth century. In their present form, they are most certainly not spontaneous compositions by traveling jongleurs (or minstrels or *Spielmänner*) but rather the work of highly educated clerical authors. These authors either made use of the well-known and popular literary paradigm of bridal-quest narrative—which they could have derived from historiography, such as Gregory of Tours' chronicle and its continuations, or from oral story-telling traditions—or they reworked the endings of already circulating bridal-quest tales. Based on hagiographic models, such as the legend of Henry and Cunegund, and under the influence of contemporary theological debates, they introduced the motif of marital chastity to these works, regardless of the fact that they were undermining the inherent logic of bridal-quest narrative.[49]

---

[48] Weinstein and Bell, *Saints*, p. 76. Examples of eleventh and twelfth-century royal saints are St. Edmund the Confessor (d. 1066; canonized 1163), St. Henry II of Germany (d. 1024; canonized 1145), St. Stephen (d. 1038; canonized 1083) and St. Emeric (or Henry) of Hungary (d. 1031; canonized 1083).

[49] A very likely model for the German bridal-quest epics was also the German *Alexius A*, see n. 38 above.

Unlike in earlier stories of bridal abduction, the brides in the German bridal-quest narratives agree to marry their wooer. The women actively support the male protagonists' bridal quest and they give their consent to the marriage.[50] The consensual nature of the marital bond is furthermore emphasized at the end of each of the works when the spouses make their consensual and simultaneous vows of chastity. They either take a vow of perpetual marital chastity on their wedding night, as in *Der Münchner Oswald* and *Orendel*, or they take a vow later in their lives to transform a marriage consummated solely for the purpose of royal progeny and succession into a spiritual marriage, as in *König Rother* and in the continuation to *Salman und Morolf*. All these marriages agree with contemporary marriage practice and they arguably served as models for the lay audience of the first indigenous, secular, vernacular German narratives.

[50] For a more detailed discussion of the woman's active participation in the bridal quest see Bornholdt, *Engaging Moments*, pp. 151–152.

"THE SPIRIT OF FORNICATION, WHOM THE CHILDREN OF THE HELLENES USED TO CALL EROS": MALE HOMOEROTICISM AND THE RHETORIC OF CHASTITY IN THE LETTERS OF NILUS OF ANCYRA

Cristian Gaspar

> "If frosts and fasts, hard lodging and thin weeds,
> Nip not the gaudy blossoms of your love..."
> (William Shakespeare, *Love's Labour's Lost* act V, scene II)

Some time during the first two decades of the fifth century AD, two young men living in Constantinople fell in love with each other. One of them mentioned this in a letter sent to an old Christian ascetic, an acquaintance of his, who at the time was leading a life of prayer and renunciation in a monastic settlement in Asia Minor, near modern day Ankara. In a reply couched in somewhat hesitating, yet unambiguous, terms, the monk told his young correspondent that he was deceived: what he felt for the other young man could not be love. It was rather a trick of the devil, for such "love" was inappropriate for a well-educated Christian nobleman. He should keep away from his "beloved," fast, and invoke God's help in order to preserve his chastity undefiled.

Beyond this apparently resolute prohibition of male homoeroticism, there is much that makes this monastic response to the problem of male same-sex relationships extremely interesting, especially if we consider it in its historical context and in comparison with other (both Christian and non-Christian) problematizations of this aspect of male sexuality. First of all, one may ask why such a relationship would be regarded as inappropriate for a young man living in the increasingly Christianized society of the Eastern Roman Empire and why it would take a monk to define it as problematic. Furthermore, one may look at the reasons put forward by the monastic advisor in order to motivate the young man to deny and repress his avowed same-sex attraction as well as at the rhetorical strategies employed in his messages to achieve this purpose. Finally, it would be necessary to investigate other contemporary sources and situate his response in its specific historical and spiritual contexts. How representative was such a rejection of male homoeroticism for the society where its proponent lived? Was it so determinate only because the man who formulated it was a Christian ascetic? Would other, less ascetic-minded, contemporaries agree with his verdict?

In what follows I intend to search for answers to some of these questions by looking at a series of texts produced in Late Antiquity in the eastern provinces of the Roman Empire during the last decades of the fourth and the first three decades of the fifth century AD. The main group of sources I will use deals with male[1] same-sex relationships (and with some other connected issues) and was authored by a Christian ascetic living in a monastic (most probably cenobitic) milieu. In addition to its more obvious value (i.e., as a primary source for the history of homoeroticism in early Christian times), this set of texts also offers a unique opportunity to analyze monastic problematizations of same-sex activities addressed to recipients living in non-monastic environments within the new Christian society, i.e. the laymen. Existing investigations of monastic attitudes towards same-sex behavior were based mainly on texts produced, intended for, and circulated within the monastic milieus. The present study attempts to take advantage of what seems to be a unique opportunity. Discussing a set of texts which, although produced by a monk, were explicitly aimed at Christian individuals living in a non-monastic context is likely to offer a necessary corrective to the existing, rather one-sided, picture of monastic attitudes towards male homoeroticism. Yet these texts have not attracted scholarly attention, despite the considerable interest they present for studying the history of homoeroticism in (Late) Antiquity and Christian attitudes towards same-sex relationships. This makes them all the more appealing, especially in a field where new original sources, virtually untouched by previous researchers, are a commodity hard to come by.

There are several possible explanations for such neglect. While there has been a virtual explosion of publications on ancient homoeroti-

[1] Sources for female same-sex relationships in monastic milieus during this period are extremely limited. This reflects the general situation of ancient female homoeroticism, which was rarely seen as problematic by the male authors to whom we owe most of the surviving sources and was, therefore, rarely discussed. For a discussion of Christian attitudes, see Bernadette J. Brooten, *Love between Women: Early Christian Responses to Female Homoeroticism* (Chicago, 1996), with relevant bibliography. Ancient Greek and Roman sources are collected in Thomas K. Hubbard, ed., *Homosexuality in Greece and Rome: A Sourcebook of Basic Documents* (Berkeley, 2003); see also Juan Francisco Martos Montiel, *Desde Lesbos con amor: Homosexualidad femenina en la Antigüedad* (Madrid, 1996).

cism starting in the 1980's,[2] these have mainly focused on Classical Greece, the Hellenistic world, and the early Roman Empire, for which most sources were well-known, properly catalogued, and readily available. A significantly smaller number of works dealing with same-sex relationships during later periods (such as the later Roman Empire, Byzantium, and the Medieval West) appeared to date.[3] Most notably, in spite of a few recent attempts, Byzantine homoeroticism remains a severely understudied topic.[4] The scarcity of sources for the Christian period, many of them improperly edited, of difficult access, and not available in modern translations is partly to blame for this. To further complicate the matter, the study of ancient and medieval sexuality seems to experience an increasing tendency towards highly theoretical and speculative discussions. Many modern scholars seem to find

---

2 Some of these will appear in the following notes; for the rest, the reader is referred to the extensive bibliographies provided in the recent works of Hubbard, *Homosexuality*, pp. 533–47 and Craig A. Williams, *Roman Homosexuality: Ideologies of Masculinity in Classical Antiquity* (New York, 1999), pp. 367–75.

3 For the Later Empire, see Eva Cantarella, *Secondo natura: la bisessualità nel mondo antico* (Rome, 1988), pp. 229 ff., and Danilo Dalla, *«Ubi Venus mutatur»: omosessualità e diritto nel mondo romano* (Milan, 1987), pp. 165 ff., as well as Aline Rousselle's "Statut personnel et usage sexuel dans l'Empire romain," originally published in 1989 and now reprinted in her *La contamination spirituelle: science, droit et religion dans l'Antiquité* (Paris, 1998), pp. 149–170. Other significant titles on medieval homoeroticism include Derrick Sherwin Bailey, *Homosexuality and the Western Christian Tradition* (London, 1955), an outdated classic offering an apologetic survey of Christian evidence; Vern L. Bullough, *Sexual Variance in Society and History* (Chicago, 1978); Michael Goodich, *The Unmentionable Vice: Homosexuality in the Later Medieval Period* (Santa Barbara, California, 1979); V. L. Bullough and James A. Brundage, eds., *Sexual Practices and the Medieval Church* (Buffalo, 1982) and Brundage's *Law, Sex, and Christian Society in Medieval Europe* (Chicago, 1987); a more detailed bibliography is provided by Warren Johansson and William A. Percy, "Homosexuality" in *Handbook of Medieval Sexuality*, Vern L. Bullough and James A. Brundage, eds. (New York, 1996), pp. 155–89; H. Lutterbach, *Sexualität im Mittelalter: Eine Kulturstudie anhand von Bußbücher des 6. bis 12. Jahrhunderts* (Köln, 1999) provides a valuable study of the early medieval penitentials in the West and summary overviews of earlier Christian attitudes towards same-sex (see esp. pp. 32–33 and 41–42). Now see also V. A. Kolve, "Ganymede/Son of Getron: Medieval Monasticism and the Drama of Same-Sex Desire," *Speculum* 73/4 (1998), 1014–67, an excellent contribution focusing on Western late medieval monastic milieus, with an accessible theoretical introduction and further bibliography.

4 See the bibliography given by Kōnstantinos G. Pitsakēs, "Η θέση των ομοφυλοφίλων στη Βυζαντίνη κοινωνία [The position of homosexuals in the Byzantine state]" in Πρακτικά ημερίδας Οι περιθοριακοί στο Βυζάντιο, 9 Μαίου 1992 (= *Les marginaux à Byzance*), ed. Chrysa A. Maltezou (Athens, 1993), pp. 170–269, esp. p. 170, preliminary note; cf. Dion C. Smythe, "In Denial: Same-Sex Desire in Byzantium" in *Desire and Denial in Byzantium: Papers from the Thirty-first Spring Symposium of Byzantine Studies, University of Sussex, Brighton, March 1997*, ed. Liz James (Aldershot, 1999), pp. 139–148, as well as other studies in that volume.

conceptual controversy and discussions of essential epistemological issues more attractive than a more traditional search for new and unexplored material. Such debates are undoubtedly important in order to build the necessary hermeneutic framework for approaching the problem of homoeroticism in pre-modern societies. Nevertheless, they also have the tendency of turning into rather sterile dogmatic clashes. Methodological sophistication is not always matched by a similar interest in searching for unexplored original sources that might offer new data and lead to subtle adjustments of established interpretations, which more often than not tend to be too rigid.[5]

However, the most important obstacle in the way of proper scholarly research into early Christian attitudes towards same-sex relationships still remains the extremely partisan nature of most investigations into this highly sensitive issue. It seems difficult, on one hand, to look at same-sex relationships during historical periods when Christianity played an important part in shaping violent official reactions to unorthodox sexual behavior without resorting to concepts such as "intolerance," "persecution," "guilt," and "responsibility." On the other hand, confessionally b(i)ased approaches to this problem will go to great lengths to exculpate the Christian Church by resorting to arguments about the "unnatural" character of same-sex relationships, which motivated, in their opinion, a "natural" reaction, a "continuous," "relentless," and "coherent" rejection of such behavior. The (ab)use of historical research of same-sex relationships as doctrinal panoply for contemporary debates concerning fundamental gay rights is likely to prevent further dispassionate and neutral research in this field, an ideal that some militant scholars nowadays consider impossible as well as undesirable. The sad example of John Boswell's pioneering work stands as a reminder of how creative energies that might have been better spent can go to waste in false debates.[6]

---

[5] Cf., for instance, Amy Richlin's "Introduction" to her book *The Garden of Priapus: Sexuality and Aggression in Roman Humour* (2nd rev. ed., New York, 1992), pp. xx–xxi, with which I strongly disagree.

[6] In his *Christianity, Social Tolerance, and Homosexuality: Gay People in Western Europe from the Beginning of the Christian Era to the Fourteenth Century* (Chicago, 1980), John Boswell tried to argue, against all evidence, that Christianity never played a major role in shaping and promoting "intolerant" attitudes towards "homosexuals" and that a Church hostile to "gay people" only emerged in the thirteenth century. Such a misguided attempt sparked a heated debate with furious reactions, often as misguided as the author's original thesis. Boswell's work, not lacking in scholarly merits but not exempt of serious blunders, was attacked from both sides by militant Christian and gay scholars. For

It will not take long to quote the few existing studies that address, mostly *en passant*, the issue of same-sex relationships in late antique monastic milieus.[7] Those dedicated exclusively to this topic are even fewer and, until recently, they amounted to little more than inventories of relevant judicial and ecclesiastic sources with minimal discussion.[8] Two more focused attempts at analyzing attitudes towards homoeroticism in Egyptian monastic texts are methodologically unreliable, and provide a highly distorting view of the original evidence.[9] Finally, I could mention two recent investigations of homoeroticism in monastic and hagiographic sources, which approach the topic from different perspectives than that of the present study.[10] Most of the work, then, it

this debate, see the extensive bibliography compiled by Paul Halsall, at http://www.fordham.edu/halsall/pwh/index-bos.html. Boswell's last book, *Same-Sex Unions in Premodern Europe* (New York, 1994), further undermined his scholarly position through a sensational misinterpretation of a Byzantine office for "spiritual brotherhood" as a liturgical ceremony meant to celebrate "the same-sex equivalent of medieval heterosexual marriage ceremony" (ibid., "Preface," p. x). I think the following lines, even if coming from Boswell's ideological opponents, fairly describe his work, which, "brilliant as it is, can best be understood as a work in the tradition of Christian Apologetics, not dispassionate scholarship, although it is written from a point of view that most other writers of Christian Apologetics could not and would not accept" (Johansson and Percy, "Homosexuality," p. 179).

7 See the few comments in Dalla, *Ubi Venus mutatur*, 161–162, the occasional references in Peter Brown's influential analysis of late antique sexuality, *The Body and Society: Men, Women and Sexual Renunciation in Early Christianity* (New York, 1988), pp. 230, 234, 308, and Aline Rousselle, *Porneia: On Desire and the Body in Antiquity*, trans. Felicia Pheasant (Cambridge, Massachusetts, 1988; originally published in French, Paris, 1983), pp. 152–156.

8 See, for instance, Phaidon Koukoulēs, Βυζαντινῶν βίος καὶ πολιτισμός, vol. 6 (Athens, 1955), pp. 506–511; Spiros Troianos, "Kirchliche und Weltliche Rechtsquellen zur Homosexualität in Byzanz," *Jahrbuch der Österreichischen Byzantinistik* 39 (1989), 29–48, and Pitsakēs, "Η θέση," which provides a good collection of texts with some insightful comments, despite his general tendency of taking sources at face value; both Koukoulēs and Pitsakēs referred to Nilus' *Ep.* 2.177, the main source explored in this paper, without analyzing it.

9 I quote here only as a negative example the unreliable book of Carlos Muriel Espejo, *El deseo negado: aspectos de la problematica homosexual en la vida monastica (siglos III–VI d. C.)* (Granada, 1991). It has been maintained, against the evidence of the sources, that homoeroticism was a late development in the monastic milieus of Egypt and a symptom of decaying quality of monastic life: see Ramón Teja, "El demonio de la sexualidad en el monacato egipcio" in *Codex Aquilarensis. Cuadernos de Investigación del Monasterio de Santa María la Real*, vol. 11 (Aguilar de Campo, 1994), pp. 21–31 and Derwas James Chitty, *The Desert a City: An Introduction to the Study of Egyptian and Palestinian Monasticism under the Christian Empire* (Oxford, 1966), pp. 66–67.

10 Cf. David Brakke, "Ethiopian Demons: Male Sexuality, the Black-Skinned Other, and the Monastic Self," *Journal of the History of Sexuality* 10.3–4 (2001), 501–35; Virginia Burrus, "Queer Lives of Saints: Jerome's Hagiography" *Journal of the History of Sexuality* 10.3–4 (2001), 442–79.

would seem, still remains to be done; and it is one of the aims of this study to suggest that this work should concentrate on identifying and analyzing more relevant primary sources before formulating general and 'definitive' conclusions.[11]

It is most unfortunate that the letter sent by Pierius, the young nobleman from Constantinople, to his monastic advisor, St. Nilus of Ancyra, has not survived. What must have been a passionate description of his erotic involvement with another young man can now be guessed only from the dry summary of his message contained in Nilus' reply.[12] It is even more unfortunate that this reply was buried in an improperly edited collection of letters,[13] of difficult access, and which is furthermore plagued by significant doubts concerning its authenticity.[14] I think

---

[11] This need was recognized by Johansson and Percy, who wrote: "[too] extensive for any one person to digest, Migne's collection of the Church Fathers, perhaps one hundred times longer than all surviving Greek and Latin texts together, needs to be scanned by computer for key words to further illuminate Patristic attitudes" ("Homosexuality," p. 180, n. 15). As I hope to show in what follows, sometimes even a simple, traditional, and careful reading will do.

[12] Nilus of Ancyra, *Ep.* 2.177 in *Patrologiae Graecae cursus completus*, ed. Jean-Paul Migne, vol. 79 (Paris, 1869), cols. 280B–285A; all further references to Nilus' letters are made to this volume with the column numbers in the *PG*. The Migne text, in fact, reproduces the text of the only complete edition of Nilus' *Letters* ever printed: *S. Nili ascetae, discipuli S. Joannis Chrysostomi, Epistolarum libri IV*, ed. Leo Allacci (Allatius) (Rome, 1668).

[13] Fortunately, this situation is about to change; a new critical edition of Nilus' letters, prepared by Georgios Fatouros and Michael Grünbart, will appear shortly in the *Corpus christianorum* series. I feel this is an appropriate occasion to thank Dr. Grünbart, who kindly agreed to share with me the relevant manuscript pages of this new edition. This enables me to quote and translate the text of Nilus' *Ep.* 2.177 and 3.43 in a much improved form when compared with that printed in the *PG* (see above, n. 12; I have retained references to Migne's reprint; cf. Georgios Fatorous, "Zu den Briefen des Hl. Neilos von Ankyra" in *L'Épistolographie et la poésie épigrammatique: projets actuels et questions de méthodologie. Actes de la 16e Table ronde organisée par Wolfram Hörandner et Michael Grünbart dans le cadre du XXe Congrès international des Études byzantines Collège de France-Sorbonne Paris, 19–25 Août 2001* (Paris, 2003), pp. 21–30, esp. p. 25 (a list of manuscripts on which the new text is based).

[14] The corpus of letters ascribed to Nilus raises serious problems of authenticity. For a detailed study of the corpus, see K. Heussi's analysis in *Untersuchungen zu Nilus dem Asketen* (Leipzig, 1917), pp. 31–123. Based on his own research as well as on that of his predecessors, Heussi established lists of all the spurious items in the collection, of the items which are doubled, of the pieces which belong to other authors, and of those which now appear as distinct items, but are probably the *membra disiecta* of larger letters. Cf. J. Gribomont: "La tradition manuscrite de S. Nil. I: La Correspondance," *Studia monastica* 11 (1969), 231–67; Alan Cameron "The Authenticity of the Letters of St. Nilus of Ancyra" *Greek, Roman and Byzantine Studies* 17 (1976), 181–96. Cameron clearly showed that a sixth-century editor interfered with Nilus' letters and is responsible for massively forging their headings, without significantly tampering with their contents. Although Cameron's conclusions certainly make imperative a careful and

it unlikely, though, that we may find an equally direct and powerful statement of same-sex love in any other late antique sources. And this is probably as close as we could get to a man involved in a homoerotic relationship expressing his ardent feelings for another man without resorting to a tantalizing display of traditional rhetoric. It would seem, Nilus wrote to Pierius, judging from

> the contents of your letter, [...] that during this month you have developed a great passion for Dionysiodorus, the *magister*'s son, so powerful and hard to bear that you do not wish either to eat or to drink or to live if you cannot see the youth who first fell in love with you...[15]

Apparently unimpressed, and probably alarmed by the candid tone of his young friend's confession, the good monk hurried to put matters straight from the very opening lines of his response. Pierius should not be deceived: "one thing is love according to God (ἡ κατὰ Θεὸν ἀγάπη), and yet another worldly and bodily friendship (ἡ κατὰ κόσμον καὶ σάρκα φιλία) of a rather brutish and irrational sort" (280B). His so-called "love" for Dionysiodorus was nothing but a relationship based on physical attraction.[16] Still worse, it was a sin, into which, so at least Nilus assumes, the young man fell unawares, lured by "the deceitful and filthiest demon who [was] set on ensnaring [his] virtuous and God-loving soul." The monk promptly exposed this demon as what he truly was, namely, "the spirit of fornication (τὸ πνεῦμα τῆς προνείας), whom the children of the Hellenes used to call Eros (ἔρωτα)" (280C). Love for another young man was sinful because the demon that inspired it, easily recognized by an experienced Christian ascetic, though not so

detailed study of individual headings, as well as of the possibly anachronistic elements introduced by the unknown editor, I am not convinced that serious doubts should be cast upon the actual contents of the letters when this presents no contradictions or anachronisms, and especially when it is in agreement with other works of Nilus of undoubted paternity. To my mind, although "the correspondence of Nilus of Ancyra" certainly "is a mess and a puzzle" as stated by Cameron (ibid., 181), its potential should not be underestimated.

15 *Ep.* 2.177, 280C; all translations unless otherwise indicated are mine.

16 This is apparent from the disparaging terminology Nilus used to refer to Pierius' sentiments: "terrible and loathsome passion" (ἔρως ὁ δεινὸς καὶ βδελυρός 281C), "the desire for the said youth" (τῆς ἐφέσεως τοῦ εἰρημένου παιδός 281D), "unseemly and shameful craving" (τῆς ἀτόπου καὶ αἰσχρᾶς ὀρέξεως 284C), "the wicked passion" (τοῦ φαύλου πάθους ibid.). The only apparent exception is the verb προαγαπάω (τὸν προαγαπήσαντά σε "who first fell in love with you" 280D), referring to Dionysiodorus, but Nilus probably reproduced here (in order to criticize) a term originally used by Pierius in his letter.

obviously dangerous to a young Christian nobleman, came from the pagan past bringing with him the threat of πορνεία, illicit sexual activity. These are, in brief, the main points on which Nilus would dwell in the rest of his letter, and which I intend to analyze in what follows.

Before proceeding, however, it is necessary to substantiate several of the assumptions already made in the summary offered above. For little that we may know about Nilus himself, it seems certain that throughout the later part of his life he lived as a Christian monk near the city of Ancyra, in Asia Minor (modern day Ankara, Turkey).[17] On the basis of the information contained in his works, I consider it plausible that he had spent his youthful years, before becoming a monk, in Constantinople. There he probably met and became close to John Chrysostom, archbishop of that city between 398 and 404 A.D. Furthermore, judging by the high-quality rhetorical skills displayed in some of his writings,[18] it is probable that Nilus had the benefit of a traditional education (παιδεία), which during the fourth and the fifth centuries A.D. was still a privilege of the well-to-do ruling elite of the Roman Empire. To this he added a profound knowledge of Christian Scriptures and a first hand acquaintance with the works of several major Christian writers of the time.[19] His profile is typical for the recently emerged Christian intellectual elite, some of whose members embraced

---

[17] Very little seems certain concerning Nilus' life, except his location in a monastery near Ancyra, his probable *akme* between 390 and 430 AD, a close but otherwise undocumented relationship with John Chrysostom, and the fact that he had an extensive rhetorical training and a solid knowledge of Christian writers. For a more detailed account of the data concerning his life, as well as for a detailed bibliography, see M.-G. Guérard, "Nil d'Ancyre" in *Dictionnaire de Spiritualité*, vol. 11 (Paris, 1981), pp. 345–56. Heussi's critical analysis of the few external sources concerning Nilus' life (*Untersuchungen*, pp. 11–30) remains fundamental. Fabrizio Conca published a critical edition of a curious text which purports to be an autobiographical account: Nilus Ancyranus, *Narratio* (Leipzig, 1983), but the attribution of this text to Nilus remains problematic despite Conca's attempts to find parallels between it and Nilus' other works (for this, see F. Conca, "Le «Narrationes» di Nilo e il romanzo greco" in *Studi bizantini e neogreci: Atti del IV Congresso Nazionale di Studi Bizantini*, ed. Pietro Luigi Leone (Galatina, 1983), pp. 349–360 and "Osservazioni sullo stile di Nilo Ancirano," in *Jahrbuch der Österreichischen Byzantinistik* 32.3 (1982), 217–25; which draws comparisons between the *Narrationes* and the treatise *De octo spiritibus malitiae*, which is certainly not by Nilus.

[18] The extent of his rhetorical training is best illustrated by a traditional panegyric he composed in honor of Albianus, an ascetic from Ancyra; see *Sanctis patris nostri Nili senioris In Albianum oratio* (*PG* 79, cols. 696–712).

[19] For the authors, both pagan and Christian, with whom Nilus was acquainted, see the discussion by Marie-Gabrielle Guérard in her valuable critical edition, Nil d'Ancyre, *Commentaire sur le Cantique des Cantiques*, editio princeps, vol. 1 (Paris, 1994), pp. 38–47; which is the sole modern critical edition, with bibliography (pp. 99–108).

and endorsed a particularly ascetic form of Christianity somewhat in spite of their thorough traditional education acquired in the schools of rhetoric, at the time still largely dominated by pagan masters.

As for Pierius, several indications point to the fact that he belonged to the privileged ruling class of late antique society, i.e., Nilus' own background before his conversion to a monastic lifestyle. The *Ep.* 2.177 bears the heading ΠΙΕΡΙΩΙ ΚΟΜΗΤΙ ΝΕΩΤΕΡΩΙ "To Pierius, the younger *comes*," and although its content offers no other evidence about the exact identity of the addressee, it makes a reference to his beloved, identified as Dionysiodorus, "the *magister*'s son" (Διονυσιόδωρον τὸν υἱὸν τοῦ μαγίστρου).[20] At the time when Nilus wrote this letter, Dionysiodorus' father probably occupied the position of *magister officiorum*, one of the most important civilian ministers at the emperor's court in Constantinople.[21] Consequently, Pierius belonged to an aristocratic Constantinopolitan family, as the fact that he had received the honorary rank of *comes* suggests.[22] Dionysiodorus' father may have held his position some time between 406 and 414, most likely during the first years of the reign of Theodosius II (412–450 AD).[23]

In addition to belonging to the aristocracy, Pierius was also a Christian, probably raised in a Christian family, as suggested by Nilus' use of phrases like "your virtuous and pious soul,"[24] "virtuous offspring of a virtuous root."[25] In any case, the extensive use of scriptural material

---

[20] *Ep.* 2.177, 280B.

[21] On the origin and the functions of this official, see A. H. M. Jones, *The Later Roman Empire 284–602: A Social, Economic, and Administrative Survey*, vol. 1 (Oxford, 1964), pp. 368–69 (hereafter *LRE*) and the thorough study by M. Clauss, *Der magister officiorum in der Spätantike (4.–6. Jahrhundert): Das Amt und sein Einfluß auf die kaiserliche Politik* (Munich, 1980), as well as the more recent overview in Roland Delmaire, *Les Institutions du Bas-Empire Romain, de Constantin à Justinien*, vol. 1, *Les Institutions civiles et palatines* (Paris, 1995), pp. 75–95.

[22] On *comes*, see Jones, *LRE*, vol. 1, pp. 104–106. Pierius found his way into the *Prosopography of the Later Roman Empire*, ed. J. R. Martindale, vol. 2 (Cambridge, 1980) (hereafter *PLRE*), p. 885 as "Pierius 3." Contrary to the *PLRE* suggestion that the heading of Nilus' letter 2.177 should be interpreted as meaning that Pierius was a *comes iunior*, I think that νεωτέρῳ merely refers to him as a young man.

[23] I have followed Clauss' interpretation; see his *Der magister officiorum*, 146 under "Anonymus 1," and the table on p. 141. Dionysiodorus is listed in the *PLRE*, vol. 2, p. 363. His father also appears as "Anonymus 26" on p. 1224; see also the table on p. 1258.

[24] Τὴν σὴν ἐνάρετον καὶ φιλόθεον ψυχήν (*Ep.* 2.177, 280C).

[25] Ἀγαθῆς ῥίζης ἀγαθὸν ὑπάρχοντα βλάστημα (ibid. 281C). This was a set phrase of the encomiastic genre; it was used by Basil the Great (*Ep.* 5.1, *In quadraginta martyres Sebastenses*, *PG* 31, col. 524), Himerius (*Or.* 46.70), and by Gregory Nazianzen in a passage

in the letter he received from the monk assumes some knowledge of both the Old and the New Testament on his part.[26] A spiritual relationship (of the type master-disciple) probably existed between Nilus and Pierius, although it is not clear how this functioned, given the geographic distance that separated them. It is certain that the young man did benefit from the monk's instruction on several occasions,[27] even if this exchange of wisdom was probably carried out only in epistolary form, not face to face as it happened with another young Christian nobleman called Domninus. He resided in Ancyra and received an extensive letter from Nilus detailing the perverse operations of the "spirit of fornication" in very similar terms to those of the letter to Pierius.[28]

Apparently, Pierius was not worried about the moral status of his involvement with Dionysiodorus, which he readily defined as "love." Whether he delivered the news about his homoerotic passion to Nilus quite casually in his letter or, even worse, wrote to ask advice on how to proceed in this situation must remain unclear as long as the original text is lost. I assume, however, that for Pierius loving another young man was not problematic, but rather something a young aristocrat might "naturally" do. Nilus seems to imply as much when alluding to "other signs and indications that are contained in the letter which you wrote

in which he makes an explicit connection between the formula (slightly reworking it) and the tradition of the *encomia* (see his *Or.* 18.5, *PG* 35, col. 989).

[26] The *Letter* to Pierius is rich in verbatim scriptural quotations and allusions, some reworked and integrated in elaborate structures in a way that denotes familiarity with the Scriptures; besides the Psalms (Ps. 30, 37, 39, 56, 65, 117, 140), which come naturally to a monk, there are quotations from the Book of Jeremiah and the Gospels of Mark and Luke.

[27] In *Ep.* 2.177, 284A Nilus speaks of "all the other sorts of relief and aid which *I often eagerly recommended to you* (πλεονάκις ὑποθέσθαι σοι προὐθυμήθην)" (emphasis added).

[28] *Ep.* 3.43 (408D–413C). Young Domninus was a member of the inner circle of the *curiales*, the wealthy ruling class which governed late antique cities (for the *principales*, as these top city-councilors are known, see Jones, *LRE*, vol. 2, p. 731). Nilus reveals that Dominus was involved with the collection of taxes when he mentions his "handling public affairs and assign[ing] tasks, as necessity arises, to public tax-gatherers" (τὰ δημόσια χειρίζων πράγματα, καὶ δημοσίοις πρακτῆρσι, καθὼς χρή, ποιῶν τὰς ἀποκρίσεις) (413A). Domninus' aristocratic background as well as his Christian faith are implied by several comments made in Nilus' letter to him: he is called "my noblest son" τέκνον ἐμὸν ἄριστον (409A) and exhorted to be worthy of "the admirable continence of [his] parents and of [his] grandfathers" τὴν τῶν πατέρων [...] καὶ πάππων θαυμαστὴν σωφροσύνην (412D). Having him close, Nilus could instruct him personally about matters such as a proper Christian attitude towards sexuality: "When you dismiss the tax-gatherers and have more time, come to me and I will tell you, face to face, more fully about the combats against fornication" (413C).

to me" (280D) by which he was able to detect the problem while his correspondent had obviously failed to do so.

A same-sex relationship, however, *was* problematic for a Christian nobleman in ways unsuspected by Pierius, whose attitude towards the Christian moral code appears to be one of candid ignorance, if not outright neglect. At the beginning of the fifth century AD, the moral code of the wealthy educated elite, to whom Pierius belonged, would have offered him a problematization of homoeroticism that still differed in many respects from Christian problematization(s). And it would have done so notwithstanding the gradual emergence during the first centuries of the Roman Empire of stricter, more ascetic pagan standards of moral behavior. These led to a gradual blurring of boundaries between Christian and non-Christian morals, a process well documented by modern research.[29] Although this austere pagan moral code probably entailed a less comfortable acceptance of homoeroticism, it was still regarded as a possible form of erotic fulfillment.[30] The simple fact that

[29] This was first argued by Paul Veyne in "La Famille et l'amour sous le Haut-Empire romain," *Annales ESC* 33 (1978), 35–63 (see also his "L'Homosexualité à Rome," *Communications* 35 (1982), 26–33; English trans. in P. Ariès and A. Béjin, eds., *Western Sexuality: Practice and Precept in Past and Present Times*, Oxford, 1985), pp. 26–35) and further documented by Michel Foucault in his influential *Histoire de la sexualité*, especially vol. 3, *Le Souci de soi* (Paris, 1984; English trans. R. Hurley, New York, 1986). Rousselle's book *Porneia: On Desire and the Body in Antiquity*, cited above, remains probably the most complete and persuasive analysis of this process. See also the extensive discussion with special reference to homoeroticism in Cantarella, *Secondo natura*, pp. 258–66. Williams, *Roman Homosexualiy*, p. 264, n. 46 aptly formulates this point: "Between the second and the fourth centuries AD there did, however, occur a gradual but decisive transformation in the realm of Roman morality, as witnessed by an increasingly ascetic approach to the body in general and sexual practices in particular. This process culminated in the problematization of all sexual activity not considered strictly necessary, i.e., not leading to procreation."

[30] In this new pagan morality "problematization and apprehension go hand in hand; inquiry is joined to vigilance" and, as a result, "sexual activity is linked to evil by its forms and its effects, but in itself and substantially, it is not an evil." This austere moral style "has trouble finding its place in the love of boys, but the latter is not therefore condemned as being contrary to nature" (Foucault, *The Care of the Self*, p. 239). Though, I believe, essentially justified, this conclusion reached by Foucault is based on his problematic and highly selective discussion of pagan sources from the first two centuries AD; for important corrections addressing the texts which contrasted the love of boys with the love of women in this period, see the important contribution of Simon Goldhill, *Foucault's Virginity: Ancient Erotic Fiction and the History of Sexuality* (Cambridge, 1995), pp. 46–111, and D. M. Halperin, "Historicizing the Subject of Desire: Sexual Preferences and Erotic Identities in the Pseudo-Lucianic *Erôtes*" in Jan Goldstein, ed., *Foucault and the Writing of History* (Oxford, 1994), pp. 19–34. Foucault's unfinished *History of Sexuality* remains an essential and most influential work; for a good overview of the critical debates around it, with special reference to the never published fourth volume

Pierius could describe his involvement as "falling in love" proves that in the aristocratic circles of Christian Constantinople some individuals still thought that women were not the only possible (or legitimate) objects of sexual attraction and that love could still go both ways. What would certainly pose a problem to them were things such as the role one played in a same-sex relationship (i.e. active or passive), the extent to which one gave in to one's passions, the consequences to one's health, and, probably most important, the reputation one might acquire as a result.[31]

It is very significant that, with one important exception discussed below, Nilus' reply was not concerned with these aspects. For the Christian ascetic, loving one's neighbor in the way Pierius did was simply out of order, because it was a sin. It went against being a Christian since it infringed God's law expressed in the Scriptures, the basis of Christian morality. Even if Nilus does not spell this out, his reference to "sin" and "wicked deed"[32] in describing Pierius' "love" is most telling. More important, the colorful and highly disparaging terms he used to

that should have dealt with early Christianity, cf. Daniel Boyarin and Elizabeth Castelli, "Introduction: Foucault's *The History of Sexuality*: The Fourth Volume, or, A Field Left Fallow for Others to Till," *Journal of the History of Sexuality* 10. 3–4 (2001), 357–74 and especially the important discussion by Jeremy R. Carette, "Prologue to a Confession of the Flesh" in *Religion and Culture: Michel Foucault* (New York, 1999), pp. 1–47; at p. 2, n. 6 Carette notes that the fourth volume of the *History of Sexuality* was almost complete before Foucault's death and a copy of it is extant in the Foucault archive.

[31] These elements appear in most descriptions of classical Greek and Roman attitudes to homoeroticism, such as K. J. Dover, *Greek Homosexuality* (2nd ed., Cambridge, 1989), Foucault's *History of Sexuality*, and D. M. Halperin's *One Hundred Years of Homosexuality, and Other Essays on Greek Love* (New York, 1990). They are central to the "constructionist" view of homoeroticism. Its proponents argue that patterns of sexual preference assume different manifestations in different societies and that no essential identity can be postulated between individuals who engaged in same-sex relationships in different historical contexts. Since sexuality itself as "an *appropriation* of the human body and of its erogenous zones by an ideological discourse" (Halperin, ibid., 25; his italics) and, therefore, a cultural construct, one cannot speak of ancient "homosexuality" (no such term existed before the late nineteenth century). It is very likely that "ancient sexual typologies generally derived their criteria for categorizing people not from sex but from gender: they tended to construe sexual desire as normative or deviant according to whether it impelled social actors to conform or to violate their conventionally defined gender roles."

[32] Nilus qualified Pierius' love twice as "sin" (τῆς ἁμαρτίας 280D, 281D), related to it as "fornication" (πορνεία 281B) and "corruption" (τῆς φθορᾶς 284A), described the acts associated with it as "bad habit" (τῆς κακῆς συνηθείας 280D), "wicked deed" (τὸ πονηρὸν ἔργον 281A), "the evil deed" (τὸ κακὸν 284A) "improper impulses" (ταῖς ἀπρεπέσι κινήσεσι 281A), and finally condemned the ensuing pleasure as "illicit" (τῆς ἀθέσμου ἡδονῆς ibid.).

refer to sexual passion and to its agent, the devil, with their emphasis on "impurity"[33] and "death,"[34] all suggest that what Pierius felt for Dionysiodorus was strongly condemned by Nilus because it trespassed against Christian moral rules as understood by a Christian ascetic.[35]

Does this mean that Nilus was "intolerant" or "homophobic"? Asked in such terms, the question is clearly senseless.[36] What Nilus condemns is not homoeroticism *per se*, which he apparently regarded as an equally available, albeit morally objectionable, option. Thus, he warned his young friend that the deceitful demon could *equally* assume the face of a male *or* that of a female in order to deceive his victim: "At first, however, he (viz. the demon) [...] instills an unsuspecting affection for some person, either familiar or foreign, *be it male or female* (ἄρρενος ἢ θηλείας)."[37] In accordance with a certain part of the Christian tradition, our ascetic rejects *all* sexual activity or, in his terms, πορνεία. This rejection illustrates a significant shift of focus in the realm of moral reflection, namely an evolution concerning what Foucault has termed

---

33 Numerous terms connoting "impurity" are used in the text of *Ep*. 2.177, some of which not attested in other patristic writings; thus, the spirit of fornication is "the most foul demon" (τὸν πολύσπιλον δαίμονα 280C), "the filthy serpent" (τοῦ ῥυπαροῦ ὄφεως 281A, 281D), and "filth-loving demon" (ὁ φιλορύπαρος δαίμων 284B); homoerotic attraction is termed "the terrible and loathsome passion" (ὁ ἔρως ὁ δεινὸς καὶ βδελυρός 281C) or "the fiercest fever of impurity" (πυρετὸν ἀκαθαρσίας λαβρότατον 281B) and those who might inspire it are "unclean youths" (τῶν ἀκαθάρτων νέων 284C).

34 What Pierius might derive from the view of his beloved is "the death of sin" (ὁ θάνατος τῆς ἁμαρτίας 281D).

35 Foucault saw this preoccupation with purity as a defining feature of Christian asceticism, which distinguished it from previous "technologies of the self:" "Dans l'ascétisme chrétien, la question de la pureté est centrale" (in the final French version of an interview with H. Dreyfus and P. Rabinow "À propos de la généalogie de l'éthique: un aperçu du travail en cours" in Michel Foucault, *Dits et Écrits 1954–1988*, vol. 4, *1980–1988*, Daniel Defert and François Ewald, eds. (Paris, 1994), p. 626).

36 Some modern scholars, who believe that there is an essential continuity between ancient forms of same-sex love and modern homosexuality, inappropriately use modern terminology in their analyses of ancient phenomena and speak of ancient "gay subcultures" and "homophobia;" this tendency is rightly criticized by Williams, *Roman Homosexuality*, pp. 218–224 and p. 261, n. 18, 355, n. 319. Some of the translations of ancient sources in Hubbard, *Homosexuality* represent an extreme case of telescoping modern concepts and terminology into the past and, implicitly, reading modern realities in a world which did not experience them. Foucault repeatedly warned against attaching attributes such as "tolerant" and "intolerant" to ancient societies: "il ne s'agit pas d'une rupture morale entre une Antiquité tolérante et un christianisme austère" ("Généalogie de l'éthique," p. 623).

37 *Ep*. 2.177, 280D. The same idea appears in the letter to Domninus: "the demon [...] starts speaking to the soul through some imaginary representations, as if from the mouth of another person, *male or female* (ἄρρενος ἢ θηλείας), and persistently urges him towards the loathsome passion" (*Ep*. 3.43, 409C).

"determination of ethical substance."[38] While for traditional Greek (and, with certain differences, Roman) morality the essential part of thc self that made the object of moral behavior and regulation was the sexual act seen in its close relation with desire and the ensuing pleasure, for Christian thinkers it was desire alone, now defined as sinful, which formed the main domain of one's moral behavior.[39]

Foucault's theoretical formulation is well borne out in Nilus' letter to Pierius, in which the good monk went to great lengths to argue that what a Christian should worry about most is carnal desire and the guilty pleasure that accompanies it.[40] These should be both extirpated[41] in order to attain a blessed state of purity, the only condition befitting a Christian young man.[42] Some of the effective means Nilus suggested for achieving this blessed purpose and fighting "the beasts of luxury"[43] came from the traditional arsenal of asceticism (severe fasting, fervent

---

[38] "The way in which the individual has to constitute this or that part of himself as the prime material of his moral conduct" (Foucault, *The Use of Pleasure*, p. 26).

[39] Since the intended fourth volume of *The History of Sexuality* called *The Confessions of the Flesh*, which was supposed to deal with Early Christianity, never appeared, Foucault left no systematic account of this evolution. His main ideas are available in several studies in brief formulations like the following: "Dans l'éthique [chrétienne], c'est le désir qui est le moment essentiel: son déchiffrement, la lutte contre lui, l'extirpation de ses moindres racines; quant à l'acte, il faut pouvoir le commetre sans même éprouver du plaisir—en tout cas en l'annulant autant que possible" ("Généalogie de l'éthique, p. 622); "du point de vue chrétien, la matière morale est essentiellement la concupiscence (*ce qui ne vaut pas dire que l'acte était sans importance*)" (ibid., p. 619, emphasis added).

[40] "The root of bodily action is the flesh-loving thought (ῥίζα τῆς κατὰ τὸ σῶμα πράξεως τυγχάνει ἡ φιλόσαρκος γνώμη)" (*Ep.* 2.177, 281D).

[41] Nilus expressed this with the help of a metaphor: "uproot [desire] completely before it could spring and sprout the evil deed and make it grow into a vigorous stem. For this purpose, you should put in good order your axes and concern yourself with [providing] fire as well as invoke plenty of help in destroying the tree of wantonness (τοῦ δένδρου τῆς ἀσελγείας). You see, if a root endures for some time, it often undermines even an extremely well built wall and [even] splits a rock" (284A).

[42] The description of this pure state appears as a climactic end to the letter: "you will be raised from the 'pit of suffering' [Ps. 39.3] through divine grace, and you will then see a novel air of chastity and a passionless, pure, and unconfused condition (καὶ κατάστασιν ἀπαθῆ τε καὶ καθαρὰν καὶ ἀσύγχυτον), as well as a most brilliant, clear sky unfolding from some foggy and dark night, so that you will be able to say: 'This is the day the Lord has made; let us rejoice and be glad in it!' [Ps. 117.24]. 'Now open for me, angels of God, the gates of justice! And, entering through these I will praise the Lord' [Ps. 117.19]. 'I will praise You, for You have answered me, and have become my salvation,' [Ps. 117.21] 'Blessed be God, who has not turned away my prayer, nor His mercy from me!' [Ps. 65.20]." (*Ep.* 2.167, 284D–285A). István Perczel kindly pointed out to me that this passage uses terminology and concepts found in the works of Evagrius, some of whose writings, after his condemnation in 553, were often circulated under the name of Nilus of Ancyra.

[43] Ibid., 280D.

prayer, psalmody).[44] These were drawn from Nilus' experience as a spiritual monastic leader and from his good knowledge of ascetic writings available at the time. Both these sources also inform his intricate psychological analyses of the mechanisms of temptation included in the letter to Pierius.[45] It is, I think, remarkable that he directed such advice to a young Christian nobleman living in the luxurious urban environment of Constantinople, a hotbed of temptation and a most unsuitable place for putting into practice an ascetic program like the one recommended to Pierius.[46] That Nilus undoubtedly expected his young friend and disciple to follow this ascetic routine is a sign of the times.[47]

Even so, Nilus must have been aware that Pierius, assuming he was inclined to follow the prescribed regime, did not live in the comforting solitude of the desert. Therefore, he conveyed to him other, more appropriate advice, based on common sense ("out of sight, out of mind"): stay away from Dionysiodorus! Incidentally, this reveals the monks' perfect acquaintance with a wide range of activities and venues that two young men in love might use to get close to each other, probably a result of his own pre-monastic experiences in Constantinople. First,

---

[44] Ibid., 284A.

[45] Ibid., 280D–281A.

[46] In a treatise entitled *Ascetic Discourse*, intended for the use of his monastic community, Nilus emphatically stated (for the benefit of his monks) that true asceticism was not possible in urban environments: "The master who has set himself on a peaceful life which lacks confrontation should be as far removed as possible from the warlike tumult and should have his habitation a long way from the confusion of the army camp" (*Ascetic Discourse* 41, *PG* 79, col. 769D). Life among people of the world is not possible for the true ascetic: "the saints ran away from the cities and avoided intercourse with the crowd, knowing that dwelling among people given to perdition is more pernicious for the soul than the disease of plague" (ibid., 60, col. 792D).

[47] Starting in last decades of the fourth century, the society of the later Roman Empire experienced a veritable "ascetic invasion" (Robert Markus), especially as more and more bishops came from ascetic milieus: "[t]hrough its monk-bishop the people was linked to a source of spiritual life with a distinctly ascetic tinge; and the model for the life of the Christian community came, naturally, to be infected by the model for the monastic life." This model presupposed an obliteration of the lines dividing ascetic and non-ascetic Christians: "in [this] scheme, the world and the flesh will always tend to fall into the Devil's domain. Standards upheld to the lay world or the secular clergy will appear as imperfect approximations to the ascetic's standards, concessions to the weak, rather than as norms appropriate to the several forms of the Christian vocation" (Robert A. Markus, *The End of Ancient Christianity* [Cambridge, 1990], pp. 202, 204; although based on Western material, this is, in principle, a valid description of the Eastern situation at the beginning of the fifth century AD).

Nilus compiled a descriptive list of day-to-day activities to be avoided *qua* morally problematic. The devil, says our monk,

> bids us to converse with that person and to spend time together, to keep company with them, to associate with the person and be at ease together, then be partners in necessary affairs and join in celebrations, as well as have fun and dine together without any licentious thought (χωρὶς λογισμοῦ πορνικοῦ). All these become foundations, bases, beginnings, and roots of sin.[48]

A second list is more prescriptive and included a strong injunction to abstain from such activities in the company of the beloved or, if this was unavoidable, to transform them into morally unobjectionable occurrences by a fierce display of *gravitas*.

> Take care and be on the lookout as much as it is in your power, for this whoremongering and wicked demon (τὸν μαστρωπὸν καὶ πονηρὸν δαίμονα). Shun the company of Dionysiodorus, and neither feast with him, nor attend gatherings together, neither eat nor drink with him. Do not spend your time in his company even if you only have in mind to accompany him for a short while. Should it somehow become necessary for you to meet with him, do not look him in the face lest through your windows (I mean your eyes) the death of sin might enter your soul as the Prophet says [Jer. 9.21]. Rather, look down unto the ground and give him answers with a serious countenance and with a stern face, and do not permit yourself to laugh or bathe together with him.[49]

Then, the scrupulous monk warned his young correspondent that, since the multifarious demon of fornication is such an accomplished schemer, he may even disregard age-old Greek assumptions about love being engendered only by beauty. Therefore, Nilus felt compelled to add:

---

[48] Ibid.; note the emphasis on the initial absence of sinful thought, which points to the main issue at stake in the whole discourse.

[49] Ibid. 281C–D. The curious epithet (μαστρωπός), which the demon of fornication earns here, and which no other patristic author (as far as I could ascertain) employed, is explained by a passage from Nilus' *Commentary on the Song of Songs*, 52 (ed. Guérard, p. 270): "divine love has no need for a pimp (οὐ γὰρ μαστροπεύεται ὁ οὐράνιος ἔρως), but comes by itself, attracted by the beauty of the soul and encouraged by virtuous deeds." On the other hand, the passage from Jeremiah quoted by Nilus is a *topos* of patristic exegesis, referring to the best way for provoking the cessation of passion—severing the sensorial input of sinful stimuli; for similar interpretations, see, for instance, Gregory Nazianzen, *Or.* 11 *PG* 35, col. 837 or his *Or.* 27.7, to quote just an example. The pagan tradition, too, was well aware of the erotic role of the eyes; see the superb passage from Achilles Tatius' *Leucippe and Cleitophon* (1.9.4) quoted and discussed in Goldhill, *Foucault's Virginity*, p. 74. This speaks of the "emanation of beauty flowing down through [the eyes] into the soul" and defines it as "a kind of copulation at a distance."

> You should also know that the enemy tempts some people not only by means of good-looking faces, but even through uncomely and disfigured faces, both female and male, instilling into the soul some sort of blind passion (ἔρωτα). Since the filth-loving demon is mischievous and multifarious, he often attempts to ensnare [us] in one way or another by means of an unseemly and shameful craving (διὰ τῆς ἀτόπου καὶ αἰσχρᾶς ὀρέξεως). Avoid, therefore, intercourse with unclean youths, be they handsome or uncomely![50]

After imparting such beneficial admonitions, Nilus could have left it at that and could have trusted his young and distant disciple to stay out of the devil's way. However, he did not, and this brings us to what, I think, is the most fascinating aspect of his *Letter* to Pierius. Nilus had no practical way of ensuring compliance with his advice; the young man was far away and this did not facilitate a proper relationship of spiritual fatherhood. We can surmise from his *Ascetic Discourse* how Nilus imagined this relationship should ideally work:

> When masters of this kind are found [viz., perfect], they need pupils ready to deny themselves and their will to such an extent that they would differ in no respect from inanimate bodies or from the material which is modeled by a craftsman, so that as the soul does whatever it thinks fit in the body, the latter should not resist it. And, as a craftsman exhibits his skill upon the material and this does not prevent him in any way from reaching his purpose, so the master will effect the skill of virtue in his submissive pupils, who do not contradict him in any respect[51]

We can safely assume Nilus would have had somewhat lower expectations from a layman; still, it is obvious that the master lacked in this case the means of control readily available to the elders of the desert or to the superiors of *coenobia*. He, therefore, had to rely on the *bona fides* of his disciple, which he skillfully tried to secure through his letter by a combined strategy of admonition and praise, flattering and

[50] *Ep.* 2.177, 284B–C.

[51] *Ascetic Discourse* 41, *PG* 79, cols. 769D–772A. This text was produced for a monastic audience and exhibits a high dose of self advertisement on Nilus' part, probably due to various internal and external challenges to his spiritual authority. A good discussion of these aspects is found in Daniel Caner, *Wandering, Begging Monks: Spiritual Authority and the Promotion of Monasticism in Late Antiquity* (Berkeley, CA, 2002), pp. 177–190; although this author tends to overrate the role played by economic factors and by competition for lay patronage in order to explain Nilus' criticism of rival monastic milieus near Ancyra.

instructing at the same time.[52] Furthermore, a clear indication of Nilus' effort to adapt his discourse to a non-monastic audience is the amount of explicit, sometimes very graphic detail about sexual arousal and its possible fulfillment included in his letters to the two young men. This stands in marked contrast with similar problematizations of sexuality extant in monastic sources composed for the benefit of other monks. Several ascetic authorities admitted that it was extremely dangerous to discuss openly (and all the more so to put down in writing) titillating details which might then spark the imagination of the audience, and give young monks food for sinful thoughts.[53] Nilus himself voiced a similar concern when he described the qualities required of a spiritual advisor, observing that

> for the one who talks about passions, even if by doing so he wipes off the stains of others, it is impossible to remain himself undefiled. Even the [simple] mention soils the thought of the speaker. [...] It is necessary that a [spiritual] master be skilled to such an extent that he should not ignore any of the enemy's devices in order that he could indicate to those who submit to his control the hidden weapons by unmasking them. He also needs to know how to predict the strategies of the adversary so that he may render victory effortless to his pupils and lead them out of combat crowned with the crown of victory. Such men are rare and it is not easy to find them.[54]

The reason for his detailed description of sexual temptation is, I think, clear. Both Pierius and Domninus, the two young men to whom Nilus was writing, lived in a world full of temptations and, unlike the safely secluded young monks with plenty of spare time at hand, the two would not have the opportunity to dwell upon sinful *thoughts*. Quite to the contrary, for them temptation for sinful *actions* was a much greater concern, since this was available at every step they took in the bustling streets of a late antique metropolis like Constantinople or Ancyra.

---

52 This is the same attitude as that mentioned by Xenophon in his *Symposium* when he speaks of the double function of the encomium; see Foucault, *The Use of Pleasure*, p. 204.

53 Elizabeth A. Clark, in response to some of Foucault's simplistic generalizations concerning Christian asceticism, observed that, in Christian ascetic circles, self-examination did not necessarily lead to public (or at least open) discussion of the findings, for fear of stirring the soul and offering food for sinful thoughts; cf. Elizabeth A. Clark, "Foucault, The Fathers, and Sex," *Journal of the American Academy of Religion* 54.4 (1988), 619–641, at 629, with examples from Evagrius and John Cassian.

54 *Ascetic Discourse* 28 (*PG* 79, cols. 756D–757A). Of course, this implies that he was indeed such a perfect spiritual guide.

Therefore, they needed to be instructed in detail about the works of the shameless demon of πορνεία. And Nilus did not recoil from providing detailed guidelines for correct hermeneutics of their desire.[55] To Pierius he wrote in few words how even an apparently innocent friendship could turn into spiritual disaster.

> At first, however, [the demon does], so to say, nothing that would be very hard to bear, but he only instills some attraction and a candid affection for some person, either familiar or foreign, be it male or female. Then, he bids us to converse with that person and to spend time together, to keep company with them, to associate with the person and be at ease together, then be partners in necessary affairs and join in celebrations, as well as have fun and dine together without any licentious thought. All these become foundation, bases, beginnings, and roots of sin. Afterwards, once a certain amount of time had passed, and it had become difficult for you to tear yourself away from that bad acquaintance, it is precisely then that the demon approaches the genital organs, suddenly ignites the flames of the body, and heats up the members until they blaze like bronze. And by shooting against your heart the fiery arrows of the thoughts of illicit pleasure, he urges [it] towards the wicked deed, setting it powerfully ablaze like the furnace of Babylon.[56]

In his letter to Domninus, he was even more explicit and painted a remarkable picture of the dynamics of sexual arousal up to its last

[55] According to Foucault's insightful intuition, this was the main task of monastic thinking on sexuality. He wrote that "la tâche du moine [...] est de controller sans cesse ses pensées, de les sonder afin de voir si elles sont pures, de vérifier qu'il ne s'y dissimule pas ou qu'elles n'occultent pas quelque chose de dangereux; et de vérifier qu'elles ne se révèlent pas autres qu'elles ont d'abord semblé, qu'elles ne sont pas une forme d'illusion ou de séduction " and "cette tâche requiert non seulement de la maîtrise, mais aussi un diagnostic de la vérité et d'illusion. Elle exige une constante hérméneutique de soi" ("Séxualité et solitude" in *Dits et écrits*, vol. 4, pp. 176–77). He was wrong, however, to think that such detailed analyses were the defining feature of *all* Christian discourses on sexuality and that monastic authorities were not concerned with sexual acts or with relationships to others (cf. ibid.: "ces techniques ne visent pas directement le contrôle effectif du comportement sexuel" with justified criticism by Clark, "Foucault," 632–33). Furthermore, Nilus' *Letter* to Pierius clearly contradicts Foucault's statement that "il est peu question des rapports homosexuels, et cela en dépit du fait que la plupart des ascètes vivent, de manière permanente, dans des communautés d'une assez grande importance numérique" (ibid.); laymen like Pierius (but the monks as well, as I will show in a future contribution) were indeed confronted with problems raised by homoeroticism.

[56] *Ep.* 2.177, 280D–281A.

consequences, alluding to or openly mentioning such things as erection, masturbation, erotic dreams, and (involuntary) ejaculation.[57]

> Now listen and be astonished at how the accursed demon will instruct in this matter even those who are not yet experienced in the disease of fornication! Often, while the youth lay in bed around midday, the demon, approaching him in complete silence as a crafty and villainous snake, starts speaking to the soul through some imaginary representations, as if from the mouth of another person, male or female, and persistently urges him towards the loathsome passion. Sometimes, attacking also the head of the youth, he chases sleep away from his eyes in order that, staying awake and having nothing to do, [the young man] might be completely engaged in the thoughts of impurity and, having indulged himself with shameful desires, he might very easily become practiced in fornication. However, if the young man comes under attack while asleep, [the demon] now approaches him through dreams, depicting sin to him accurately, touching his [sexual] organ and kindling an inflammation. Another one he makes see the image of a person with the face of some man or of some woman and this [he performs] in a fashion which is both unsuspected and hard to recognize, hinting at nothing, so to say, sexual, but displaying [merely] a simple friendship and an insatiable affection. Nevertheless, the demon's intention in all this charade does not have an honest purpose, but a wicked one. To some he warmly and quite openly suggests that they put into practice the desire of their heart. Some other he draws towards pleasure by having him converse with youths of the same age, and yet another he drags out of the entrenchment of divine continence through some sort of illicit acts which are better left unspoken.[58]
>
> The demon does not depict the passion only in dreams in an impure and most shameful manner. Nay, often even when a man is awake [the devil] makes him see with [the eyes of] his mind men and women impurely meeting, so to speak, for sinful purposes and engaging in sexual intercourse. And, again, it can also happen sometimes, when one is actually praying in church, that [the devil] both excites the genital organs, by igniting them with an inflammation, and pierces the heart with improper thoughts. And there are also times when he causes the one whom he is tempting to suffer even an emission [of sperm] because of [that person's] keen enjoyment. And often, as he had made a large quantity of sperm accumulate in the loins, when one urinates the urine brings forth with it this sperm to the effect that some people, scared and dismayed [by this occurrence] will fall into despair and loss of heart. Some others the

[57] This is what Foucault referred to as "[le] problème de l'érection," namely, "l'ensemble des mouvements internes qui s'opèrent depuis cette chose quasi imperceptible qu'est la première pensée jusqu'au phénomène final [...] de la pollution" ("Séxualité et solitude," pp. 177–78).

[58] *Ep.* 3.43, 409B–D.

terrible and shameless one tempts most frequently especially during the holy feasts.[59]

In writing to Pierius (and to Domninus) about such delicate matters, Nilus was imparting on them some of the wisdom he had acquired as a monastic leader. He also assumed the position of an external authority that tried to shape and influence the moral behavior of a subject into complying with an established moral code. The monk appealed to the two young men urging them to embrace what effectively amounts to complete sexual renunciation (a highly valued item in the ascetic Christian moral code). He tried to ensure compliance by a twofold appeal to values which do not immediately strike the reader as typically Christian.

The first is glory, good fame, and the appreciation others will show for a continent young man, that is, if his abstinence from same-sex relationships confirms and enhances his noble family's prestige. Pierius should be most concerned about this because his liaison with Dionysiodorus, Nilus wrote, would certainly harm him. "For the reputation of this young man is not of the best, and it is necessary to avoid the suspicions that his company might bring upon you" (281D). It is hardly suitable for a nobleman like Pierius, "virtuous offspring of a virtuous root" (281C) to shame his family's good name by failing to control his lust, that "worldly and bodily friendship of a rather brutish and irrational sort" (280B) he felt for Dionysiodorus.[60] Nilus trusted that, after all, his young friend was not one of those people "who are bent on pleasure and who are careless about the punishments to come and about that universal tribunal" and whom "the spirit of fornication, whom the children of

---

59 Ibid., 413A–B. The mention of involuntary ejaculation raises interesting problems concerning ritual purity and abstaining from communion, for which see the detailed study by David Brakke, "The Problematization of Nocturnal Emissions in Early Christian Syria, Egypt, and Gaul," *Journal of Early Christian Studies* 3 (1995), 419–60. Nilus speaks of the same problem in a long letter (*Ep.* 2.140, *PG* 79, cols. 258D–264C) sent to a monk, although there the focus is quite different; instead of concrete details about the mechanism of sexual arousal, Nilus insists on the sinful thoughts, the means to fight them, and the dangerous temptation to fall into despair and deny God's forgiving grace after sinning, at which he merely hinted in his *Letter* to Domninus (see 261B–C).

60 Nilus thus draws a distinction between Christian love (here ἀγάπη) and worldy, i.e., non-Christian friendship (φιλία), which is qualified as fit for beasts (κτηνώδης) and irrational (ἄλογος). Comparison with irrational animals, among which same-sex behavior was supposedly unknown and, therefore, "unnatural" played an important part in Greek and Roman problematizations of homoeroticism; see the recent discussion in Williams, *Roman Homosexuality*, pp. 231–244 with further bibliography.

the Hellenes used to call Eros, quite openly and rapidly and without any effort drags into the pit of wantonness" (280C).

Nilus drew a very sharp distinction between the crowd, which gives in without a fight to its irrational appetites, and the valiant few who choose to fight their sexual urges, thus revealing their self-mastery and their superior nature. By appealing to Pierius' pride of belonging to this "natural" elite of society, Nilus skillfully manipulates this feeling (which is hardly Christian and even less monastic)[61] in order to convey to him that compliance with the Christian (ascetic) moral code and elite membership are not mutually exclusive. This comes out even more clearly in his *Letter* to Domninus, the young city-councilor.

> For you are inspired both by your birth and by your most virtuous choice (τῇ καλλίστῃ προαιρέσει), and strive to offer unceasingly to God the admirable continence of your parents and of your grandfathers, scorning the beauties of life, fasting each day and adorning yourself with prayers and charitable deeds as well as preserving your purity amidst a thousand things that might defile it.[62]

By his skilful antitheses, Nilus established a stark contrast between the few who consciously adopt a superior lifestyle and the many who remain content with their beast-like condition. These he depicts as the others, the crowd (οἱ πολλοί), forever "bellowing under the sting of pleasure" and who "[do] not wish to contemplate or consider the realm of virtue and its dominion."[63] These are the cowards who put up no fight, show no fortitude, gain no victory. They are the ones who, as Nilus wrote elsewhere, betrayed true Christian values by failing to rise up to the ascetic lifestyle Christ had set as a paradigm for all his

[61] Christian monastic tradition is almost unanimous in condemning asceticism or moral behavior practiced with an eye to what others might say about it. However, in (textual) practice, seeking good fame does not always appear reprehensible; on this topic, see Maud Gleason, "Visiting and News: Gossip and Reputation-Management in the Desert," *Journal of Early Christian Studies* 6.3 (1998), 501–21. Nilus himself, when writing the panegyric for Albianus, did not hesitate to use the language of Homer's epics to describe a monk who "has been admired by the inhabitants of that place even after his death and until this very day, and his glorious fame is being sung (καὶ κλέος αὐτοῦ ἀοίδιμον ᾄδεται)" (*PG* 79, col. 705B). Cf. extensive analysis of such rhetorical uses of "fame" applied to Christian ascetics in Cristian Gaspar, "Theodoret of Cyrrhus and the Glory of the Syrian Ascetics: Epic Terminology in Hagiographic Contexts (II)," *Archaeus. Études d'Histoire des Religions* 4. 4 (2000), 151–178, especially 163–77.

[62] *Ep.* 3.43, 412D–413A.

[63] Ibid., 412D.

true followers, that "image of a most virtuous way of life."[64] A true nobleman by birth, Pierius is invited to become a true nobleman by choice by entering the ranks of Christian elite.[65]

The second argument is even more manipulative, although in less obvious ways. It plays with the concept of "passivity," an essential component of Greek and Roman images of masculinity.[66] If people will praise Pierius for his continence, just imagine what they would say if they found out that he gave in to his guilty passion to Dionysiodorus! Nilus does not explicitly link Pierius' same-sex attraction with a passive position in a possible sexual intercourse, something abhorrent to a young freeborn Roman male. He does, however, insinuate, mainly by the language he uses, that giving in to guilty pleasure would make Pierius loose his mastery of himself, the active position central to the traditional definition of masculinity with which he and his peers most probably operated. Enslavement (if only spiritual) to passion would undermine his masculinity and make him less of a man, a mere toy for the demon of same-sex lust. Assuming the young man's posture after his fall, Nilus described this enslavement in metaphoric terms: "But I am caught like a lion for slaughter, and I am led in chains like a dog, and like a bird into the trap, and I am burning with the fiercest fever of impurity" (281B). He also used a very telling image to suggest the probable result of this submissiveness: "I am surrounded by a wall of shameful passion (τῷ τῆς αἰσχροπαθείας τειχίσματι)" (ibid.), with

64 *Ascetic Discourse*, *PG* 79, col. 721D. In a particularly harsh condemnation, he even assimilated those who did not practice the same strict standard of Christian life to Christ's traitors: "It was not only Judas," he wrote, "who betrayed our Lord by thinking slightly of the divine judgement. Even Christians who do not fulfill the divine laws are reckoned as traitors, since they disdain [these laws] and impose their own will, following rather their own wicked wishes" *Ep.* 2.100 (*PG* 79, col. 245).

65 Against Foucault, Elizabeth A. Clark rightly argued that "the values that Foucault assigned to elite Greek males re-emerge, transformed, in the theorizing of the desert monks. For the monks, combat against the self is the primary task. Self-mastery has been transformed into a holy war" ("Foucault," 631). This view emphasizes continuity between classical Greek ideals of self-mastery and Christian asceticism, which was denied by Foucault. As Clark observed, Foucault's characterization of Greek sexual values ("a free male practices self-domination or self-mastery in order to create a life more brilliant than that of his fellow humans, and his elitist ethic is accompanied by a quest for self-knowledge, for 'truth'") is a very appropriate description of Christian asceticism.

66 This is argued most cogently in Williams, *Roman Homosexuality*. For classical Greek views of passivity, see Foucault, *The Use of Pleasure*, pp. 204–14 and the sources referred to in Hubbard, *Homosexuality*, pp. 8–14.

αἰσχροπαθεία literally meaning "suffering that which is shameful." The most powerful formulation appears in the *Letter* to Domninus.

> It is impossible for pleasure ever to remain calm or be appeased in those who have been subjugated and defeated by her. On the contrary, like some barbarian mistress, she afflicts [them] with the wounds of sexual intercourse and unceasingly demands her tribute, constraining even by force those who, by their failures, have become her slaves, and allowing almost no respite to those subjected to her. [...] And freedom does not appear easily, since men are eager to serve evil quite willingly day and night, willfully allowing themselves to be defeated by corruption and always loving the poison of pleasure.[67]

Cowardice, defeat, captivity, voluntary enslavement, servitude to a barbarian,[68] and a woman at that, all play upon the same opposition *active* vs. *passive* which characterized classical Greek male ideals, both in the sexual and in the social sphere.[69] In the game of power (over the self, over the others, over the demons), Nilus employs the same opposition and appeals to the same ideal.

How effective this strategy probably was will appear if we take a look at other sources on homoeroticism close in time to Nilus' *Letters*. Most of these exhibited the same obsessive concern with sexual passivity that freeborn citizens might engage in (of their own free will or otherwise). Such sources suggest that this was a matter of utmost importance, which shaped (aristocratic) male perceptions of same-sex relationships at the turn of the fifth century AD.

First, there is the imperial legislation: on two occasions during the fourth century Christian emperors issued laws against male prostitutes, i.e., men willing to adopt a passive role in same-sex intercourse for material gain.[70] One of these, directed against male prostitutes working

[67] *Ep.* 3.43, 412D–413A.

[68] In the *Ascetic Discourse*, the tempting demon is also presented as the Barbarian (τόν βάρβαρον), whom the monks are supposed to chase away "through chastity and abstinence" (διὰ σωφροσύνης καὶ ἐγκρατείας) (*PG* 79, col. 805C).

[69] On the isomorphism between sexual and social dominance in the traditional Greek moral code of the male elite, see Foucault, *The Use of Pleasure*, pp. 71–77. Nilus was not the only one to play upon the connotations submission and giving oneself up to the rule of inferiors still evoked in Late Antiquity. On this, see the excellent study by Kate Cooper, "Insinuations of Womanly Influence: An Aspect of Christianization of the Roman Aristocracy," *The Journal of Roman Studies* 82 (1992), 150–64.

[70] Legislation issued by Christian emperors concerning same-sex behavior starts with a constitution issued by emperor Constans in 342 (*Codex Theodosianus* 9.7.3). This condemned men who submitted to other men as a woman would in somewhat obscure terms (*cum vir nubit in feminam*), which have been variously interpreted. Discussions

in Rome, connected, much in the same way Nilus would do, passive homoeroticism with failing masculinity. The author of a law issued in the name of Theodosius I argued that submitting to another male not only affected Roman individuals who agreed to such unspeakable deed, but brought disgrace upon "the city of Rome, mother of all virtues." The mere presence of passive individuals who forfeited the essence of their masculinity for material gain stained the Eternal City and insulted the manly force of its initial founders.[71] Death penalty by burning alive was prescribed "so that all should understand how sacred the dwelling of a virile soul must be."[72] If these two early laws referred explicitly to male prostitutes, in 438 the compilers of the vast legal corpus known as the *Codex Theodosianus*, also included, along with the constitution of Constans from 342, a shortened version of the law from 390. In its new wording, which was to take precedence over all existing legislation on the matter, the law now referred not to passive male prostitutes, but to passive males generally:

> All those, through whose crime a male's body is treated as a female [body] and is compelled to suffer the passivity specific to the other sex, in fact have nothing that would differentiate them from women; they will pay for a crime of this kind through the avenging flames in full view of the people.[73]

by Dalla, *Ubi Venus mutatur*, pp. 167ff and Cantarella, *Secondo natura*, pp. 224–26 are fundamental. See also, Williams, *Roman Homosexuality*, p. 362, n. 5. This law does not refer to "homosexual marriages," *pace* Boswell, *Christianity*, p. 123.

71 *Non patimur urbem Romam virtutum omnium matrem diutius effeminati in viro pudoris contaminatione foedari et agreste illud a priscis conditoribus robur fracta molliter plebe tenuatum*; the text of this constitution was preserved as *Collatio legum Mosaicarum et Romanarum* 5.3 (ed. Riccobono, vol. 1, p. 481) and, in a significantly altered version, as *Codex Theodosianus* 9.7.6. See Dalla, *Ubi Venus mutatur*, pp. 170–74 and Cantarella, *Secondo natura*, pp. 226–230.

72 *Vt universi intellegant sacrosanctum esse debere hospitium virilis animae* (*Collatio* 5.3.2); Peter Brown's comments ("for the first time in history, in 390, the Roman people witnessed the public burning of male prostitutes, dragged from the homosexual brothels of Rome" *Body and Society*, p. 383) are certainly apt to create dramatic effect, but not altogether accurate: we do not know of any public execution of this kind actually carried out under this law.

73 *Codex Theodosianus* 9.7.6; The increasingly severe stand imperial legislators took towards passivity is duly noted by Dalla, *Ubi Venus mutatur*, p. 183 ("riteniamo che [...] ispessitasi la severità, la norma sia servita nel V secolo a reprimere anche l'omosessualità passiva in genere") and Cantarella, *Secondo natura*, p. 230. This trend culminates with two laws of Justinian (*Novellae* 77 issued in 538 and 141 from 559), where involvement in same-sex activities is punished by mutilation and death regardless of the role assumed. This blanket condemnation was followed by active persecution; for an account of this see Dalla, *Ubi Venus mutatur*, pp. 185–214, who speaks of "repressione totale."

It is important to note that repressive measures against same-sex activities seem to become harsher and more extended in time probably in connection with the increase of Christian influence on the imperial household. An ascetic emperor like Theodosius II, praised by ecclesiastical historians for converting his imperial palace into a monastery, was more likely to condone a general condemnation of passive males, while his predecessors had legislated exclusively against passive male prostitutes.[74]

Death was not only the punishment for sexual submission to another male; it was, sometimes, by far preferable to it. A rhetorical declamation composed by Libanius (314–393 AD), the famous sophist of Antioch, argued as much.[75] Notwithstanding the fictitious topic it addresses,[76] I think this text is quite relevant for the present inquiry. Such declamations were intended to serve as didactic material in the schools of rhetoric that still trained educated members of Late Roman intellectual elite at the end of the fourth century AD. As such, they did not serve as mere "storehouses of technique and felicitous wording"[77] from which many a Roman nobleman drew the substance of his own speeches when appearing in public. They also offer precious indications about

[74] Cantarella (*Secondo natura*, pp. 264–65) made a very important observation: Christian morality, especially that preached in ascetic circles, was more likely to endorse a condemnation of both parties engaged in a same-sex relationship, regardless of their role (active or passive) on scriptural authority and as a result of its Jewish heritage, which was openly hostile to any type of homoeroticism. Roman emperors, however, even if they were Christians, had to legislate for a society whose morals condemned only the passive male. In these circumstances, "che possibilità di successo avrebbe avuto un intervento legislativo che si fosse posto in totale, aperto e insanabile contrasto con la morale popolare," that is to say, "con un'etica sessuale tuttora ispirata, fondamentalmente, all'esaltazione della virilità intesa comme capacità di sottomettere [?]"

[75] *Declamatio* 42 in Libanii *Opera*, ed. R. Foerster, vol. 7, *Declamationes 21–51* (Leipzig, 1913), pp. 400–430.

[76] "A tyrant asked a neighboring city to deliver a beautiful young man to him, and threatened war if he did not get him. The city agreed to go to war. As the tyrant came and besieged the city, the young man's father killed him and threw him down from the walls. The tyrant departed and the father is now being charged with murder." This was a popular topic, it seems, in the schools of rhetoric; besides Libanius' *Decl.* 42, two other texts treating similar imaginary cases survive: one earlier in Latin (Calpurnius Flaccus, *Decl.* 45, second century AD) and another one, later, in Greek (Choricius of Gaza, *Decl.* 9, first half of the sixth century AD). The latter replaced the boy with a girl, presumably reflecting the fact that, in those days, same-sex love was no longer suitable as a schoolbook topic; for a similar exclusion of same-sex content from a collection of "erotic" letters dated to the end of the fifth century, see W. G. Arnott, "Pastiche, Pleasantry, Prudish Eroticism: the Letters of 'Aristaenetus'," *Yale Classical Studies* 27 (1982), 291–320, especially 314–15.

[77] D. A. Russell, *Greek Declamation* (Cambridge, 1983), p. 81.

the attitudes and mentalities instilled into the minds of young men who attended those schools and then went on to become city-councilors, civil servants, military governors or, more and more frequently, Christian bishops and monastic leaders. A young man like Pierius, for instance, was expected to read such texts, and take them as models for his own compositions. The well-educated Nilus had probably done the same in his own youth. By studying them, we can obtain, as a reputed connaisseur of the genre put it, "an idea of the values and prejudices that teachers assumed or encouraged."[78]

In his *Declamation* 42, Libanius spoke in defense of a father accused of murdering his own son rather that have him submit to the lust of another male, a tyrant who, madly in love with the youth, threatened to make war against the city unless he got what he wanted. For the fictitious father there was, apparently, no dilemma; "after all, rape is unbearable while death is not, so let the city be saved together with his chastity!"[79] Undefiled chastity is seen here as the supreme value, an ideal with which many Christians would have heartily agreed. Many of the arguments Libanius developed in his discourse to defend the fictitious father's course of action would deserve a detailed analysis. Hoping to return to them elsewhere, I will concentrate on only one of these, which is particularly relevant to the present topic. What was so painful about the boy's fate if he had been allowed to go and live with the tyrant who was in love with him? For his father, the answer was clear: a fate worse than that of a slave. "My child, however, was not going to be a slave, even if this is terrible enough. No, he would have been forcefully deprived of his manhood and reckoned among women..."[80] And worse still would follow once the prime of his youth had passed and he had ceased to be sexually desirable for the tyrant.

> What wife could I give him after that? How could he dare educate his own children? And how could he attend any religious celebration or any games or any sacrifices? Would he not loose his very name and acquire a new one derived from his outrage? A fine life, indeed, would that be if he did not dare as much as look into the eyes of his own slaves![81]

---

[78] Ibid., p. 22.

[79] Libanius, *Decl.* 42.15, p. 409.

[80] Ibid., 42.41, p. 422.

[81] Ibid., 42.42, p. 423; this is echoed by Nilus in *Ep.* 2.38, addressed to a certain Asclepiodotus: "What is the use for you to command to your slaves when you are yourself enslaved by your passions like some harsh mistresses?"

To be sure, the father imagined by Libanius belongs to a timeless, fictitious world much more like the Athens of Pericles than the later Roman Empire. Some of the consequences associated by the Antiochene sophist with a violent deprivation of masculinity were, in fact, borrowed from a speech composed in the fourth century BC, *Against Timarchus* of Aeschines.[82] Nevertheless, it is not far-fetched to believe that some opinions of Libanius' own contemporaries, be they Christian or not, were also mirrored in his *Declamation* 42. We know, from Libanius' outraged remarks, that many adult citizens of Antioch indulged in same-sex relationships with young boys and men, some of whom were his own students.[83] Early in his teaching career in Constantinople, Libanius himself had been accused of trying to seduce some of his young students. Although this accusation was probably based on nothing more than malicious slander, it nevertheless caused him to be driven out of the capital and then, once his "reputation" caught up with him, from Nicomedia, where he had subsequently settled as a teacher of rhetoric.[84] Libanius mentioned as something natural the existence of male prostitutes in a speech aimed at defending actors who played in mime shows against various accusations of immorality, including that of being covert male prostitutes.[85] John Chrysostom, whom Nilus

[82] The classic analysis of this speech is Dover, *Greek homosexuality*, pp. 19–109; for an English translation of relevant passages and recent literature, see Hubbard, *Homosexuality*, pp. 118–121, 131–153. It soon became a rhetorical *topos* to undermine an opponent's credibility by insinuating that he had submitted in his youth sexually to another male; see, Williams, *Roman Homosexuality*, pp. 173–75 and 334, n. 69. Libanius uses this *topos* on several instances: see *Or.* 37.3, 4.15 ff., and 39.5–6, which subverts the authoritarian appearance of a certain Mixidemus as a judge by dwelling on his lack of masculinity due to the fact that he had been passive in same-sex relationships.

[83] On male homoeroticism at Antioch in the last decades of the fourth century A.D., see the sources collected and discussed by A.-J. Festugière in his *Antioche païenne et chrétienne: Libanius, Chrysostome et les moines de Syrie* (Paris, 1959), pp. 195–210.

[84] This story is reported by Eunapius (*Vitae sophistarum* 17.1.7–8, ed. G. Giangrande [Rome, 1956], p. 82), who speaks of an "accusation concerning young men" (διαβολῆς [...] περὶ τὰ μειράκια). Libanius never detailed the circumstances of his expulsion from Constantinople, but it is likely that they were connected with these charges of pederasty (see Robert J. Penella, *Greek Philosophers and Sophists in the Fourth Century AD: Studies in Eunapius of Sardis* (Leeds, 1990), pp. 102–103).

[85] Libanius, *Or.* 64.39 dating from 361; ed. R. Foerster, vol. 4, p. 444: male prostitutes, presumably describing a contemporary situation: "those make a bad use of their own [masculine] nature and do not deny the name they acquired from submitting to the most shameful things;" 64.48 (pp. 450–51) speaks of young men who, although surrounded by good teachers and watchful parents managed to find a way to give in to the request of their lovers. In contrast to these, Libanius adds, "I myself know some young men better looking than Hyacinthus, who, although far away from their

greatly admired and who had been Libanius' pupil—his *best* pupil, some say—before converting to Christianity and asceticism, complained in one of his early works (between 378–386 AD) that Christian men in Antioch enjoyed sex with young boys much more than going to the whores, although they certainly should have known better.[86] The phenomenon was there; attitudes towards it were in many respects similar to those of fifth-century Athenians: it was shameful for a young man to submit sexually to another male.[87] A more ascetic stance is, perhaps, what characterizes Libanius' time and this is reflected in the basic argument of *Declamation* 42: chastity is a young man's best treasure to be defended even at the cost of one's life. For the loss of one's masculine (i.e., dominant) status by sexual submission to another male is something to be loathed and avoided. The death of sin, as Nilus would have called it, brings eternal shame while fame won through chastity is everlasting. In Libanius' words, spoken by the young man about to die by his father's hand, "chastity will make a fine tombstone for me!"[88]

It is in this context, I argue, that we can better understand Nilus' *Letter* to Pierius, the assumptions on which it is based, and the skillful use our good monk made of these assumptions. Nilus' rejection of male homoeroticism is undoubtedly a result of his adherence to the

parents and [entrusted] to permissive guardians" nevertheless managed to stay chaste and adds: "I will not even mention here the chastity shown by young men who were orphans lest anyone suspect I am setting myself as an example" (a fine opportunity for self-advertising not missed by Libanius, who became an orphan early in his youth).

[86] "But these persons who are, so to speak, 'rational,' who have had the benefit of divine instruction, who say to others what should be done and what should not be done, and who have heard the scriptures which have come down from heaven—these men have intercourse more fearlessly with young boys than with prostitutes!" (*Adversus oppugnatores vitae monasticae* 3.8 as translated in John Chrysostom, *A Comparison Between a King and a Monk / Against the Opponents of the Monastic Life*, trans. David G. Hunter [Lewiston, NY, 1988], p. 142.) Festugière dryly comments: "Si l'on devait prendre ces mots à la lettre, il semblerait que les chrétiens d'Antioche n'eussent pas été moins pédérastes que les païens" (*Antioche*, p. 208, n. 2); Pierius' experience in Constantinople does not leave, I think, too much room for doubt.

[87] Libanius told his pupils that love for a youth was not something even an active lover should make public if he was an honorable man. This is what he said about his amorous tyrant in *Decl.* 42.33 (p. 418): "Great and powerful was the love (ἔρως) which burnt him, and oppressed him, and did not let him breathe. How can we tell? He spoke out the very things he should have kept secret. And he did it through a public embassy! A thing unheard of: a young man's beauty was requested through an embassy!"

[88] ἐγὼ δὲ ἕξω καλὸν τὴν σωφροσύνην ἐντάφιον (*Decl.* 42.56, p. 430). Calpurnius Flaccus also has a memorable *dictum* in this context: *perit homo sed pudor vivit* "the young man perished, but chastity lives on!" (*Decl.* 45; *The Declamations of Calpurnius Flaccus*, ed. Lewis A. Sussman [Leiden, 1994], p. 82).

moral code of Christianity, which unambiguously condemned males who engaged in sexual relationships with other males. At the same time, though, same-sex relationships are only an incidental object of this rejection, its true target being (illicit) sexual activity *tout court*. Such a wholesale condemnation is best explained as a consequence of the ascetic view of Christian morality which Nilus the monk tried to enforce upon Pierius the young nobleman.

To do so, he recommended the traditional ascetic practices so aptly caught in Shakespeare's lines quoted at the beginning of this study. And this was to be expected from a monastic mentor. At the same time, Nilus did not overlook other available means. My analysis has shown, I believe, that in order to carry conviction, Nilus selected and used rhetorical strategies meant to appeal to Pierius' sense of belonging to the ruling elite rather than to his faltering sense of Christian duty. He stimulated his correspondent's desire for good reputation and played upon his fears of losing dominant status through sexual passivity. The ultimate message Nilus tried to convey was that sexual abstinence, an element of moral behavior highly regarded by late antique Christians and pagans alike, could be construed as the sign of a superior lifestyle, a perfect means of defining an individual's elite status. Being a shared value, abstinence offered a solution of continuity for individuals with traditional elite mentalities who had to adapt to the new moral environment of the Christian Roman Empire. Men like Nilus, whom many of us today may dislike, played an important part in this process. It is of them that Nietzsche once wrote: "One would deceive oneself utterly if one presupposed any lack of intelligence among the leaders of the Christian movement: oh, they are clever, clever to the point of holiness, these good church fathers!"[89]

Works cited

Primary Sources

John Chrysostom, *A Comparison Between a King and a Monk / Against the Opponents of the Monastic Life*, translated with an Introduction by David G. Hunter (Lewiston NY, 1988).

The Declamations of Calpurnius Flaccus, text, translation, and commentary by Lewis A. Sussman (Leiden, 1994).

[89] Friedrich Nietzsche, *Twilight of the Idols*, in *The Portable Nietzsche*, ed. and trans. Walter Kaufmann (New York, 1954), p. 651.

Eunapii *Vitae sophistarum*, ed. Giuseppe Giangrande, Typis publicae officinae polygraphicae, Rome, 1956.
Fontes iuris Romani antejustiniani, ed. Salvatore Riccobono et al., 2nd revised ed. (Florence, 1968).
Libanii *Opera*, ed. Richard Foerster, vol. 4, *Orationes 51–64* (Leipzig, 1908); vol. 7, *Declamationes 21–51* (Leipzig, 1913).
Nil d'Ancyre, *Commentaire sur le Commentaire sur le Cantique des Cantiques*, editio princeps, ed. Marie-Gabrielle Guérard, vol. 1 (Paris, 1994).
Sancti Nili ascetae, discipuli S. Joannis Chrysostomi, Epistolarum libri IV, ed. Leo Allacci (Allatius), Typis Barberinis, Rome, 1668; reprinted in *Patrologiae Graecae cursus completus*, vol. 79, ed. Jean-Paul Migne, cols. 81–582, Migne, (Paris, 1869).
Sancti patris nostri Nili senioris In Albianum Oratio, in *Sancti patris nostri Nili Abbatis Tractatus seu opuscula*, ed. Josephus-Maria Suarez, Typis Barberinis, Rome, 1673; reprinted in *Patrologiae Graecae cursus completus*, vol. 79, ed. Jean-Paul Migne, cols. 696–712, Migne (Paris, 1869).
Sancti patris nostri Nili Tractatus de monastica exercitatione, in *Sancti patris nostri Nili Abbatis Tractatus seu opuscula*, ed. Josephus-Maria Suarez, Typis Barberinis, Rome, 1673; reprinted in *Patrologiae Graecae cursus completus*, vol. 79, ed. Jean-Paul Migne, cols. 720–809, Migne (Paris, 1869).
Theodosiani libri xvi cum constitutionibus Sirmondianis, ed. Th. Mommsen, 3rd ed., vol. 1, part 2 (Berlin, 1962).

Modern Literature

Arnott, William Geoffrey, "Pastiche, Pleasantry, Prudish Eroticism: the Letters of 'Aristaenetus'," in *Yale Classical Studies* 27 (1982): 291–320.
Bailey, Derrick Sherwin, *Homosexuality and the Western Christian Tradition* (London, 1955).
Boswell, John Eastburn, *Christianity, Social Tolerance and Homosexuality: Gay People in Western Europe from the Beginning of the Christian Era to the Fourteenth Century* (Chicago, 1980).
——, *Same-Sex Unions in Pre-modern Europe* (New York, 1994).
Boyarin, Daniel and Elizabeth A. Castelli, "Introduction: Foucault's *The History of Sexuality*: The Fourth Volume, or, A Field left Fallow for Others to Till," in *Journal of the History of Sexuality* 10.3–4 (2001): 357–74.
Brakke, David, "The Problematization of Nocturnal Emissions in Early Christian Syria, Egypt, and Gaul," in *Journal of Early Christian Studies* 3 (1995): 419–60.
——, "Ethiopian Demons: Male Sexuality, the Black-Skinned Other, and the Monastic Self," in *Journal of the History of Sexuality* 10.3–4 (2001): 501–35.
Brooten, Bernadette J., *Love between Women: Early Christian Responses to Female Homoeroticism* (Chicago, 1996).
Brown, Peter Robert Lamont, *The Body and Society: Men Women, and Sexual Renunciation in Early Christianity* (New York, 1988).
Brundage, James A., *Law, Sex, and Christian Society in Medieval Europe* (Chicago, 1987).
Bullough, Vern L., *Sexual Variance in Society and History* (Chicago, 1980).
Bullough, Vern L. and James A. Brundage, eds., *Sexual Practices and the Medieval Church* (Buffalo, NY, 1982).
Burrus, Virginia, "Queer Lives of Saints: Jerome's Hagiography," in *Journal of the History of Sexuality* 10.3–4 (2001): 442–79.
Cameron, Alan, "The Authenticity of the Letters of St. Nilus of Ancyra," in *Greek, Roman and Byzantine Studies* 17 (1976): 181–96.
Caner, Daniel, *Wandering, Begging Monks: Spiritual Authority and the Promotion of Monasticism in Late Antiquity* (Berkeley CA, 2002).
Cantarella, Eva, *Secondo natura: La bisessualità nel mondo antico* (Rome, 1988).

Carette, Jeremy R., "Prologue to a Confession of the Flesh," in idem, ed., *Religion and Culture: Michel Foucault*, 1–47 (New York, 1999).
Chitty, Derwas James, *The Desert a City: An Introduction to the Study of Egyptian and Palestinian Monasticism under the Christian Empire* (Oxford, 1966).
Clark, Elizabeth A., "Foucault, The Fathers, and Sex," in *Journal of the American Academy of Religion* 54.4 (1988): 619–641.
Clauss, Manfred, *Der magister officiorum in der Spätantike (4.–6. Jahrhundert): Das Amt und sein Einfluß auf die kaiserliche Politik* (Münich, 1980).
Conca, Fabrizio, "Le «Narrationes» di Nilo e il romanzo greco," in *Studi bizantini e neogreci: Atti del IV Congresso Nazionale di Studi Bizantini*, ed. Pietro Luigi Leone, 349–360 (Galatina, 1983).
——, "Osservazioni sullo stile di Nilo Ancirano," in *Jahrbuch der Österreichischen Byzantinistik*, 32.3 (1982): 217–25.
Cooper, Kate, "Insinuations of Womanly Influence: An Aspect of Christianization of the Roman Aristocracy, " in *The Journal of Roman Studies* 82 (1992): 150–64.
Dalla, Danilo, *"Vbi Venus mutatur": omosessualità e diritto nel mondo romano* (Milan, 1987).
Delmaire, Roland, *Les Institutions du Bas-Empire Romain, de Constantin à Justinien*, vol. 1, *Les Institutions civiles et palatines* (Paris, 1995).
Dover, Kenneth James, *Greek Homosexuality*, 2nd ed. (Cambridge MA, 1989).
Espejo Muriel, Carlos, *El deseo negado: aspectos de la problematica homosexual en la vida monastica (siglos III–VI d. C.)* (Granada, 1991).
Fatouros, Georgios, "Zu den Briefen des Hl. Neilos von Ankyra," in *L'Épistolographie et la poésie épigrammatique: projets actuels et questions de méthodologie. Actes de la 16e Table ronde organisée par Wolfram Hörandner et Michael Grünbart dans le cadre du XXe Congrès international des Études byzantines Collège de France-Sorbonne Paris, 19–25 Août 2001*, 21–30, Centre d'études byzantines, néo-helléniques et sud-est européennes—E.H.E.S.S (Paris, 2003).
Festugière, André-Jean, *Antioche païenne et chrétienne: Libanius, Chrysostome et les moines de Syrie* (Paris, 1959).
Foucault, Michel, *The History of Sexuality*, vol. 2, *The Use of Pleasure*, translated by R. Hurley (New York, 1985; repr. 1990).
——, *The History of Sexuality*, vol. 3, *The Care of the Self*, translated by Robert Hurley (New York, 1988).
——, "À propos de la généalogie de l'éthique: un aperçu du travail en cours," in *Dits et Écrits 1954–1988*, vol. 4, *1980–1988*, eds. Daniel Defert and François Ewald, 609–31 (Paris, 1994).
——, "Séxualité et solitude," in *Dits et Écrits 1954–1988*, vol. 4, *1980–1988*, eds. Daniel Defert and François Ewald, 168–78 (Paris, 1994).
Gaşpar, Cristian, "Theodoret of Cyrrhus and the Glory of the Syrian Ascetics: Epic Terminology in Hagiographic Contexts (II)," in *Archaeus. Études d'Histoire des Religions* 4. 4 (2000): 151–178.
Gleason, Maud, "Visiting and News: Gossip and Reputation-Management in the Desert," in *Journal of Early Christian Studies* 6.3 (1998): 501–21.
Goldhill, Simon, *Foucault's Virginity: Ancient Erotic Fiction and the History of Sexuality* (Cambridge, 1995).
Goodich, Michael, *The Unmentionable Vice: Homosexuality in the Later Medieval Period* (Santa Barbara CA, 1979).
Gribomont, Jean, "La tradition manuscrite de S. Nil. I: La Correspondance," in *Studia monastica* 11 (1969): 231–67.
Guérard, Marie-Gabrielle, "Nil d'Ancyre," in *Dictionnaire de Spiritualité*, vol. 11, 345–56 (Paris, 1981).
Halperin, David M., *One Hundred Years of Homosexuality: And Other Essays on Greek Love* (New York, 1990).

——, "Historicizing the Subject of Desire: Sexual Preferences and Erotic Identities in the Pseudo-Lucianic *Erôtes*," in *Foucault and the Writing of History*, ed. Jan Goldstein, 19–34 (Oxford, 1994).
Heussi, Karl, *Untersuchungen zu Nilus dem Asketen* (Leipzig, 1917).
Hubbard, Thomas K., ed., *Homosexuality in Greece and Rome: A Sourcebook of Basic Documents* (Berkeley CA, 2003).
Johansson, Warren and William A. Percy, "Homosexuality," in *Handbook of Medieval Sexuality*, eds. Vern L. Bullough and James A. Brundage, 155–89 (New York, 1996).
Jones, Arnold Hugh Martin, *The Later Roman Empire 284–602: A Social, Economic, and Administrative Survey*, vol. 1 (Oxford, 1964).
Kolve, V. A. "Ganymede/Son of Getron: Medieval Monasticism and the Drama of Same-Sex Desire," in *Speculum* 73.4 (1998): 1014–67.
Koukoulēs, Phaidon, Βυζαντινῶν βίος καὶ πολιτισμός, vol. 6 (Athens, 1955).
Lutterbach, Hubertus, *Sexualität im Mittelalter: Eine Kulturstudie anhand von Bußbüchern des 6. bis 12. Jahrhunderts* (Köln, 1999).
Markus, Robert A., *The End of Ancient Christianity* (Cambridge, 1990).
Martindale, John Robert, *Prosopography of the Later Roman Empire*, vol. 2 (Cambridge, 1980).
Montiel, Juan Francisco Martos, *Desde Lesbos con amor: Homosexualidad femenina en la Antigüedad* (Madrid, 1996).
Nietzsche, Friedrich, *Twilight of the Idols*, in *The Portable Nietzsche*, translated and edited by Walter Kaufmann. (New York, 1954).
Penella, Robert J., *Greek Philosophers and Sophists in the Fourth Century A.D.: Studies in Eunapius of Sardis* (Leeds, 1990).
Pitsakēs, Kōnstantinos G, "Η θέση των ομοφυλοφίλων στη Βυζαντινή κοινωνία" in Πρακτικά ημερίδας Οι περιθωριακοί στο Βυζάντιο 9 Μαίου 1992 (= *Les marginaux à Byzance*), ed. Chrysa A. Maltezou, 169–269 (Athens, 1993).
Richlin, Amy, *The Garden of Priapus: Sexuality and Aggression in Roman Humour*, 2nd revised ed. (New York, 1992).
Rousselle, Aline, Porneia: *On Desire and the Body in Antiquity*, translated by Felicia Pheasant (Cambridge MA, 1988).
——, "Statut personnel et usage sexuel dans l'Empire romain," in *La contamination spirituelle: science, droit et religion dans l'Antiquité* (Paris, 1998).
Russell, Donald Andrew, *Greek Declamation* (Cambridge, 1983).
Smythe, Dion C., "In Denial: Same-Sex Desire in Byzantium," in *Desire and Denial in Byzantium: Papers from the Thirty-first Spring Symposium of Byzantine Studies, University of Sussex, Brighton, March 1997*, ed. Liz James, 139–148 (Aldershot, 1999).
Teja, Ramón, "El demonio de la sexualidad en el monacato egipcio," in *Codex Aquilarensis. Cuadernos de Investigación del Monasterio de Santa María la Real*, 11 (1994): 21–31.
Troianos, Spiros, "Kirchliche und Weltliche Rechtsquellen zur Homosexualität in Byzanz," in *Jahrbuch der Österreichischen Byzantinistik* 39 (1989): 29–48.
Veyne, Paul, "La Famille et l'amour sous le Haut-Empire romain," in *Annales ESC* 33 (1978): 35–63.
——, "L'Homosexualité à Rome," in *Communications* 35 (1982): 26–33.
Williams, Craig A., *Roman Homosexuality: Ideologies of Masculinity in Classical Antiquity* (New York, 1999).

THE CRY OF EDEN

Rafael Chodos

It is believed that, the narrative of the Garden of Eden was composed approximately three thousand years ago, part of what Old Testament scholars call "the primeval history" of Genesis, which begins with the story of the six days of the creation of the world and ends with the story of the Tower of Babel.[1] Relatively soon after this story was composed, it was written down and became part of the Five Books of Moses, which were already crystallized and largely canonized by the seventh century BC.[2] While we are not sure when these texts began to be recited or read aloud in synagogues and places of assembly, still it appears that they took on a kind of authority relatively early in their life-cycle and that people who heard this story even at the end of the first millennium BC thought of it less and less as a story and more and more as a statement of doctrine.[3] We might say that these parts of the Bible progressed early in their life-cycle from religious literature to sacred text.

[1] This primeval history may be distinguished from the patriarchal history which begins with God's call to Abram in chapter 12 and ends with the fulfillment of His promise to give the Land of Canaan to Abraham's descendants, in the Book of Joshua. Modern Bible scholars commonly refer to the Hexateuch, the Five Books of Moses plus the Book of Joshua, as one literary unit woven together from the primeval history and the patriarchal history, along with various priestly texts which concern themselves with temple practice, sacrifices, purity ordinances, and social and political governance—and the work of the so-called "Deuteronomist," who repackaged much of the earlier material. See S. R. Driver, *An Introduction to the Literature of the Old Testament* (New York, 1897; repr. New York, 1956); Gerhard von Rad, *Genesis: A Commentary* (Philadelphia, 1972); and Claus Westermann, *Genesis 1–11: A Continental Commentary*, trans. John J. Scullion, 1 (Minneapolis, 1994). Also the FOTL Project at Claremont (George W. Coats, *Genesis, with an Introduction to Narrative Literature*, The Forms of the Old Testament Literature, 1 [Grand Rapids, Mich., 1983]).

[2] See the account in 2 Kings 22–23, the story of Josiah and the discovery of the "Book of the Law."

[3] See Rolf Knierim, *The Task of Old Testament Theology* (Grand Rapids, Michigan, 1995), pp. 57 ff., discussing "The Interpretation of the Old Testament": "...biblical texts are...theological texts" (p. 67). I am "dancing over" the rich methodological complexities which he discusses there because I have a different purpose.

In spite of its antiquity, the story of the Garden of Eden is scarcely mentioned in the Prophets and other writings. When Isaiah and Jeremiah were lamenting Israel's forsaking of God's covenant—an idea that was firmly grounded in the Pentateuch—they did not mention Adam's sin; this aspect failed to become part of their theological armory.[4] Centuries later, in rabbinic times, only a few of the many themes which the story weaves together seem to have caught the Jewish imagination: the theme of man being created in God's image, which is the most important and is related to the theme of man's place in the divine hierarchy, and issues of the relationship between man and woman as well as that between man and the rest of the environment.[5] It is of interest that, apparently, it was not until the Christian era that disobedience, original sin, and the fall from grace became central to the interpretation of the Garden of Eden story.

The present study offers an explication of this narrative. Rather than look forward from the story through the succeeding three thousand years of commentaries and interpretations, we will approach this narrative as a response to what came before it.

Firstly, it should be stated that religious narratives have a life-cycle. As the ancient epic says, "For how long do we build a house? For how long do we seal a document?"[6] Stories which were compelling to our ancestors often lose their power to move us. The tensions and deep conflicts which they addressed, the resolutions they offered, sooner or later may lose their currency. This no doubt is why no one retells today the Sumerian story of Inanna, the Babylonian Ishtar, who chose the shepherd Dumuzi as her husband in preference to the farmer.[7] At the time this story was first told, perhaps as long ago as about 3500 BC, there must have been conflict in the community about whether to live

[4] Isaiah 51, "He will make her wilderness like Eden...," and several references in Ezekiel—not to Adam's sin but to the contrast between Eden and a wilderness. The fact that the theme of disobedience is not mentioned later, except in Ezekiel 28 relating to the King of Tyre, is also remarked by James Barr, *The Garden of Eden and the Hope of Immortality* (Minneapolis, 1993), as well as other commentators.

[5] There is of course discussion among the rabbis of Adam's transgression, and of the disobedience of Eve and the Serpent. But it is not the principal theme in Jewish discourse.

[6] Words of Utanapishtim to Gilgamesh, in *The Epic of Gilgamesh*, trans. Maureen Gallery Kovacs (Stanford, California, 1989), p. 93.

[7] See translation in Diane Wolkstein and Samuel Noah Kramer, *Inanna, Queen of Heaven and Earth* (New York, 1983). The source text for this particular work is just one of many ancient texts in which the same stories are told.

by raising flocks or by farming, and the story set this conflict up in symbolic terms; then, through well-crafted poetry and the recounting of Inanna's careful examination of the advantages of both enterprises, resolved it in favor of sheep-farming.[8] The story has historical, but not emotional, interest. Further, its religious interest is difficult to trace; we might, perhaps view it as a myth, which is true for the rest of the Gilgamesh cycle.

Who cares today about the Hulupu tree which Inanna wanted to cut down for its wood, but which was guarded by a snake at its base, and in which Lillith had made her home, and atop which a fearsome bird had made its nest?[9] When Gilgamesh heard Inanna weeping over her inability to cut down this tree, he and his bosom friend Enkidu determined to go into the garden of Humbaba and cut it down themselves—a heroic project in which they were gloriously successful; and Inanna rewarded Gilgamesh for his efforts.

The epic proceeds with the story of this same Enkidu, the wild man, who first appears in the Gilgamesh cycle naked, unshaven, and utterly uncivilized, who lives with the animals, and he has no language. He frightens passers-by on the road, and they complain to Gilgamesh, who comes up with a plan: the temple prostitute should go to Enkidu, take off her clothes, spread herself before him, and seduce him. This the prostitute does, and Enkidu spends six days and seven nights with her, in a constant state of arousal. Then he begins to speak; he shaves, he dresses himself, he becomes Gilgamesh's best friend, he goes to the court with Gilgamesh and accompanies Gilgamesh on many heroic adventures. Ultimately the two of them come into the garden of Humbaba, where the Hulupu tree was. But in order to gain access to it, one of them had to die. The gods decided that Enkidu would die; Gilgamesh would live, occasioning much grief to Gilgamesh, who laments Enkidu bitterly, refusing to bury his body for seven days and seven nights.[10]

What might induce one today to read about the feast attended by Inanna and Enki the Sumerian god of wisdom, at which they drank

---

[8] Echoes of this same polarity are found in the story of Cain and Abel (Genesis 4,2).

[9] There are different versions of this story; I am reporting the one centered on Inanna. The "standard" Gilgamesh story does not mention Inanna; instead (Tablet II) Gilgamesh hears of the Cedar Forest and the monster Humbaba and sets out simply to make a name for himself.

[10] This is from the Old Babylonian version in Stephanie Dalley, trans., *Myths from Mesopotamia* (Oxford, 1989), p. 149.

beer to excess, and Enki, in the best of spirits, gave to Inanna all the *me*, the arts and cultural developments over which he was master? He gave her the high priesthood, the staff, the art of shepherding, kingship, the dagger and the sword, the art of prostitution, the art of kissing the phallus. All of these gifts he had loaded onto his boat—the Boat of Heaven—and Inanna sailed away in that boat toward Uruk, her home town. And when he awoke from his drunken stupor, Enki asked his servants, "Where are my treasures? Where is the priesthood? Where is the kingship? Where is the art of shepherding? Where are the dagger and the sword?" And his servants told him that he had given all the treasures to Inanna, that she was on the Boat of Heaven, had left the harbor, and was sailing on her way back to Uruk. Immediately Enki tried every device to recover the *me* but he was unsuccessful. Inanna's boat came safely into the harbor of Uruk and all the treasures were unloaded there. When Enki realized that the deed was done, he blessed Inanna and the City of Uruk, and said, "May my holy treasures remain forever in the City of Uruk!"

The Gilgamesh stories, all but one (the story of the flood which was known dimly to Josephus),[11] had for the most part disappeared until they were only recently excavated and resuscitated.[12] Tablets on which parts of the story were written in cuneiform script were discovered toward the middle of the nineteenth century; during the last seventy years Sumerian and Babylonian literatures were made available in English translation.[13] Further, it is possible that fragments of different retellings of these stories may have recently been found,[14]—but the stories themselves were lost for millennia. But there are traces in the stories of the Old Testament. The narrative of the Garden of Eden involves many of the same characters in the same configurations: a tree whose fruit

[11] There was a Babylonian priest named Berossus, who lived at the beginning of the third century BC, who wrote a history of Babylonia for the Greeks, but his book is lost. However, a later author, Polyhistor, knew of it and retold the flood story, and Polyhistor's account was known to Josephus (*Antiquities of the Jews* 1.3.6). But the rest of the Gilgamesh cycle was lost to memory.

[12] Kovacs, introduction to *Epic of Gilgamesh* (see above, n. 6); also Samuel Noah Kramer, "Archaeology and Decipherment," chapter 1 in *The Sumerians: Their History, Culture, and Character* (Chicago, 1963).

[13] The preface and introduction in John Gardner and John Maier, *Gilgamesh Translated from the Sin-Leqi-Unninni Version* (New York, 1984), give a good short history of the rediscovery of Gilgamesh.

[14] There is an interesting map of the "finds" in the Middle East in M. L. West, *The East Face of Helicon* (Oxford, 1997), p. 591.

has magic power, situated in a special garden, guarded by a serpent, in which a woman lives. We can see traces of Dumuzi in the story of Cain and Abel; the Noah narrative echoes the Babylonian account of the flood with the central character of Atra-Hasis.

Ancient stories recede but they leave seeds. Just as Glaucus said to Diomed when they met on the field of battle, "As a generation of leaves so is the generation of men: leaves which the gentle wind carries to the ground; but in the forest they are reborn and become strong again in their time" (*Iliad* 6.144–148).

It is possible that the story of the Garden of Eden was a relatively new story when the earliest Old Testament texts were compiled, with tensions that were not completely resolved, capturing a signal moment in religious consciousness—the product of a passionate religious sensibility and the trace of a tortured religious struggle. In order to achieve resolution as a statement of doctrine, the narrative must be burdened with interpretations and dogma which were perhaps never intended. In this process one may become blind to the ineffably beautiful, even *wild* quality which the narrator himself, and his contemporary audience, must have found most appealing. Let us continue with first observations.

In the Books of Genesis and Exodus one may discern two different authors whose contributions were combined in the final redaction. One used ELOHIM to refer to the divine presence, and the other speaks of YAHWEH. The Garden of Eden account is part of the Yahwistic material; judging from the high craft displayed in the narrative we can assume authorship by a professional storyteller. It is believed that a type of entertainment was to listen to stories told to the accompaniment of lyres or other stringed instruments.[15] While such stories may have been originally transmitted orally, like the Homeric epics, we know that in Babylonia as early as 1650 BC, official scribes were employed to write down the Gilgamesh cycle.[16]

---

[15] William Foxwell Albright, *Yahweh and the Gods of Canaan* (Winona Lake, Indiana, 1994), p. 2, discussing whether verse or prose is the earlier form in the OT; Howard N. Wallace, "The Yahwistic Source and Its Oral Antecedents," chap. 2 in *The Eden Narrative*, Harvard Semitic Monographs 32 (Atlanta, 1985).

[16] W. G. Lambert and A. R. Millard, introduction to *Atra-Hasis: The Babylonian Story of the Flood* (Oxford, 1969; repr. Winona Lake, Indiana, 1999), pp. 7 ff. Similar scribal schools existed in the mid-second millennium BC in Egypt—as shown by the materials collected in Miriam Lichtheim, *Ancient Egyptian Literature*, 2, *The New Kingdom* (Berkeley, 1976), pp. 7 and 167. For a very detailed account of the early profession of scribe in Mesopotamia, see Giuseppe Visicato, *The Power and the Writing* (Bethesda, Maryland, 2000).

This story however does not appear to have been a retelling of an older narrative; at least we do not have an antecedent. The story differs from that of the Flood, a retelling of what must have been a well-known story, ca. 1000 BC. Noah shares a structure with the Babylonian Atra-Hasis, the Sumerian Utanapishtim, and the Greek Deucalion and Pyrrha. But the Garden of Eden appears noticeably, to have been original when composed.[17]

The story appears to have been written down quickly after it was composed, so that it makes the impression of being relatively fresh, as is seen by comparing it with the narrative of the six days of creation and the Genesis account of the flood. The emotional coloring of those other stories is flat and monotone; the narrative lines one-directional. There is little variety in diction and almost no change in rhythm, believed to be indicative of antiquity, of retelling and re-editing by generations of redactors before being written down to become part of the so-called Hexateuch.

The Story of the Garden of Eden is full of different emotional colorings, and has a changing and skillfully modulated rhythm. The beginning segment with Adam giving names to the beasts, while God sits by and watches, is warm and sunny; it is a scene of domestic tranquility, perhaps of a parent enjoying the first efforts of a young child. But the mood changes palpably when we come to the serpent's conversation with Eve, changing again with God's interviews with Adam, Eve, and the Serpent, and the subsequent utterances by God. The pace quickens, the tension mounts, the sense of intricacy comes to the fore.

This sense of intricacy is due to the fact that the story has four speaking parts, which in itself sets it quite apart from most of the other

---

[17] Although the story appears to have been original, still it is not perfectly clear that we have a single narrator here. Like most of the stories in the Old Testament—particularly in the Pentateuch, which is its oldest part—this story may be a palimpsest: something overwritten, like a collage, but made to appear as if it were a single story line. Commentators have conjectured that the two trees in the center of the garden may represent different literary traditions and the melding of two independent story lines. Also, the short interlude in which Adam gives names to all the animals may be a later interpolation since the core story might be told without that material: Westermann, *Genesis 1–11* (see above, n. 1), pp. 186–190. See also Barr, *Garden of Eden* (see above, n. 3), and Wallace, *Eden Narrative* (see above, n. 15). But there is the possibility that the two trees were there from the beginning; the "naming scene" may have a different source.

narratives of Genesis: the Creation story has only a narrator, the story of Cain and Abel has two speaking parts, in the story of the Flood, the narrator and God speak while Noah acts but utters not one word. The boast of Lamech is another one-actor narrative, and the story of the Tower of Babel involves no particular characters or personalities, but rather utterances of people who are presented as stereotypes. The Garden of Eden involves four characters who interact in a coherent way; they are given consistent personalities and an effort is made to have their dialogue develop in accordance with their characters. In fact, the story exhibits the three classical unities of time, place, and action: it all takes place in the Garden, apparently in a single day, and there is only one plot sequence involved. The garden itself is used almost as a stage; the story begins with God placing man in the Garden, and it ends with the expulsion at which point everyone leaves the Garden—including God himself.

The "brush strokes" which our narrator deploys are varied in thickness and texture and the description of the garden itself is vague. God planted all trees that were pleasing to look at and bearing good things to eat, and more than that, little is said. The command which God gives to Adam is set forth without explanation or elaboration, namely, that there are two trees in the center of the garden, and man is forbidden to eat of one of them. There is little elaboration until the conversations between the serpent and Eve, and then between Yahweh and his creatures where, by contrast, we observe lively detail and an accelerated rhythm.

This narrator employs two conspicuous narrative "conceits": first, the conceit of the garden itself. This is a garden in which God walks in the cool of the afternoon, portrayed as a wealthy landowner who is able to plant a garden near his home. This is perhaps God's "vacation home," for we know that, in general, God dwells in Heaven. But he brings the man whom He had just formed into the garden, "to work it and watch over it"—*l'ovdah u'lshomrah*. Adam is a single, particular, man with allegorical meaning as "all of us." The intimate garden setting must have seemed frightening to the narrator and his audience since it held up the possibility of man's direct encounter with God. (An image from science fiction movies in which there is an alien being on the space craft comes to mind: God walks in the garden just like the alien being moves through the ventilators.) The second obvious conceit is the four rivers into which the one river was parted: Pishon, Gichon, Hidekel, and P'rat. P'rat is obviously the Euphrates, and the Hidekel is therefore probably the Tigris. But Gichon and Pishon, which water lands far away from Mesopotamia—such as Ethiopia and Havila (in Northern Arabia)—are most probably fictive names used as geographical locators, much as if one were to describe a place which exists at the juncture of the four rivers, the Nile, the Yalu, the Amazon, and the Mississipi. It is a garden at the center of the world—at the *omphalos ges*.

The narrator's name and personal circumstances are of course lost to us, but from the fact that he lived when and where he did we may assume that he was familiar with the many religious traditions which were coming into contact with each other at that time: The Sumerian stories of Gilgamesh and the deities with which he interacted such as Enki, Anu, Enlil, Ishtar or Inanna, some at least 2000 years old, some ca. 3000 years old. The mythologies of Egypt must also have been known to him, because Egypt had invaded that part of the world and had occupied it more than once during the second millennium, and there were caravan routes operating between Egypt and Mesopotamia all through the second and first millennia BC.[18] We can suppose that our author was also aware of the relatively new religious mythologies of Asia Minor and Greece, roughly during the period of narration.[19] There is the fact of cultural reciprocity. The road that leads from Mesopotamia to Greece is the same road that leads from Greece to Mesopotamia.

The genre of The Garden of Eden additionally sets up a cluster of expectations, and, whether deliberately or unconsciously, the narrator either fulfills or disappoints them. A "genre confusion," which appears to be present a sign of deep-seated disquietude. One can observe three identifiable genres, intermingling, and carried off with remarkable success.

First and foremost the account deals with theft, through that act of theft, an attempt to gain power, also exemplified in the Greek story of Prometheus in that Prometheus stole fire from the gods and gave it to man. For this act of effrontery he was punished; but through his sacrifice man obtained fire and all the other useful arts related to it,

---

[18] William Foxwell Albright, *From the Stone Age to Christianity*, 2nd ed. (Garden City, New York, 1957).

[19] See West, *East Face of Helicon* (see above, n. 14). It collects many particular instances of Greek borrowings from Mesopotamian sources. Recent scholarship is building a convincing case for the proposition that Greek myth and religion were heavily influenced by Mesopotamian sources.

such as metallurgy. But the Prometheus myth is not the only example of such a plot. Gilgamesh, too, stole the wood from Humbaba's tree. We may also discern the same basic theme in the medieval legends about the Holy Grail.

In all these stories the person who steals precious things from the gods is a hero, not a villain. Though punished, his basic posture is heroic, and the tone of the story is fundamentally optimistic. One interpretation is that in the Genesis account Adam takes something that belongs to God, namely, the fruit of the tree of the knowledge of good and evil. Eating it, he gains the knowledge it represents. He is punished, too, but is not blamed by the narrator, nor does God carry out the punishment that was threatened; It did not come about that "on the day you eat of that fruit you shall surely die."[20] Instead, Adam and Eve walked out of the garden, and God even made garments of skin for them.

The next genre we can discern here is the genre of a case report; that is, a prohibition, a violation, a court scene in which the truth is brought out through the process of cross-examination, followed by a decree of punishment. The narrator takes the time to develop each of the elements of this genre fully, and the court scene is particularly vivid. God in this case acts as a Middle Eastern prince would act investigating misconduct by his employees. He acts as interrogator and judge in the matter. He examines Adam first; and then Eve. The narrator appears to imagine the actual questions and answers as they would occur in a courtroom in which the skillful interrogator seizes on an unintended admission, "Who told you that you were naked? Have you eaten of the tree whereof I told you not to eat?" Adam now points the finger at Eve, and she in turn points the finger at the serpent. There is nothing more to be said or asked. God now pronounces the judgments.[21]

---

[20] One of the Midrashic explanations of this seeming contradiction is that Adam ate the fruit on a Friday and died on a Friday. This is just as convincing, surely, as Augustine's passionate but silly argument that Adam actually "died" at the moment that he disobeyed God's command. But the possibility of a "spiritual" death is a third, more plausible, and more accepted explanation.

[21] Or recites what sound like wisdom poems from 2000 years before: laments about the harshness and limitations of life. Similar laments can be found in the poetry of the Sumerians and Babylonians. Several Sumerian laments have been found: not just Gilgamesh's lament for his dead friend, Enkidu, but the more formal laments for cities which have been destroyed, the source genre for the biblical book of Lamentations. See laments for the cities of Urim, Sumer, Nubrug, and Enidug. Also, see the so-called "Dialogue of Pessimism" and "Song of the Righteous Sufferer" reproduced

The last discernible genre is the aetiology, a story which explains how a certain state of affairs came to exist. The aetiology always begins with an assumption, or perception of the way the world is, and it makes its point by offering an explanation of how things got to be that particular way. This genre is evoked clearly in Gen. 2.24, where the narrator tells us that Eve was created from Adam's rib, writing "Therefore shall man leave his father and his mother and cling to his wife, and they shall be as one flesh." We may see a more ambiguous aetiology in the story of how Adam gave names to all the creatures. Aetiology is evoked again when God pronounces what are usually called "judgments" against the Serpent, Eve, and Adam, at Genesis 3,14 and following. Those judgments, or "oracles", have a descriptive quality. They are in verse, which is not true of the rest of the narrative, and they are much longer than the usual form of "judgment", which is typically short.[22] In fact, it may not be accurate to see them as "judgments" at all. In the Hebrew, two of them begin with the phrase, "*ki [asita et hadavar hazeh]*...," which is not really the standard formula for pronouncing judgment in those passages of the Old Testament attributed to the Yahwist. Instead, the formula is "*ya'an ki*..." or "*ya'an asher*...," the formula which appears in the more obviously "judgmental" passages, (Genesis 22.16, the Angel to Abraham at the binding of Isaac, Leviticus 26.43, God's threat to those who break His statutes, Numbers 20.12, God passing judgment against Moses for his striking the rock in the desert rather than merely speaking to it). The Hebrew connective "*ki*" has many different meanings such as an intermediate between the obviously aetiological "*al ken*" in Genesis 2.24 and "*ya'an ki*" in the later passages just mentioned, meaning, "even as you have done this-and-that, so shall such-and-such a result follow and such-and-such a state of affairs come about." Viewed as an aetiology, then, these "judgments" constitute poetic descriptions of the sorry state of affairs which the narrator set out to explain, or, in other words, laments. The fact that this story combines three different genres into one story line is part of what gives it its special qualities, namely, complexity, and even humor, or irony, which results from the

---

in W. G. Lambert, *Babylonian Wisdom Literature* (Oxford, 1960; repr. Winona Lake, Indiana, 1996).

[22] Judgments are typically short and to the point: "he shall be put to death," "he shall pay treble damages," etc. See, for example, Exodus 21 in which many "judgments" or statutes are articulated, and the short judgments in Hammurabi's code.

deliberate mixing of genres, and the deliberate departure from generic norms, such as in Apuleius' story of the *Golden Ass*. Similarly Don Quixote trades deliberately on genre confusion, since the protagonist's personal profile does not fit the expectations raised by the genre of the hero knight who goes out in search of adventure. But there is much more to the story of the Garden of Eden that brings both humor and, certainly, irony to the fore.

Firstly, the command not to eat of the fruit of the Tree of the Knowledge of Good and Evil: cannot this command be viewed as humorous or ironic? One asks, What is the point of this prohibition?

Secondly, the account of the naming of the animals. This has a humorous ring to it, where the narrator tells us, "And whatsoever Adam called every living creature, that was the name thereof."

Thirdly, the pun on the Hebrew word, "erom" for "naked" when it applies to Adam and Eve, and for "subtile" when it applies to the serpent, is a humorous device.

Fourthly, the serpent's sly question to Eve, "Has God forbidden you to eat of the fruit of every tree in the garden?" has a deliberate naivete to it, which we might view as ironic and humorous.

Fifthly, the fact that the serpent—the lowly serpent—is ironically, able to see the truth about the tree and that it is he who tells it to Eve.

Sixthly, Adam points the finger at Eve, and then she points the finger at the serpent; the pacing of the dialogue in that section of the story might be seen as humorous.

Seventh, ironically, God does not carry out the sentence He originally threatened—the sentence of immediate death.

Eighth, the fact that God makes clothes of skin for the pair.

Ninth, the fact that at the end of the story, everyone leaves the garden of Eden—Adam, Eve, and God himself, so that the narrative "stage" is left unexpectedly empty—this, too, might be seen as a form of irony.

There are some deeper points about the genre confusion: firstly, seen as a Prometheus type, the narrative departs from the genre in two important respects. Adam is not a hero, a giant; he is not particularly clever, beautiful or strong, rather an "ordinary person", who happened to be in the right place at the right time. Secondly, his manner of "stealing" the fruit which belongs to the God is not through strength or feat of arms or even of cleverness, rather, Eve hands him a piece of the fruit and he eats it, a passive rather than an active thief.

Considered as a story of "crime and punishment," the narrator departs from the usual genre in an obvious manner. Rather than relating the story of one person's transgression and subsequent punishment, the normal format of a case report, God seems to pass judgment on three defendants at once—a demonstration of unparalleled forensic virtuosity. This combining of three different case reports into one might be seen as humorous, with a further question: of what the serpent did to deserve his punishment, if indeed it was a punishment, since what he said to Eve was the truth.

All these observations might incline us to say that the mood of this story is fundamentally humorous.[23] Yet, after all, the dominant mood of this story is not comic or ironic, there is irony here in the service of something quite different. The cry of Eden is, after all, profoundly serious. It is well-known that like dreams, religious narratives arise in response to tensions and discomfitures. Freud's pioneering work, *The Interpretation of Dreams*,[24] purports to explain all dreams as wish-fulfillment, but later theorists and practitioners have enlarged the sources of dreams from mere "wishes" to all sorts of tensions and problems which arise in daily life and are somehow worked out and resolved in the dreams. The symbolic resolution which the dream presents resolves the tensions which gave rise to it—but it requires sensitivity, and often guesswork, to discover what the tensions were and what symbolic language the dream used to resolve them.

Freud postulated a difference between what he called the "dream thoughts" and the "dream content"—which is to say, the dream itself—and then he identified two major mechanisms employed in the dream, namely condensation and displacement. The dream content itself (as remembered upon awakening) is a laconic, highly economical expression of the much more voluminous "dream thoughts," and the elements of the dream thoughts are usually displaced in the dream itself, that is, arranged in diffferent orders and relationships.

The narrator of the Garden of Eden, like all those who produce great religious narratives, could be considered to be a kind of dreamer; but his dreams were of a character different from that of the dreams that Freud analyzed. Most of us dream in response to personal ten-

---

[23] J. William Whedbee's recent book, *The Bible and the Comic Vision* (Minneapolis, 2002), argues that the humorous dimension of the Bible is important.

[24] First published in 1900. Sigmund Freud, *The Interpretation of Dreams*, ed. and trans. James Strachey (New York, 1998).

sions, problems, and disturbances: our relationships are not satisfactory; our jobs are giving us trouble; we have money worries, or personal ambitions. Our dreams are ours not just because we have them, but because they spring from sources which are of interest primarily to our own selves.

But great religious narratives like this one spring from a different kind of source. The dreamer has transcended his personal circumstances. He is extremely sensitive to the larger problems, disturbances, difficulties, and tensions in the ambient culture in which he lives. His discomfort does not come from worries about his relationships, or employment, or personal ambitions: no, this kind of narrator responds to deep-seated conflicts between the largest cultural vectors in his world.[25]

The narrative he forms is quite like the dreams we ordinary people have: it, too, is a condensed, symbolic resolution—or attempted resolution—of the conflicts and tensions he senses. But as it comes out of his lips, he tries to adjust it to conform to the requirements of the genres with which he is familiar. His hearers appreciate his narrative, and adopt it as their own, if it presents a satisfactory resolution of tensions that they feel as well. They could not themselves have formed the narrative because that requires great genius; but many people can recognize the narrative when they hear it.

It must be emphasized that the period in which our narrator composed this story was one of close cross-cultural encounter, with an interchange of Sumerian as well as Babylonian religious ideas, dominant at that time in that part of the world,[26] but presenting radically different models of the relationship between man and god. For example, the Babylonian myth of the creation of man begins with the gods complaining that the work they must do to feed themselves and house

---

[25] Cf. J. Harold Ellens *Jesus as the Son of Man*, Occasional Papers of the Institute for Antiquity and Christianity 45 (Claremont, Calif., 2003). Instead of focusing exclusively on what Jesus' hearers—and later interpreters—must have understood the phrase to mean, Ellens focuses on Jesus' understanding of the term, and to elicit this he focuses on Jesus' own psychological processes which, he points out, must have undergone a development over the course of his life. The argument here is similar: a focus upon what the narrator himself must have felt about his own story.

[26] The Canaanite religion, involving the myths of Baal and Dagon, could have been in the narrator's mind, but it was heavily influenced by Mesopotamian sources. See Albright, *Yahweh and the Gods of Canaan* (see above, n. 15), and in any event, the narrator must be supposed to have been hostile to it, as the religion of the nation being conquered; whereas the older Babylonian and Egyptian traditions, and the newest Greek tradition, were not "politically incorrect."

themselves has become onerous, and that they have created man to do this work for them.[27] Mankind became unruly, noisy, and troublesome, so the gods sent the flood to destroy them. Only one righteous human was saved, Atra-hasis; all the rest perished. But then the gods realized how much they missed not having humans around to do their work for them, so they agreed that the human race could be replenished, but this time they made sure that the humans would be better organized so that there would be no more noise and annoyance.

On the other hand, the Sumerian view of man's life was that he was created by the gods to serve them, that he lived at their sufferance, and that upon his death he would descend into a lifeless state in the nether world, far away from the gods.

The Egyptians—at least by the time of the Middle Kingdom, leading perhaps up to the century of the narration of the Garden of Eden—had a different notion of man's destiny. Man was on a journey toward eternity. At his earthly death he would come before the assembly of the gods and be judged. If his soul were found pure enough—that is, not burdened with the dust of this world, and not heavier than the feather of *ma'at*, truth—it would go to what they called "lightland," a place of eternal joy. If not, he would not be allowed to complete his journey and he would suffer death—the curse of nothingness.

During life, the gods dealt with men exclusively through the priests and pharaoh, who were their viceroys on earth. From the earliest times in Egypt the king was seen as a god, and he was surrounded by an elaborate priestly and royal hierarchy. Until much later, the Egyptian world of the court and temple was completely separate from the world of the common man. As a result the general view was that the gods did not interact directly in human affairs but always watched from afar, keeping tabs on humans' activities and waiting to settle the score on the day of judgment for each soul. Humans owed obedience to the gods and to the laws of the pharaoh. The consequence of disobedience was that the soul could not complete its journey to eternal life.[28]

The fundamental similarity of the Greek pantheon to the Babylonian and Egyptian pantheons is hard to ignore. In all three cases we have families of gods, some of whom are stronger than others, and they have

[27] See Lambert and Millard, *Atra-hasis* (see above, n. 16). Tablet I begins, "When the gods, like men, bore the work and suffered the toil..."

[28] See any of the many translations of the Book of the Dead, e.g. in Lichtheim, *New Kingdom* (see above, n. 16), pp. 119 ff.

disagreements with each other which have their impacts on mankind. But Greek religion exhibited, from the earliest times, a different mood and personality from what we find in Babylonia and Egypt. We might even say that the Greek view of the gods was more playful; the gods walked on earth, sometimes even in disguise, and one needed to be alert to detect them. Prayer to the gods could be very personal—not merely propitiation or sacrifice on a timeclock, and not always communal or institutional. The Greek often uttered specific prayers arising out of specific personal circumstances. When, at the beginning of the Iliad, Agamemnon laid "harsh words," *krateron mython*, on the aged priest of Apollo, Chryses, and refused to return Chryses' daughter to him, the poet tells us that Chryses left the council of the Achaians and walked along the shore of the loud-roaring sea—*Be d'akeon para thina poluphloisboio thalasses*—and he prayed to Apollo to avenge the wrong done to him. Apollo heard his prayer (*eklue* is the Greek word) and responded to it directly, picking up his bow and his arrows and sitting a hillside shooting at the Achaians for nine days, sinking their ships and killing them. Finally Agamemnon recanted and returned the daughter of Chryses to her father. This type of personal prayer differs noticeably from what we see in Egypt, where the prayers were formalized and predictable, delivered on a seasonal schedule. And it was different also from what we seem to have in Babylonia, where the prayers also were ritualized.

The Old Testament offered a new view of the relationship between man and God—original, legal, and different entirely from any of the three views just described. The shortest way to describe this relationship is as a covenant—although the word "covenant" is too simple because there were different covenants. There was a covenant with Noah, a covenant with Abraham, followed by a covenant with the whole people of Israel; all slightly different from one another. But the intensely legal idea of a contractual or voluntary bond, with obligations running in both directions, is common to all these covenants, and it was this legal notion toward which the Hexateuch was moving.

Like all religious innovators, the narrator of the Garden of Eden seems restless, dissatisfied, and rebellious. What he rebelled against most definitively was the Babylonian notion that man exists as a slave to God. While he did not completely reject the idea that man was lower than the gods, yet he dreamed of a different relationship which might still be plausible—a relationship in which obedience might not be necessary. In the Old Testament account, the image of gods walking on earth—which was finding a new kind of expression in Asia Minor and Greece—as well as the notion of God as a Judge, which notion was already fully developed in Egypt—were combined.

First, the notion that God created just one man appears to be unique in ancient Near Eastern mythologies. The other creation stories involve the creation of the *race* of men, an example of the condensation Freud identified. Man's experience of God is condensed into one man, Adam, in one place, Eden.

Second, the story begins with the words, "God placed the man in the Garden, to work it and to keep it." *L'ovda ul'shomra.* This phrase has a distinctively legal ring to it, similar to "to have and to hold," *habendum et tenendum*, from Roman law. This phrase was probably a legal formula used to establish the relationship of tenant farmer or steward. God set man in His garden as the steward there, to tend it and keep it.[29] In addition, the 60th law in the Code of Hammurabi reads as follows: *If anyone give over a field to a gardener, for him to plant it as a garden, if he work at it, and care for it for four years, in the fifth year the owner and the gardener shall divide it, the owner taking his part in charge.* The phrase "If he work at it and care for it..." is the same legal formula that can be observed in the narrative of the Garden of Eden.[30] In the southern parts of Babylonia, in the third millennium BC, all land remained the possession of the community, the city-state, which leased it to tenant farmers. In the northern part of Babylonia, all land belonged to the king, who allowed private individuals to cultivate it for his benefit.[31] By the second millennium, land leases and tenures had developed into something a bit more flexible, but throughout those centures it remained a common, standard arrangement that the tenant worked

---

[29] Note the opening verses of Isaiah 5 in which there is an implied catalog of the tasks a tenant had to carry out in order to clear and work a vineyard, as well as the connection of "served... and kept..." in Hos. 12.12. But the Code of Hammurabi is the most convincing parallel.

[30] I am using the L. W. King translation here (*The Letters and Inscriptions of Hammurabi*, ed. and trans. L. W. King, 3 vols. [London, 1898–1900]). I reject, of course, the Midrashic reading which suggests that the actual object of the verb *l'shomrah* is "the Sabbath"—since the biblical narrative has just finished telling us how, on the Seventh Day, God ceased from work and rested. See Midrash Rabbah on Genesis.

[31] Piotr Steinkeller, "Land-Tenure Conditions in Third-Millennium Babylonia: The Problem of Regional Variation," in *Urbanization and Land Ownership in the Ancient Near East*, Michael Hudson and Baruch A. Levine, eds., Peabody Museum Bulletin 7 (Cambridge, Mass., 1999).

the land in exchange for a fraction of the produce.[32] So the trees that God had planted, and all the fruit of them, belonged to God. They were planted for God to eat. Yet the standard arrangement for stewards and tenant farmers was that the steward could take a fraction of the fruit for himself. This was his pay.

Under the Code of Hammurabi, the penalty for stealing property of the temple or the king, and for receiving such property, was death. Law 6 in sequence: *If any one steal the property of a temple or of the court, he shall be put to death, and also the one who receives the stolen thing from him shall be put to death.* The penalty for a steward who stole from his master varied according to what was stolen and who was stolen from. For stealing fodder or farm implements, the hands were to be cut off.[33] For stealing actual cattle, he was to be torn to pieces. And of course for a tenant who failed to pay the rent, whether by failing to transmit to the landowner the full portion of produce agreed, or by overeating himself, the penalty included cancellation of the lease and loss of his tenancy.

The arrangement God made with Adam—"of all the trees you may eat, except of this one that grows in the center"—deviated from the standard arrangement: one of the trees was to be left alone and Adam did not have the right to eat any of its fruit—yet he was required to tend it. The death penalty for violation of his fiduciary duty was probably imposed because the garden was temple or court property.

Because he had been given dominion over all the beasts, including the serpent, and since Eve herself, made from his rib, was his to name and command, Adam was responsible for their actions "on his watch." And the command which bound him bound them as well. This aspect of the story harks back to ancient legal concept of the responsibility of a community for the bad acts of its members. We see vestiges of this notion in Deuteronomy 21, which involves the discovery of a corpse lying in open fields; the city closest to the corpse is required to sacrifice a heifer to cleanse itself. And we can find a similar notion expressed in the 109th law in Hammurabi's Code: "If conspirators meet in the house of a tavern-keeper and these conspirators are not captured and delivered to the court, the tavern-keeper shall be put to death." Adam

[32] See Piotr Steinkeller, *Third-Millennium Legal and Administrative Texts in the Iraq Museum, Baghdad*, Mesopotamian Civilizations 4 (Winona Lake, Indiana, 1992), pp. 13, 23, 24, 84, 98–99; and Hammurabi's Code, Laws 40–50, 60–65.

[33] Hammurabi's Code, Law 253.

was responsible to police behavior in the Garden and the responsibility for misconduct fell on all.

God, Yahweh, walks in the garden and speaks directly to Adam. For this reason, Spinoza included Adam in the list of "prophets", that is, persons who spoke directly with God.[34] But we may perhaps see in this image, which is more personal and intimate than any other image of Yahweh in the Hexateuch, an infiltration of the Greek idea that the gods walk among men from time to time. In this account, Yahweh acts in some respects like a Greek divinity.

Further, the serpent from the Hulupu tree, which was coiled around it to prevent Gilgamesh and others from drawing nigh, is now transformed in our narrator's dream into an intelligent creature who persuades Eve to eat, becoming a caduceus-like symbol, instead of a menacing symbol. Eve herself now brings the fruit to Adam.

What of the nakedness of Adam and Eve? This has parallels in the story of Enkidu, the friend of Gilgamesh, Enkidu the wild man. According to the standard Gilgamesh texts, Enkidu was created as a double of Gilgamesh; the wild other. But through the good offices of the temple prostitute, Enkidu is civilized. He puts on clothes and becomes Gilgamesh's close friend, goes to court with him, and together they engage in heroic exploits.

It is possible that the narrator had the character of Enkidu in mind when he writes that Adam and Eve were "naked but not ashamed." Nakedness here bespeaks simply lack of civilization, and "shame" is a difficult word, particularly in the Hebrew: "*v'lo yitboshashu*"—*bet, shin* is the root, and the *shin* is doubled. *Busha* means shame in later Hebrew;[35] but the word is also related to the word "*lovesh*", *lamed, bet, shin*—the word which means simply to wear clothing.[36] The point is that Adam and Eve were, like Enkidu, unclothed and utterly "uncivilized". God makes skins for them and "puts clothing on them"—*vayalbishem*. That means simply: now they are civilized.

---

[34] Baruch Spinoza, *Tractatus Theologico-Politicus (Gebhardt Edition, 1925)*, trans. Samuel Shirley, 2nd ed. (Leiden, 1991), p. 80. This work was first published anonymously in Hamburg in 1670.

[35] Cf. Psalms 89.45; Ezekial 7.18; Micah 7.10; Obadiah 10.

[36] This use of the *lamed* as a verb-maker is found also in the word for bread, *lechem*, which comes from the two-letter root *chet* plus *mem* 'warmth'. So we find *hamam*. See Ibn Ezra on this word, who calls it an *ayin/vav* root and cites *yitbonen* and *binah*.

The "tree of knowledge of good and evil" is thus our narrator's transformation of the Sumerian notion of "*me*"—all the arts of civilization, which Inanna took from Enki and brought to the city of Uruk. These were possessions of the gods, and man obtained them through some act of betrayal, or heroism, or trickery, or—for the legal mind of our narrator—simple breach of fiduciary duty.

The narrator here dreams of God as a judge, as Osiris in the Egyptian Book of the Dead. But although the judgment is meant to take place on the day of death, no immediate death is imposed but, rather, the curse of mortality. Yet the association of the day of judgment with the day of death, so strong in Egyptian belief and crucial to the development of the legal notions underlying covenant, reward, and punishment in the Hexateuch is preserved in our story.

Again, there is a parallel between the Garden of Eden and Enki and Inanna; once the Boat of Heaven had reached the harbor of Uruk, Enki realized that the *me* had come into the possession of man. Instead of being angry he blessed the city of Uruk and prayed that the *me* would remain there forever. Yahweh reacts in a similar fashion. Realizing that Adam and Eve have now eaten of the tree of knowledge, he makes them clothes and dresses them, and goes out of the garden with them.

But like Gilgamesh, Adam is unable to escape the bonds of mortality. He cannot eat of the tree of life. He is barred from the garden so that he cannot become fully like God. In this way, the boundary between man and God remains fundamentally impermeable; man in God's image is possible, but man as the equal of God—that is not to be.[37]

We have attempted to explore the meaning of this account to its narrator, who, together with his audience, was certainly moved by it. His story interfaced and integrated all the religious traditions of his day, fusing mystery traditions, stories of death and rebirth, and Greco-Roman and Jewish themes into one compelling religious narrative. We can identify what kind of cry this narrator uttered; it was of course a cry of anguish, a lament; but it was also a cry of exultation and discovery—discovery of a new kind of relationship between man and God, and exultation at the notion that man might at last be free of the burden of servitude to the gods.

[37] Barr, *Garden of Eden* (see above, n. 4), discusses the notion of "eternal life" and its relationship to this story.

The story is often thought of as the account of "man's first disobedience," but "disobedience" is a very clumsy word for the breach of fiduciary duty of which Adam was guilty. The fact is, the narrator apparently did not agree that disobedience was necessarily negative. After eating the fruit, Adam and Eve lived, and left the garden; God went with them, and history began to unfold.

For this narrator, man is not God's slave and he is not even to be God's tenant farmer or steward. No, man will have his own lands where he will be master. Yes, it is true, that land will bring forth only thorns and thistles and he will have to struggle to earn his way; his wife will have pain in childbirth—all the lamentable conditions of human existence will be upon him. Yet he will not be a slave, and he will suffer no punishment for disobedience. Nor will he live in ignorance, no, he ate of the fruit of the tree of knowledge; and for this narrator, that was the condition that needed to be satisfied in order for man to enter into conversation with God.

For what kind of relationship could mankind possibly have with God if one did not know "Good and Evil"? It is possible to consider the "knowledge of good and evil" as the equivalent of all the arts of civilization, as the Sumerian *me*. This narrator subscribed to the notion presented in the Atra-hasis story, that the gods would not permit humans to exist if they remained unruly and noisy; the gods required them to become civilized if they were to live upon the earth. But this account transformed the relationship between god and man from one of abject servitude to a true relationship.

Obedience to God's commands, and adherence to His statutes and commandments, the honoring of the covenant—all this is an important theme throughout the Hexateuch, and particularly in the Yahwistic portions. The next story, of Cain and Abel, is about the first murder; and the general decadence of the human race is told through the story of the boasting Lamech and then of the Flood. The Yahwist's preoccupation with the idea of obedience reached its culmination in the narrative of the binding of Isaac. In *City of God* (14,15) Augustine compares the disobedience of Adam to the pious obedience of Abraham: it would have been so easy for Adam to obey God's command. He was not required to *do* anything; all he had to do was avoid eating the forbidden fruit. But he could not do even this, while Abraham was commanded to do something infinitely more difficult, namely, to sacrifice his only son; and Abraham obeyed. For this, the Yahwist says, God promised to reward him by "multiplying his seed."

It is interesting to ask why this account remained a part of the biblical canon? It remained because of the prominence it gives to the creation of man in God's image, and because of the need to have a rational history which begins with creation and moves through the initiation of man's relationship with God.[38] Furthermore, the story is a preview of the pattern of patriarchal history: Adam was steward over the Garden, but he was expelled. Later God would give the whole land of Canaan to the descendants of Abraham—a land flowing with milk and honey. The loss of one garden and the promise of another; there is a resonance there which the redactors of the Hexateuch must have wanted to preserve.

But our narrator was a radical and although his powerful story was preserved, its central ideas were rejected by the redactors of the Hexateuch and the rest of the Old Testament because they were too extreme. His notion that man was not to be the servant of God is acceptable; as was the idea that man was not even to be a steward of God's land. But his notion that man could disobey God, that he could be master of his own land, that there was dignity in being independent of God, and that God's love for him was somehow unconditional—those ideas were too much for the early Hebrews. All they could reach instead was the legal notion of covenant: a contract, or feudal, reciprocal bond, in which man gave his obedience in exchange

[38] The sixteenth-century mystic Isaac Luria focused on the fact that the story of Adam follows the story of the first Sabbath, and he seems to have been puzzled by the different accounts of the creation of man contained in Genesis 1.27 and 2.7. Luria did not know that the two stories were combined from different sources, the "Elohistic" and the "Yahwistic." Instead, he focused on the moment right after the work of the Six Days had concluded and imagined that after all the noise and commotion of the six days' work of creation had died down, a great silence fell upon the world—a silence different from that which had existed before the First Day. This new silence Luria called the *Tzimtzum*—which means *contraction*: God who filled the Universe as a *plenum*, the "*Ein Sof*," now contracted himself to allow the "*Sefirot*"—the four worlds of Creation—to fill the space.

In the *Tzimtzum* the only sound that could be heard was the slightly heavier breathing of God who was now fatigued from his labors. In the silence of the *Tzimtzum* the birds had wings but they did not yet fly; the fish did not yet swim; the animals did not yet eat or walk; the sap did not yet move in the trees. Everything was potential and history had not yet begun. Even mankind, although male and female had been created on the Sixth Day, was not yet actuated. It was in the quivering silence of the *Tzimtzum* that God took His rest on the Seventh Day, and it was out of the shimmering silence of the *Tzimtzum* that the narrator of the story of the Garden of Eden raised his electrifying cry. (Luria did not write anything, but his teachings were written down by his followers. This *midrash* on the silence of the *Tzimtzum* is my own).

for God's promise—of a specific land, then of glory, and finally of eternal reward. The audacious vision of a relationship with God which did not require obedience, subsided into the then-new and overarching legal structure of the covenant.

The early Christians gave the Eden narrative a different interpretation, beginning with Paul's idea, expressed in Romans, chap. 5, vv. 12 ff., that Jesus was a second Adam, signalling a new epoch for all mankind. Expanding upon Paul's idea Augustine gave expression to the notion of original sin. Adam's sin corrupted the human race, and as a result, it is only Grace that can provide redemption.

But Augustine's interpretation actually could also be interpreted as a regression from the notion of covenant, back into the theology of the third millennium BC, in which man was seen as abjectly lower than God. If not for Augustine's refined and intensely beautiful writing, and the strength of his struggle to resolve the conflicts that were important to him—between the pagan world and early Christian thought—as well as powerful demonstration that he made in his own life of the possibility of coming closer to God, it would have been quite obvious that his interpretation of the Eden story was at odds with the intentions of the narrator. Augustine, who was not familiar with Gilgamesh, offered his hearers a new, sophisticated, refined, way to fall back into the ancient attitude of abject servitude toward God which, I believe, is not inherent in the Genesis account.

Augustine, of course, has been discussed and criticized. The idea of original sin has not been universally received.[39] And contrary perhaps, to Augustine,[40] the sin described in the story was not the sexual act: the mere fact that the Hebrew word "to know" (*yod—dalet—ayin*) refers both to an act of mentation and to carnal knowledge does not mean that Adam's eating of the fruit was a sexual awakening. Instead, the tense of the Hebrew "*yada*" rather than "*vayeda*" in chapter 4, verse 1, suggests that Adam's "knowing" of Eve took place in the Garden. The eleventh-century commentator, Rashi, pointing this out, writes that Eve was already pregnant with Cain and Abel before she ate the fruit.

---

[39] See Elaine Pagels, *Adam, Eve, and the Serpent* (New York, 1988), for a history of the struggle over this doctrine to the time of Augustine. Cf., as well F. Regina Psaki, ed., *The Earthly Paradise: The Garden of Eden from Antiquity to Modernity* (Binghamton, N.Y., 2002).

[40] See, e.g., *City of God* 14.20.

There is also the possibility that one of the fundamental assumptions of the Christian interpretation—that we all long to return to the Garden, that the Garden is the target of intense *nostalgia*, that we all want to live there eating the fruits and good things—this notion, too, is rejected by the narrator, since the Garden is never mentioned again. Even God leaves it and locks the door behind Himself.

It is then an interpretation that the story of the Garden of Eden is not the story of man's fall; no, the only character in the story whose elevation changes perceptibly is God Himself, who comes down from Heaven to be with Adam in the garden. From the narrator's point of view, the story is surely about the *ascent* of man from Eden; about the willingness to accept moral responsibility for one's actions and for the actions of those near him, and about the transformation in man's legal status from tenant farmer or steward to land owner.

The fate which befell the Epic of Gilgamesh may befall the Bible as we know it. Folklore may be transformed into cultic mythology, which is to say, mythology associated with religious practice. Religious literature may itself become sacralized, as is the case with the Bible, as well as the Koran in which the telling becomes fixed in stone, becoming a defining text for its community. As sacred text, it becomes the object of mimesis,[41] in turn, perhaps, entering a genre of literature.[42]

Yet the story of the Garden of Eden, I will suggest, remains compelling and has a future for two reasons. First, its lament: the accuracy of its observations about how people act, how they tend to evade responsibility, and what the human condition is—those observations are as accurate today, and the lament is just as moving today, as when the story was brand-new. And second, the narrator's central theological ideas—that the relationship with God might be something different from what had been assumed for so many centuries; that the mere imbalance of power between man and God, and the fact that God is the Creator and we are the Creatures, might not imply that man owes God obedience. As the realization becomes more urgent that God needs our help to complete His act of Creation—the very idea from which Atra-hasis starts, but which our Eden narrator has refined so exquisitely—and that there

---

[41] Cf. Dennis R. MacDonald, *The Homeric Epics and the Gospel of Mark* (New Haven, 2000); Dennis R. MacDonald, ed., *Mimesis and Intertextuality in Antiquity and Christianity* (Harrisburg, Pennsylvania, 2001).

[42] Cf. Jack Miles, *God: A Biography* (New York, 1995), and *Christ: A Crisis in the Life of God* (New York, 2001).

is no set of commands which God has already uttered to which we must be obedient, but that He craves to be in conversation with us as we engage with Him to complete the work of creation—as all these new ideas take hold in our hearts, this ancient story might continue to function as a sacred text.

INDEX